THE TRAGEDY OF
AMERICAN DIPLOMACY

BOOKS BY WILLIAM APPLEMAN WILLIAMS

American-Russian Relations, 1781–1947

The Shaping of American Diplomacy, 1750–1970

The Tragedy of American Diplomacy

The Contours of American History

The United States, Cuba, and Castro

*The Great Evasion: An Essay on the Contemporary
Relevance of Karl Marx*

The Roots of the Modern American Empire

*From Colony to Empire. Essays in the Development
of American Foreign Relations* (Ed.)

THE TRAGEDY OF
AMERICAN DIPLOMACY

William Appleman Williams

SECOND REVISED AND ENLARGED EDITION · A DELTA BOOK

FOR CORRINNE

A DELTA BOOK
Published by
DELL PUBLISHING CO., INC.
1 Dag Hammarskjold Plaza
New York, N.Y. 10017

Delta ® TM 755118, Dell Publishing Co., Inc.

ISBN: 0-440-59007-8

Published by arrangement with World Publishing Company
and with the author.

Printed in the United States of America

Second Revised and Enlarged Edition
15   14   13

ISBN: 0-385-29070-5

AUTHOR'S PREFATORY NOTE
This second revised edition was prepared during August 1971.

*I am deeply grateful to Wendy M. Tomlin
for her encouragement and assistance.*

CONTENTS

This is a time for searching criticism, all right,
but for criticism of the whole society.
JAMES RESTON, 1958

We are never so much the victims of another,
as we are the victims of ourselves.
JULIUS LESTER, 1970

How do you ask a man to be the last man
to die for a mistake?
JOHN FORBES KERRY, 1971

INTRODUCTION: HISTORY AND THE

We find genuine tragedy . . . only in that destruction which does not prematurely cut short development and success, but which, instead, grows out of success itself.

Breakdown and failure reveal the true nature of things. In failure, life's reality is not lost; on the contrary, here it makes itself wholly and decisively felt. There is no tragedy without transcendence.

This transformation may go the way of deliverance, where man rises to supreme reality through conquest of the tragic. Otherwise this transformation may go the way of decline into irresponsible aestheticism of the spectator: man distracted, drifting, falling off into nothingness.

KARL JASPERS, TRAGEDY IS NOT ENOUGH.

TRANSCENDENCE OF THE TRAGIC

The tragedy of American diplomacy is aptly symbolized, and defined for analysis and reflection, by the relations between the United States and Cuba from April 21, 1898 through April 21, 1961. The eruption of two wars involving the same two countries in precisely the same week provides a striking sense of classical form and even adds the tinge of eeriness so often associated with tragedy.

After three years of pressure culminating in an ultimatum, the United States declared war against Spain on April 21, 1898. The generally avowed objectives were to free Cuba from Spanish tyranny, to establish and underwrite the independence of the island, and to initiate and sustain its development toward political democracy and economic welfare.

During the subsequent 63 years, the United States exercised continuous, extensive influence in and over all aspects of Cuban affairs. This ongoing intervention produced some positive results. The advantages Cuba enjoyed as an American protectorate rather than a Spanish colony were significant and beneficial. Sugar production was modernized and increased. Some public utilities and other improvements associated with the basic sugar economy were gradually provided. And in the city of Havana, Americans and Cubans developed one of the business and entertainment centers of the Western Hemisphere.

As Cuba planted, harvested, refined, and sold more sugar,

it enjoyed slow and sporadic economic development. A modest number of Cubans improved their personal and group economic welfare. Furthermore, some of the forms and mechanisms of representative government were established and legalized, and some of the resulting institutions put out shallow roots into Cuban thought and culture. Reforms were instituted that helped stabilize Cuban politics and contributed to the elementary and routine kind of law and order necessary for moderately efficient economic activity. On rather widely separate occasions, small segments of the Cuban population participated in a consequential way in the process of representative government. And perhaps most important of all, the Cubans were encouraged—and exhorted—to define their future in terms of the kind of democracy and prosperity provided in the United States.

Yet when measured by the Cubans in the course of their daily experiences, or by outsiders concerned to discover and evaluate the results of American control, there was clearly a continuing, even increasing disparity between the actuality and the rhetoric. For the United States dominated the economic life of the island by controlling, directly or indirectly, the sugar industry, and by overtly and covertly preventing any dynamic modification of the island's one-crop economy. It defined clear and narrow limits on the island's political system. It tolerated the use of torture and terror, of fraud and farce, by Cuba's rulers. But it intervened with economic and diplomatic pressure and with force of arms, when Cubans threatened to transgress the economic and political restrictions established by American leaders.

That sad result was not the result of malice, indifference, or ruthless and predatory exploitation. American leaders were not evil men. They did not conceive and excuse some dreadful conspiracy. Nor were they treacherous hypocrites. They believed deeply in the ideals they proclaimed, and they were sincere in arguing that their policies and actions would ultimately create a Cuba that would be responsibly self-governed, economically prosperous, and socially stable and happy. All, of course, in the image of America.

Precisely for those reasons, however, American diplomacy contained the fundamental elements of tragedy. It held within itself, that is to say, several contradictory truths. Those truths, allowed to develop according to their own logic without modification by men who understood that process and acted on their knowledge, would ultimately clash in a devastating upheaval and crisis.

There was first the truth of American power. Measured in relative or absolute terms, the United States has possessed overweening power in relation to Cuba, a power it has exercised vigorously and persistently.

There was secondly the truth that the use of that power failed to create in Cuba or in its relationship with America a reality that enjoyed any persuasive correlation with the ideals avowed as the objectives of the power. American policy makers did not honor their avowed commitment to the principle of self-determination, and they did not modernize and balance the Cuban political economy.

A third truth resulted from that deployment and use of American power. Gradually, but with increasing momentum, Cubans evolved a coalition of groups committed to important changes in their society. In turn, that objective implied significant modifications in Cuba's relations with the United States. Though this coalition included reformers and moderate conservatives, it drew most of its verve and drive from noncommunist radicals. Their dedication and courage in actively opposing the Batista regime sustained and strengthened the general movement, and ultimately won them recognition as the symbol and positions as the leaders of the campaign for a new and better Cuba.

The convergence and interaction of these three truths produced the Cuban crisis of 1959–1961. Rather than contributing to general and beneficent transformation of Cuban society during the years after 1898, American power and policy produced instead a Cuban and an American crisis that characterized and symbolized the underlying tragedy of all American diplomacy in the twentieth century. In Cuba, the half-century confrontation of the contrasting truths finally erupted in a militant social revolution conceived and designed to establish—*in fact and in the present*—the kind of Cuban society and development that American diplomacy had promised since 1898.

The Cuban Revolution of 1959–1960 was neither plotted,

planned, nor manufactured for export in the Soviet Union. Neither Russian troops nor Russian arms played any role in its success in deposing the Batista regime, or in establishing its authority throughout Cuba. Cuban communists discounted and opposed the revolution until after it had succeeded.

Once triumphant behind the leadership of Fidel Castro and the 26th of July Movement, the Cuban Revolution was conditioned by two factors: on the one hand, the internal politics of the Cuban revolutionary coalition; on the other, the dynamic effect of American power and policy upon that Cuban struggle. It is possible, though very improbable, that the radical wing of the Cuban coalition would have secured its ultimate control of the revolution even if American policy had been more tolerant, more imaginative, and more helpful. But American policy was none of those things. As a result, so creating the fourth truth and contributing to the tragedy, American policy interacted with the politics of the Cuban coalition in a way that strengthened the radicals. It probably also pushed them much further to the left than they had originally hoped or intended to go.

Two contradictory features characterized the early American response to the revolution. The surface pattern of formal (though noticeably cool and reserved) correctness was interpreted by many observers as a tactical approach to some accommodation to the new circumstances. But beneath that veneer, and clearly discernible from the outset, there was a fundamental antagonism toward the revolution and its commitment to extensive but nondoctrinaire changes in the status quo.

Coming to dominate American thinking and policy within a year, that opposition presented itself in the rhetoric of anticommunism and the cold war. In turn, that ideology served both as justification for a hostile posture and as rallying-cry for strong measures. Undemocratic and arbitrary actions which on a much broader, more vicious level had been accepted and tolerated as routine under the Batista and earlier regimes were suddenly in a truly revolutionary situation advanced as proof that Cuba had become a Soviet puppet. And all Cuban moves toward controlling or nationalizing the powerful and extensive American property holdings in the island evoked similar outcries—and the first thoughts and discussions of retaliation.

In this respect, as in others, the American outlook on Cuba typified a general inability to comprehend and come to terms with two aspects of revolutions per se. Americans gained neither understanding nor perspective, for example, from the knowledge that during the American Revolution their own Founding Fathers arbitrarily confiscated British and colonial property. And they overlooked or discounted almost completely the economic and psychological needs of poor countries. Those requirements could be met only through extensive aid or through measures of nationalization.

Just as a good many early American fortunes, *and considerable capital for general development*, were obtained through confiscation and other arbitrary measures, so in the twentieth century the new, poor countries were prompted to employ similar devices. And neither the Americans in the 1770s (or the early 1800s), nor the Cubans in the 1960s, felt secure and confident about their respective independence until the economic power of their former overlords had been brought under control. But all such considerations were conveniently evaded through the device of explaining everything as the diabolical work of Cuban communists and the Soviet Union.

When initially advanced, and for many months thereafter, the stereotype of Soviet influence or control was grossly at odds with the facts. Yet persistently and subtly advocated by official American leaders, and crudely merchandized as news or expert opinion by the mass media, it became the accepted picture and explanation of Cuban affairs. American policy based upon and derived from that mistaken view produced two grave and tragic consequences. In Cuba, American rhetoric and policy weakened the moderate elements in the revolutionary coalition and simultaneously strengthened the radicals. They also pushed those radicals further along their own revolutionary path and into an increasingly close relationship with the Soviet Union. In the United States, such Cuban developments intensified the original antagonism, served as convenient if distorted proof for the a priori assertion of Soviet influence, and hardened the resolve to oppose the revolution. A momentum toward violence was thus established and sustained.

The United States first tried economic and political weapons to weaken and subvert the Castro Government. Then, after those measures failed, the United States invaded Cuba by

proxy on April 17, 1961, in an effort to overthrow and replace that government by force of arms. The counter-revolutionary forces that waded ashore in the Bay of Pigs were
financed, armed, trained, and guided in their operation by
private and official American leaders. The action was a blatant
violation of the treaty system that the United States had
solemnly created to govern international relations in the Western Hemisphere, and a violation of its own neutrality laws.
It was likewise a callous negation of avowed American principles by President John Fitzgerald Kennedy (who was fond
of using the rhetoric of idealism).

Those aspects of the invasion, along with other characteristics of the episode, heightened the aura of terror that was
developing around American foreign policy. One of the most
unnerving features was the extensive elitism that had become
ingrained in the policy-making process. The assault on Cuba
was conceived, planned, and implemented by a small group of
men in the executive department. They opened no general
dialogue with members of the Congress (even in private conversation), and expended great effort and exerted great pressure to avoid any public discussion or debate.

That degree of elitism, which goes far beyond the delegation of power and authority required to execute public policy,
began to develop under President William McKinley. The
decision to acquire all the Philippines at the end of the war
against Spain was made by a small group of insiders; and
military intervention in China was initiated by executive order.
President Theodore Roosevelt dramatized the continuing concentration of power in the executive department with these
arrogant remarks about his intervention to control the Panama
canal route: "The vital work . . . was done by me without
the aid or advice of anyone . . . and without the knowledge
of anyone. I took the Canal Zone."

President Woodrow Wilson further extended such elitism
during World War I: covertly changing policy on loans to
the Allies, and intervening with force against the Bolshevik
Revolution without Congressional authority. In a similar way,
President Franklin Delano Roosevelt maneuvered behind the
scenes to aid England and France against Nazi Germany and
Imperial Japan (including the use of American armed forces)

at a time when the American public was seriously divided over the question of becoming involved in those conflicts.

The requirements of secrecy during World War II enlarged the power of the men at the top to make decisions without general debate. The practice of informing a few chosen Congressional leaders of a policy just before it was put into operation was developed as a substitute for the kind of dialogue and compromise that characterizes meaningful democracy or representative government. President Harry S Truman used that technique in winning support for his program of global opposition to revolutionary movements at the end of the war. He likewise refined the technique of announcing and defining issues in such a way as to place critics on the defensive as men and women who seemed to be challenging traditional American values and objectives.

Elitism consolidated those gains, and took new ground, during the Korean War crisis of 1950–1952. The decision to intervene was made without public discussion. Women and men in their living rooms, as well as their Congressional representatives, were simply confronted with the information that Americans were engaged in combat against communists. The provisions of the Constitution were evaded by calling the war a police action, and, for the more sophisticated, by arguing that the Congressional commitment to the United Nations included an obligation to resort to force.

During those years, moreover, the Central Intelligence Agency enlarged its power and freedom to undertake various self-selected interventionist projects around the world. It deposed premiers, installed counter-revolutionary governments (and aided other such movements), and in all probability assassinated various men and women it considered dangerous or troublesome. The invasion of Cuba, in which the CIA played a major role, was but another—if a major—stride down the road away from responsive and responsible self-government in the United States.

That in itself generates terror. The kind of terror that Karl Jaspers implies when he speaks of the destruction which grows out of success, and of the possibility that tragedy can lead to decline rather than transcendence. Such terror became ever more omnipresent during the subsequent missile confrontation with the Soviet Union (which also involved Cuba) and the grossly unjustified intervention in Santo Domingo. Then came the deceitful and manipulative climax of the intervention in the Vietnamese revolutionary civil war.

That ultimate manifestation of the tragedy and the terror of American foreign policy began with encouragement to Ho Chi Minh as a way of defeating Imperial Japan. Then the emphasis shifted to helping France maintain its position in Indochina in order to be sure of French support against the Soviet Union in Europe. And to securing access to the raw materials—and the potential customers—of Asia. Those commitments were deepened when the Chinese Communists won power. Grants of money to France led to talk about nuclear weapons and then, when the French were defeated, to discussions about how to contain the Vietnamese who would very probably use a free election to self-determine themselves out of the orbit of western capitalism.

The answer to that problem was for the elite to abandon elections. That done, the CIA agents became the new ward heelers. Then, terror of terrors, the acceptance of the philosophy that power and freedom erupt from the muzzle of a gun. And so a few experts became 15,000 advisors under fire in the field; and those mushroomed into more than half a million men, a bombing campaign that surpassed the air assault on Nazi Germany and Imperial Japan, a chemical attack that destroyed children as well as vegetation and animals, and an appalling barbarism among young Americans. All in the name of assistance, reform, and self-determination.

Thus, even by itself, the elitism generated terror about what was done as well as about how the decisions were made. Such dismay was deepened by the elite's self-isolation from the nature of reality, by its loss of the power of critical thought, by its exaggerated confidence in American economic strength and military might, by its own arrogance and self-righteousness, and by its messianic distortion of a sincere humanitarian desire to help other peoples. Even the American public came more and more to be considered as simply another factor to be manipulated and controlled in the effort to establish and maintain the American Way as the global status quo.

Yet, in truth, the attitudes and the outlook of the public also contributed to the sense of terror about American foreign relations. For, beginning with the depression of the 1870s, an increasing number of farmers and urban businessmen, and even workers, came to favor and support American overseas expansion. Others acquiesced in the imperial policy as it was developed and acted upon. Many such citizens thought this expansion would improve their own economic condition, or strengthen the national economy. Another group wanted to strike a blow for freedom, either by blocking the expansion of European powers or by extending America's activity as a world reformer. Or both. And still others, caught up in the nationalistic or patriotic support for the government that is common in all societies, or perhaps sublimating their frustrations about life in America, provided additional support for the active expansionists. By the 1890s, therefore, most Americans generally favored an expansionist policy, though they might disagree about specific actions.

Beginning with the rise of Jacksonian Democracy during the 1820s, moreover, Americans steadily deepened their commitment to the idea that democracy was inextricably connected with individualism, private property, and a capitalist marketplace economy. Even the great majority of critics sought to reform existing society precisely in order to realize that conception of the good system. The small minority that wanted to change central features of the capitalist political economy, or replace it with a new order, was viewed as an odd bag of quixotic idealists, ignorant dreamers, or dangerous radicals—or all three. And foreigners who had created and preferred a different way of life were considered inferior or backward—proper subjects for education and reform in the American Way.

Those two characteristics of public involvement in foreign policy were firmly established by the time of the Bolshevik Revolution in Russia. The general support for American expansion created, ironically, the power base for the increasing elitism among the policy-makers. And the antagonism toward other approaches to organizing society, and toward other value systems, provided fundamental backing for an anti-revolutionary policy.

Whatever the periodic outbursts of opposition to the basic

strategy of expansion and intervention, or even to specific manifestations of that outlook, the policy-making elite felt steadily more confident of being able to generate or manipulate effective support or acquiescence among the general public. By the 1950s, indeed, the ultimate touch of terror had appeared. Not only could the elite answer critics by explaining that it could not change course because of popular support for existing policy, but even the reformers within the elite believed and acted upon that reading of political reality. The political system was thus immobilized as a process of peaceful change.

Seen in historical perspective, therefore, what we are accustomed to call the Cold War—meaning the confrontation between the United States, the Soviet Union, and the People's Republic of China, between 1943 and 1971—is in reality only the most recent phase of a more general conflict between the established system of western capitalism and its internal and external opponents. That broader view not only makes it possible to understand more clearly why American foreign policy has been criticized by conservatives as well as radicals but also provides a fuller grasp of the long struggle by China (and other nations) against being reconstructed as a part of the western capitalist system. It should also deepen our determination to break free of the assumptions, beliefs, and habits that have carried us so close to the abyss of thermonuclear war.

It is not enough to be more prudent, more flexible, and more efficient. We have now to cut to the bone and scrape the marrow of our traditional outlook. Nothing is more painful or more demanding in human affairs. But we can take heart from the knowledge that such action is the source of individual self-realization and true national greatness.

Only a few Americans in positions of influence or leadership demonstrated that kind of bedrock courage prior to 1965. It was customary for such spokesmen, even when they recognized and described the difficulties, to call merely for more vigor and efficiency in the prosecution of traditional programs and policies. But Walter Lippmann repeatedly and patiently explained some of the root causes of the crisis in American diplomacy, and went on to suggest cogent if often unpopular alternatives. And a few other commentators such as James Reston wrote in a similar vein.

Another striking example was provided by foreign service officer George Frost Kennan. At the end of World War II, Kennan played a key role in developing the containment policy toward the Soviet Union and other radical movements. That policy was predicated upon the assumption that, because of its great relative economic advantage and its absolute monopoly of atomic weapons, the United States was powerful enough to force the Soviet Union to change fundamentally its entire system. But within a decade, Kennan so modified that unrealistic estimate as to call repeatedly and with some eloquence for an end to the rigidity and single-track diplomacy that he had done so much to initiate.

Senator J. William Fulbright has been even more impressive. Beginning in the late 1950s, he initiated a keen and sophisticated critical evaluation of American diplomacy from his position on the Senate Foreign Relations Committee. His talent for asking searching questions and his ability to work through to relevant answers earned him a reputation as one of the nation's most perceptive critics of foreign policy.*

In his vigorous and unqualified condemnation of the Cuban invasion at a top-level meeting held before the initial landing, for example, Fulbright revealed himself as a man of magnificent personal and political courage and as a man who grasped the full dimensions of the tragedy of American diplomacy. He flatly asserted that the proposed attack was morally, legally, and practically a grave mistake: certain to cause incalculable negative consequences whether or not it succeeded in its immediate objective of initiating the overthrow of the Castro Government. Fulbright also questioned the judgment of the proponents of the invasion in arguing that Castro's Cuba posed a serious threat either to the military security or to the vital national interests of the United States. But even if that argument were granted, Fulbright insisted that the means would subvert the ends of American diplomacy. And that was his key insight into the general as well as the immediate crisis.

Fulbright's powerful performance at the meeting on Cuba can be more fully understood against the background of his earlier analysis of the difficulties underlying American foreign

* Fulbright is perhaps the best example of the enlightened conservative as critic of American foreign policy. My respect for his position does not imply agreement with him on all foreign or domestic issues.

policy. Writing late in 1958, he advanced his central points with unusual clarity and candor. "If there is a single factor which more than any other explains the predicament in which we now find ourselves, it is our readiness to use the spectre of Soviet Communism as a cloak for the failure of our own leadership." Quite aware of Russia's challenge to American leadership, and in no way disposed to discount or evade that issue, Fulbright nevertheless insisted that it was crucial "to ask ourselves some very searching questions." "We must stop thinking about these problems in terms of a stereotyped view of the world," he concluded. "We must abandon the clichés and reconsider all our assumptions."

He then acted to break open the clichés employed by the elite. The drastic escalation of the intervention in Vietnam undertaken by President Lyndon Baines Johnson through the winter of 1964–1965 generated a wrenching awareness of the tragedy and the terror of American foreign policy among a small group of students, professors, and concerned citizens. They struggled, through the tactics of teach-ins and non-violent demonstrations, to dramatize the issues, to arouse the public, and to force the policy-making elite to open a consequential dialogue with the citizenry. Their efforts did arouse many students, but most others were slow to break free of the chains of tradition. The critics did not muster the power to force a strategic confrontation with the elite.

Then Fulbright used his position as chairman of the Senate Committee on Foreign Relations to launch a nationally televised inquiry into the war. The maneuver was skillfully conceived and beautifully executed: he pushed the issue into the daily experience and consciousness of the body politic and revitalized the essential process of serious, sustained dialogue. He forced the policy-making elite on the defensive (though their power was sufficient to mount an effective rear-guard action), he transferred his respectability to the larger body of critics (despite the periodic outbursts of violence that scared many citizens), and he gave other politicians reason to believe that their consciences might win votes (though that kind of confidence in the essence of democracy took a bit longer to materialize). It was a notable achievement.

Fulbright did not go on, however, to "reconsider all our

assumptions." That involves, of necessity, a re-examination of the history of twentieth-century American foreign relations (and the relationship between foreign policy and the domestic economy). In proceeding according to that intellectual strategy we first confront directly what happened. We learn the ideas and the actions of the men who made or influenced policy, and the consequences of those events at home and abroad. Second, at the end of such a review of the past, we return to the present better informed. Finally, that increased knowledge and understanding may help us to muster the nerve to act in ways that can transform the tragedy into a new beginning.

For history is a way of learning, of getting closer to the truth. It is only by abandoning the clichés that we can even define the tragedy. When we have done that, we will no longer be merely acquiescing in the deadly inertia of the past. We will have taken the first and vital step in making history. Such a re-examination of history must be based upon a searching review of the way America has defined its own problems and objectives, and its relationship with the rest of the world. The reason for this is simple: realism goes nowhere unless it starts at home. Combined with a fresh look at Soviet behavior, such an understanding of American policy should help in the effort to outline new programs and policies designed to bring America's ideals and practical objectives closer to realization.

In the realm of ideas and ideals, American policy is guided by three conceptions. One is the warm, generous, humanitarian impulse to help other people solve their problems. A second is the principle of self-determination applied at the international level, which asserts the right of every society to establish its own goals or objectives, and to realize them internally through the means it decides are appropriate. These two ideas can be reconciled; indeed, they complement each other to an extensive degree. But the third idea entertained by many Americans is one which insists that other people cannot *really* solve their problems and improve their lives unless they go about it in the same way as the United States.

This feeling is not peculiar to Americans, for all other peoples reveal some degree of the same attitude toward the rest of the world. But the full scope and intensity of the American version is clearly revealed in the blunt remark of former

Secretary of State Dean G. Acheson. He phrased it this way in explaining and defending the American program of foreign aid as it was being evolved shortly after the end of World War II: "We are willing to help people who believe the way we do, to continue to live the way they want to live."

This insistence that other people ought to copy America contradicts the humanitarian urge to help them and the idea that they have the right to make such key decisions for themselves. In some cases, the American way of doing things simply does not work for other people. In another instance it may be satisfactory, but the other society may prefer to do it in a different way that produces equally good results—perhaps even better ones. But even if the American way were the *only* effective approach, the act of forcing it upon the other society —and economic and political pressure are forms of force— violates the idea of self-determination. It also angers the other society and makes it even less apt to accept the American suggestion on its own merits. Hence it is neither very effective nor very idealistic to try to help other people by insisting from the outset that they follow closely the lead and the example of the United States on all central and vital matters.

The same kind of difficulty arises in connection with the economic side of American foreign policy. The United States needs raw materials and other goods and services from foreign countries, just as it needs to sell some of its own goods and services to them. It might be able literally to isolate itself and survive, but that is not the issue. Not even the isolationists of the late 1920s and early 1930s advocated that kind of foreign policy. The vital question concerns instead the way in which America obtains what it needs and exports what it wants to sell.

Most Americans consider that trade supplies the answer to this problem. But trade is defined as the exchange of goods and services between producers dealing with each other in as open a market as it is possible to create, and doing this without one of them being so beholden to the other that he cannot bargain in a meaningful and effective way. Trade is not defined by the transfer of goods and services under conditions established and controlled largely by one of the parties.

Here is a primary source of America's troubles in its economic relations with the rest of the world. For in expanding its own economic system throughout much of the world, America has made it very difficult for other nations to retain their economic independence. This is particularly true in connection with raw materials. Saudi Arabia, for example, is not an independent oil producer. Its oil fields are an integrated and controlled part of the American oil industry. But a very similar, if often less dramatic, kind of relationship also develops in manufacturing industries. This is the case in countries where established economic systems are outmoded or lethargic, as well as in the new, poor nations that are just beginning to industrialize. American corporations exercise extensive authority, and even commanding power, in the political economy of such nations.

Unfortunately, there is an even more troublesome element involved in the economic aspect of American foreign policy. That is the firm conviction, even dogmatic belief, that America's *domestic* well-being depends upon such sustained, ever-increasing overseas economic expansion. Here is a convergence of economic practice with intellectual analysis and emotional involvement that creates a very powerful and dangerous propensity to define the essentials of American welfare in terms of activities outside the United States.

It is dangerous for two reasons. First, it leads to an indifference toward, or a neglect of, internal developments which are nevertheless of primary importance. And second, this strong tendency to externalize the sources or causes of good things leads naturally enough to an even greater inclination to explain the lack of the good life by blaming it on foreign individuals, groups, and nations. This kind of externalizing evil serves not only to antagonize the outsiders, but further intensifies the American determination to make them over in the proper manner or simply push them out of the way.

The over-all result of these considerations is that America's humanitarian urge to assist other peoples is undercut—even subverted—by the way it goes about helping them. Other societies come to feel that American policy causes them to lose their economic, political, and even psychological independence. The people in such countries come to feel that they are being harmed rather than helped. That inclines them to resort to political and economic retaliation, which only intensifies and further complicates a problem that is very complex at the outset. Thus the importance of trying to understand how the contradictions in American policy have developed. If that aspect of the problem can be resolved, perhaps then it will be possible to evolve a program for helping other people that is closer to American ideals and also more effective in practice.

But it is wise to avoid deluding ourselves even before we begin. "History writing," as Sir Lewis Namier has observed, "is not a visit of condolence." History is a mirror in which, if we are honest enough, we can see ourselves as we are as well as the way we would like to be. The misuse of history is the misuse of the mirror: if one uses it to see not only the good in the image, but to see the image as all good. As Oliver Cromwell spoke to England, so history speaks to all men: "I beseech you, in the bowels of Christ, consider that ye may be mistaken." The courage to accept that challenge is the precondition of winning even a chance to transform the tragedy into a new opportunity for great achievement.

THE TRAGEDY OF
AMERICAN DIPLOMACY

CHAPTER ONE

I. THE TRANSFORMATION OF THE
EXPANSIONIST OUTLOOK

Our people are decided in the opinion that it is necessary for us to take a share in the occupation of the ocean . . . and that line of policy be pursued which will render the use of that element as great as possible to them. . . . But what will be the consequence? Frequent wars without a doubt. . . . Our commerce on the ocean and in other countries must be paid for by frequent war.

THOMAS JEFFERSON TO JOHN JAY, 1785

A continuance of the present anarchy of our commerce will be a continuance of the unfavorable balance on it, which by draining us of our metals . . . [will bring our ruin]. In fact most of our political evils may be traced up to our commercial ones, and most of our moral to our political.

JAMES MADISON TO THOMAS JEFFERSON, 1786

The question is, whether small or extensive republics are more favorable to the election of proper guardians of the public weal; and it is clearly decided in favor of the latter.

JAMES MADISON, 1787

IMPERIAL ANTICOLONIALISM

[*Our success*] *furnishes a new proof of the falsehood of Montesquieu's doctrine, that a republic can be preserved only in a small territory. The reverse is the truth.*

THOMAS JEFFERSON, 1801

We have just commenced exporting, yet the home market is even now completely glutted in many articles. . . . We shall be compelled to diminish our production unless a foreign market can be found.

PRAIRIE FARMER, 1843

We in the West . . . want the world's wide market.

REPRESENTATIVE WILLIAM WATSON
WICK OF INDIANA, 1846

It is clear that much the most important factor in maintaining the commercial prosperity of the United States during the recent past has been its agricultural industry. It is further clear that if the commercial prosperity of the country is to be maintained in the future it must continue to find abroad a market for its surplus agricultural products.

EDITORIAL IN *Bradstreet's*, 1884

*We are rapidly utilizing the whole of our continental territory.
We must turn our eyes abroad, or they will soon look inward
upon discontent.*

REPRESENTATIVE JOHN ADAM KASSON
OF IOWA, 1881

*We are now on the threshold, in my judgment, of a develop-
ment outward, of a contest for the foreign commerce of the
world.*

SENATOR PRESTON B. PLUMB
OF KANSAS, 1884

*A silver standard, too, would make us the trading center of
all the silver-using countries of the world, and these countries
contain far more than one-half of the world's population.*

WILLIAM JENNINGS BRYAN, 1893

America's traditional view of itself and the world is composed
of three basic ideas, or images. One maintains that the United
States was isolationist until world power was "thrust upon it,"
first to help Cuba, then twice to save the world for democracy,
and finally to prevent the Soviet Union and other Communist
regimes from overwhelming the world. Another holds that,
except for a brief and rapidly dispelled aberration at the turn
of the century, America has been anti-imperialist throughout
its history. A third asserts that a unique combination of economic power, intellectual and practical genius, and moral rigor
enables America to check the enemies of peace and progress—
and build a better world—without erecting an empire in the
process.

Not even Joseph Stalin maintained that America's record in
world affairs was exactly the reverse of this common view, and
for Americans to do so would be to mistake a candid and
searching re-examination of their own mythology for a tirade
of useless self-damnation. The classical ideas about American
foreign policy are not all wrong: the United States did come
to full, active involvement in international affairs by degrees;

it has been anti-imperialist in some respects at certain times; and periodically it has consciously acknowledged various limitations on its power.

But those truisms do not offer much insight into, or much guidance for understanding, the dynamic nature of American foreign relations. It is both more accurate and more illuminating to realize that the successful revolution which began in 1775 and culminated in 1783 established the United States as a world power which sought and played a very active role in international affairs. The War of 1812 offers a revealing example of that strength. Although the United States suffered the embarrassment of having the Capitol in Washington burned, and failed in its grandiose objective of conquering Canada, it nevertheless fought the British Empire to a negotiated settlement that secured American ambitions west of the Mississippi. Spain recognized the meaning of that victory, and in 1819 conceded without a fight a huge strip of real estate extending from the Gulf of Mexico to the Pacific Ocean. And in the Monroe Doctrine of 1823, Americans boldly asserted their claim to predominance throughout the entire Western Hemisphere.

The vigorous expansionism manifested in the Monroe Doctrine was only the continuation and maturation of an attitude held by the Revolutionary generation. Americans thought of themselves as an empire at the outset of their national existence —as part of the assertive self-consciousness which culminated in the American Revolution. Though at first it may seem surprising, when contrasted with the image of isolationism which has been accepted so long, in reality that early predominance of a pattern of empire thought is neither very strange nor very difficult to explain. Having matured in an age of empires as part of an empire, the colonists naturally saw themselves in the same light once they joined issue with the mother country.*

* This early expansionist outlook, and its relation to classical and mercantilist thought, is discussed in the following studies: T. A. Bailey, "America's Emergence as a World Power: The Myth and the Verity," *Pacific Historical Review* (February, 1961); L. Baritz, "The Idea of the West," *American Historical Review* (April, 1961); A. B. Darling, *Our Rising Empire, 1763–1803* (New Haven: Yale University Press, 1940); R. W. Van Alstyne, *The Rising American Empire* (New York: Oxford University Press, 1960); C. Vevier, "American Continentalism: An Idea of Expansion, 1845–1910, *American Historical Review* (January, 1960); and

However natural, attractive, and exhilarating, such a commitment to empire nevertheless posed a serious dilemma for the Founding Fathers. Political theory of that age asserted the impossibility of reconciling democratic republicanism with a large state. Up to the time of the American Revolution at any rate, the British could remain ignorant of—or evade—that issue. Self-governing Englishmen never had to cope with the problem of integrating their conquests into their domestic social and political economy. Americans were not so fortunate, for any expansion they undertook immediately enlarged the mother country. Led by James Madison, they sought to resolve the contradiction between their drive for empire and their politics by developing a theory of their own which asserted that democratic republicanism could be improved and sustained by just such an imperial foreign policy.

Probably taking his cue from David Hume, an Englishman who attacked Montesquieu's argument that democracy was a system that could work only in small states, and from British mercantiles such as Francis Bacon, Thomas Mun, and James Steuart, Madison asserted that expansion was the key to preventing factions—themselves primarily the result of economic conflicts—from disrupting the fabric of society. Institutional checks and balances could help, and were therefore necessary, but they were not enough in and of themselves. Expansion was essential to mitigate economic clashes by providing an empire for exploitation and development, and to interpose long distances (and thus difficulties and delays in sustaining initial antagonisms) between one faction and the rest of the nation and the government itself.

Madison thus proposed, *as a guide to policy and action in his own time*, the same kind of an argument that the historian Frederick Jackson Turner formulated a century later when he advanced his frontier thesis, which explained America's democracy and prosperity as the result of such expansion. Madison's theory was shared (or borrowed) by many other American leaders of his time. Thomas Jefferson's thesis that democracy and prosperity depended upon a society of land-

---

W. A. Williams; *The Contours of American History* (Chicago: Quadrangle Books, Inc., 1966), and *The Roots of the Modern American Empire* (New York: Random House, 1969).

holding and exporting freemen was a drastically simplified version of the same idea. Perhaps Edward Everett of Massachusetts most nearly captured the essence of the interpretation and argument in his judgment that expansion was the *"principle* of our institutions." In 1828–1829, Madison himself prophesied a major crisis would occur in about a century, when the continent had filled up and an industrial system had deprived most people of any truly productive property. His fears proved true sooner than he anticipated. For in the Crisis of the 1890s, when Americans *thought* that the continental frontier was gone, they advanced and accepted the argument that continued expansion in the form of overseas economic (and even territorial) empire provided the best, if not the only, way to sustain their freedom and prosperity.

That response to the crisis was not simply the result of a few imperial spokesmen imposing their ideas upon the rest of American society. Indeed, the industrial, financial, and political leaders of the metropolis who directed the new imperial thrust after 1896 had been significantly influenced in their own thinking by the agricultural and commercial interests that had pushed expansion for many generations. And, to an important degree, such metropolitans were responding as men who wanted to secure and consolidate their political control of the system.

From the outset, for example, colonial Americans had viewed the acquisition of more land as a primary way of solving their problems and fulfilling their purposes. That perpetual force for expansion (along with a more narrow possessiveness) contributed much to the campaign to drive the Indians ever further west, to the pressure to declare war on Great Britain during the winter of 1811–1812, to the determination to tear Texas and California away from Mexico, and to grab as much as possible of the Pacific Northwest.

Once a pioneer began to produce surpluses, moreover, he became a farm businessman looking for markets.* At any given moment, those who had just climbed that step on the ladder of entrepreneurial success sold their extra produce in the nearest village; and some never moved beyond the local market.

---

* I have explored this part of the story more fully in *The Roots of the Modern American Empire* (New York: Random House, 1969; paper, 1970).

Others, though they were larger operators, also relied on the domestic consumer. But tobacco and cotton farmers needed foreign markets from the outset, and the number of food producers whose surpluses went abroad increased steadily after the turn of the nineteenth century.

By the late 1830s, if not earlier, a decreasing number of farmers knew who *really* bought their surplus production. It might go down the road to the town trader and be consumed by his friends. But it might just as easily be shipped to a larger trading center. Yet it could also fill the belly, or cover the back, or go into the pipe of someone in another country. The American agricultural businessman was being ever more fully integrated into the world capitalist marketplace, and he soon realized that he had to sell more abroad if he was going to prosper.

The growth of farm exports benefited the traders and shippers who had always been deeply involved in market expansion, and who had never hesitated to pressure the government for active assistance and protection. By the end of the Civil War, those two groups had developed an even greater interest in overseas markets for agricultural surpluses. Their concern was soon supplemented by the similar involvement of the processors of crude foodstuffs, the directors of the booming railroads, and the southerners who developed a rough cotton textile industry. The reasons were simple: the explosive growth of commercial agriculture in the north and west created a surplus of massive proportions. Beef and pork, as well as wheat, were soon streaming abroad in what seemed to be an always rising river of exports. And the recovery of cotton production re-created that traditional surplus at a time when new competitors had entered the marketplace. As for the railroads, they viewed the export trade as crucial to their profits.

The most perceptive economic and political leaders of the metropolis, men like August Belmont, Senator James Gillespie Blaine, and the editors of key business and financial journals, promptly recognized the implications of those developments. They realized that the farm businessmen (and those pioneers who were becoming such entrepreneurs) constituted a majority of the politically active population. That meant it was vital to provide markets for such agricultural surpluses if they were to maintain—let alone consolidate—the power of the metropolis. They also understood that such exports played a vital part in the functioning of the metropolitan economy, as well as in the life of the individual farmer. The wrenching depression of the 1870s dramatized those points, and awakened other metropolitan leaders to the arrival of a new day: the industrial sector of the economy would soon need such foreign markets for its own profits. Not only did some firms like Rockefeller launch campaigns to penetrate world markets, but agricultural exports were crucial in the recovery of the system from the depression.

Such awareness was intensified by the uneven performance of the economy during the 1880s (and the disaffection thus generated among farm businessmen) and by the action of almost every European nation to limit the impact of American agricultural exports on its own economy (and its social structure). The agriculturalists demanded vigorous government assistance to keep old markets open and to find and penetrate new markets. They agitated for the regulation of railroads in order to retain more of the market price as profit. They attacked aliens and other foreigners who owned land in the United States, developing their own grass roots version of the argument that the frontier was the key to prosperity and welfare long before Professor Turner offered his more sophisticated version of that theme.

And they became ever more vociferously insistent, and emotionally aroused, to force metropolitan leaders to remonetize silver as part of the nation's currency system. That action, they maintained, would open the markets of Latin America and Asia (the Chinese would be converted from rice to wheat), undercut Great Britain's dominance of world trade (in general, as well as in wheat and cotton), and provide an effective demonstration of America's power and right to lead the world into a new era.

From the point of view of the metropolis, the threat from the provinces and the needs of its own economy began to converge. A great many farm businessmen were in trouble, and if they voted together they could control national policy. There was, in truth, a crisis before the Crisis of the 1890s. It was primarily defined by the challenge posed by the agricultural majority to the metropolitan businessmen, financiers and politicians—and their allies in the provinces—who had generally run the country since the Civil War. And, to heighten the sense of urgency, more and more influential metropolitan businessmen were calling for overseas economic expansion.

Such confrontations ultimately assume a sharp political form (even in societies that do not institutionalize their politics in some form of representative government), and that process began to develop in the United States at the end of the 1880s. Farm businessmen turned more purposefully and energetically to political action. The talk about a third party among members of the Northern and Southern Alliances, as well as the older Patrons of Husbandry, led on to the organization of the People's—or Populist—Party. Others, inspired by such men as William Jennings Bryan, chose to strike for control of the Democratic Party. The outlook of the established leaders of that organization, typified by the narrowly metropolitan outlook of President Grover Cleveland, was unequal to the challenge. Many, perhaps most, of these men accepted the inevitability of overseas economic expansion; but they were strongly inclined to approach it conservatively as a need of the maturing industrial part of the economy that would be met as part of a natural process which it was unwise to force.

That opened the way for the agricultural expansionists within the Democratic Party to seize the initiative. Republicans like Blaine and Benjamin Harrison recognized the resulting danger to their position: if they could not divide the farm businessmen, then the metropolis would lose its power and authority. Those men, and others within the Republican Party, also believed in the necessity of overseas economic expansion for the industrial-financial sector of the political economy. And so they boldly whacked the future on its bottom. They risked a destructive fight within the party, and the loss of upcoming elections, to commit the Republicans to a policy of expansion. That was their strategy: hopefully for prompt victory; surely for ultimate triumph.

Their approach provides a good example of the relevance of History—of how one can gain a sense and a feeling of the long view, of how to read the forces of one's own time, and of how to act to order and direct that momentum. The point is *not* that their answer is right for our time. It is rather that they had developed a historical perception that informed their understanding of their immediate reality, and that they were not put off by the possibility of short-term defeat.

Blaine and Harrison successfully committed the metropolitan Republican leadership to a foreign policy of overseas economic expansion. That approach, in their view, would win the urban businessmen, hold a crucial segment of northern and midwestern agricultural businessmen, and adapt the traditional American outlook to new circumstances. They won in the short-run—the election of 1888. They lost the next rounds—the elections of 1890 and 1892. And they won in the long-run—the decision for imperial expansion during the Crisis of the 1890s, the elections of 1896, 1900, 1904, 1908, and the total commitment of the Democratic Party under Woodrow Wilson to a policy of global expansion.

II. THE CRISIS OF THE 1890s AND THE TURN TO IMPERIALISM

As our manufacturing capacity largely exceeds the wants of home consumption, we shall either have to curtail the same by shutting up a great many establishments or we shall have to create a fresh outlet through export.

Iron Age, 1877

A foreign market becomes more and more necessary.

Bradstreet's, 1883

I am an exporter, I want the world.

CHARLES L. LOVERING, MASSACHUSETTS
TEXTILE EXECUTIVE, 1890

I believe, gentlemen, that the time has come for the United States as a great nation to take its place as one of the great commercial nations of the world.

POPULIST JERRY SIMPSON, 1894

If Cuba were free she would pass under American trade influences.

People's Party Paper, 1896

We want our own markets for our manufactures and agricultural products; we want a foreign market for our surplus products. . . . We want a reciprocity which will give us foreign markets for our surplus products, and in turn that will open our markets to foreigners for those products which they produce and which we do not.

WILLIAM MC KINLEY, JANUARY 1895

American factories are making more than the American people can use; American soil is producing more than they can consume. Fate has written our policy for us; the trade of the world must and shall be ours.

ALBERT J. BEVERIDGE, APRIL 1897

It seems to be conceded that every year we shall be confronted with an increasing surplus of manufactured goods for sale in foreign markets if American operatives and artisans are to be kept employed the year around. The enlargement of foreign consumption of the products of our mills and workshops has, therefore, become a serious problem of statesmanship as well as of commerce.

THE DEPARTMENT OF STATE, APRIL 1898

In the field of trade and commerce, we shall be the keen competitors of the richest and greatest powers, and they need no warning to be assured that in that struggle, we shall bring the sweat to their brows.

SECRETARY OF STATE JOHN HAY, 1899

Even protectionist organs are for free trade in China, where freedom is for the benefit of American manufacturers. Even anti-Imperialists welcome an Imperial policy which contemplates no conquests but those of commerce.

London Times, 1900

The Crisis of the 1890s was a major turning point in American history. It marked the close of the age of Jacksonian Laissez Nous Faire, and provided the setting for the death scene of the individual entrepreneur as the dynamic figure in American economic life. At the same time, it marked the triumph of a new system based upon, characterized by, and controlled by the corporation and similar large and highly organized groups throughout American society.

Initiated by the failures of the Philadelphia and Reading Railroad, and the National Cordage Company, early in the year, and symbolized by Industrial Black Friday of May 5, the Panic of 1893 quickly developed into a severe and double-cycle depression that lasted until 1898. "Never before," judged the *Commercial and Financial Chronicle* in August 1893, "has there been such a sudden and striking cessation of industrial activity. . . . Mills, factories, furnaces, mines nearly everywhere shut down in large numbers . . . and hundreds of thousands of men [were] thrown out of employment."

By the end of the first year, some 500 banks and 15,000 businesses had failed. One owner explained it very bluntly: "You have done business for nothing and still there has been no business." As for the farmers, railroad magnate James J. Hill reported on the basis of a survey throughout his empire that "very few of the farmers have any money, and the local banks are unable to help them." In mid-summer, 1894, there were 4,000,000 unemployed, and the editor of *Railroad Age* admitted that "never was human life held so cheap." Though the pathetic march of Coxey's Army, and the bitter failure of the Pullman Strike, became the symbols of the resulting unrest and violence, there were 30 other major strikes in progress at the time of the more famous railroad crisis in Chicago.

Because of its dramatic and extensive nature, the Crisis of the 1890s raised in many sections of American society the specter of chaos and revolution. Conservatives and reformers came to share the same conviction that something drastic had to be done, not only to solve the immediate problem, but to prevent the recurrence of such crises. That an expansionist foreign policy would provide such relief and prevention rapidly became an integral and vital part of all but an infinitesimal segment of the response to the general crisis. The issue that in a few years developed into what in the 1950s would have been called a Great Debate concerned *not* whether expansion should be pursued, but rather what *kind* of expansion should be undertaken.

This broad support for expansion, and particularly overseas economic expansion, rested upon agreement among conservatives and liberals (even many radicals joined in for a few
years), and Democrats and Republicans, from all sections and
groups of the country. A strong majority agreed that foreign
policy could and should play an important—if not crucial—
part in recovering from the depression of the 1890s and in
forestalling future difficulties.

This consensus was based on two ideas. The first, held by
manufacturers, farmers, merchants, and most other entrepreneurial groups in the economy, explained the depression and
social unrest as the result of not having enough markets for
their specific product—be it steel, shoes, or sows. Hence each
group looked at foreign policy as a means of obtaining markets
for its merchandise or services. That attitude, and the resulting
agitation for vigorous action, was apparent during the dispute
in 1894–1896 with Great Britain over the boundary between
Venezuela and British Guiana.

The militant stand taken by President Grover Cleveland
and Secretary of State Richard Olney did upset bankers in
New York (along with some in Boston), but most industrial
and commercial leaders throughout the country backed the
assertion of American predominance in the Western Hemisphere. And a bit earlier, in a less well-known episode, businessmen such as William Rockefeller of Standard Oil had
urged the Cleveland Administration to intervene boldly in the
Brazilian Revolution of 1893. Determined to protect and expand the trade with Brazil that was beginning to develop,
Cleveland deployed ships of the United States Navy in a way
that helped defeat the rebels who were opposed to the pattern
of unequal economic relations with America.

In both cases, Cleveland's action verified the striking pre-
diction made in 1893 by the editors of the Omaha *Bee News*.
Commenting upon his inauguration, they had welcomed Cleveland as one who could be relied upon "to promote as far as
possible the 'Manifest Destiny' doctrine." Cleveland's handling
of the American-conceived and executed revolution against
Queen Liliuokalani in Hawaii (1893) followed the same pattern. While he withdrew the proposed treaty of annexation
from consideration by the Senate, he did not carry through
on restoring the Queen to power. Instead, he recognized the

American-dominated Republic of Hawaii that was established on July 4, 1894, and maintained American naval forces in the islands.

Despite the narrower and more orthodox outlook he had revealed during the 1880s, therefore, Cleveland became significantly more openly expansionist during his second term as president. Several factors help explain his increased vigor. He had always agreed about the desirability of larger markets (and easier access to raw materials) for the metropolis, and the deepening economic troubles undoubtedly made him more willing to act directly and forcefully in support of that policy. And, though he was unresponsive to most agrarian reform proposals, he knew he faced a growing revolt within the Democratic Party and he could hardly have missed the appeal of the Republican campaign for market expansion. Finally, he was a strong, though not jingoistic, nationalist.*

From the time he entered the White House in 1893, Cleveland was subjected to a rising clamor for vigorous overseas economic expansion, and to ever more troublesome political problems. Agreeing with labor leader Samuel Gompers that "the great storehouses are glutted," the sometimes radical farm leader "Sockless" Jerry Simpson argued that the "surplus must seek foreign markets." Flour millers agreed, as did the wool manufacturers, the large industrial leaders who organized the National Association of Manufacturers in 1895, and spokesmen for the National Live Stock Exchange. Editorials and articles in *Scientific American, Engineering Magazine,* and *Iron Age* supported the same solution. And the *United States Investor* concluded that "an outlet for surplus stocks becomes an imperative necessity." Such agitation and pressure had become so general and insistent by the end of 1897 that the Department of State began to print and distribute its consular reports, which it described as being prepared "for the benefit of American industries seeking foreign outlets," on a daily schedule.

The second idea about expansion was much broader and took account of the particular outlook of all special interests.

---

* Here consult W. LaFeber, *The New Empire* (Ithaca: Cornell University Press, 1963); T. J. McCormick, *China Market, America's Quest for Informal Empire, 1893–1901* (Chicago: Quadrangle Books, 1967); and M. Plesur, *America's Outward Thrust, Approaches to Foreign Affairs, 1865–1890* (DeKalb: Northern Illinois University Press, 1971).

It explained America's democracy and prosperity in the past as the result of expansion across the continent and, to a lesser degree, overseas into the markets of the world. Either implicitly or explicitly, depending on the form in which it was presented, the idea pointed to the practical conclusion that expansion was the way to stifle unrest, preserve democracy, and restore prosperity.

The generalization about the relationship between expansion, democracy, and prosperity became most well-known as the frontier thesis advanced by the historian Frederick Jackson Turner. Turner first presented his argument in a formal paper before the American Historical Association in December, 1893, but in 1896 he published a version of his interpretation for the general public in the *Atlantic Monthly*. "For really three centuries the dominant fact of American life has been expansion," he explained, and then went on to suggest that "the demands for a vigorous foreign policy, for an interoceanic canal, for a revival of our power upon the seas, and for the extension of American influence to outlying islands and adjoining countries, are indications that the movement will continue."

Although Turner's formulation of the argument that prosperity and representative government were tied causally to expansion became the most generally known version, the central idea was put forward with but minor variations by many other intellectuals during the same years. One such figure was Captain Alfred Thayer Mahan, who began his career as a naval strategist with anti-expansionist ideas. He first held that expansion would lead to centralized government and huge armaments, which would in turn promote wars, repression, and ultimately revolution. But his reading in mercantilist thought of the seventeenth and eighteenth centuries, and the economic difficulties and political unrest in the United States after 1888, combined to change his mind. Becoming a vigorous expansionist, he championed a big navy on the grounds that the United States had to move outward "to seek the welfare of the country." And though he often clothed his arguments in the rhetoric of Christianity and the White Man's Burden, Mahan essentially derived his proposals from what he termed "the importance of distant markets and the relation to them of our own immense powers of production."

Still another such expansionist intellectual was Brooks Adams, brother of the more famous Henry Adams and close friend of such political leaders as Theodore Roosevelt, Henry Cabot Lodge, and John Hay. Reasoning in terms that purported to be valid for all known civilizations, Adams insisted that expansion was the key to wealth and welfare and concluded that the United States would stagnate if it did not consolidate its position in Latin America and push on across the Pacific to make Asia an economic colony. And finally, such expansionism was also implicit in the writings of William Graham Sumner, an economist and sociologist who believed almost fanatically in the virtue and viability of the old order of laissez faire individualism.

Those big ideas about expansion evoked responses from different ideological and political groups in the country. Turner's statement of the frontier thesis, for example, appealed to the wing of the reform movement which favored using antitrust laws and political reforms to preserve democracy and prosperity.* Adams, on the other hand, had his largest following among other reformers who accepted the large corporation and the giant banks but wanted the national government to regulate and control them in behalf of the general welfare.

Sumner's role is more difficult to judge. For one thing, his influence was connected with that of Herbert Spencer, the British philosopher of laissez faire. For another, and unlike Turner and Adams, Sumner did not himself advocate an expansionist foreign policy. But one of his central ideas asserted that it was "the opening of the new continents and the great discoveries and inventions which have made this modern age. . . . The chief source of new power, however, has been the simplest of all, that is, an extension of population over new land." This explanation implied further expansion, just as his defense of laissez faire sanctioned such action as a natural right. In any event, Sumner's influence—whatever it amounted to—affected the more conservative section of American society which insisted that the principles and practices of laissez faire offered the best answers to all economic and social problems.

Those specific pressures and general ideas in favor of ex-

---

* Ultimately, of course, Turner affected the thinking of all groups; and from the beginning he attracted the enthusiastic interest of Theodore Roosevelt.

pansion rapidly gained strength after 1890. By 1895, many individuals and groups were stressing the importance of expansion as a way to solve domestic economic problems. The editors of *Harper's* magazine outlined the approach rather bluntly as early as 1893. "The United States will hold the key," they explained, "unlocking the gates to the commerce of the world, and closing them to war. If we have fighting to do, it will be fighting to keep the peace." Others saw expansion as a way to avoid labor unrest—or even revolution. "We are on the eve of a very dark night," warned businessman F. L. Stetson in 1894, "unless a return of commercial prosperity relieves popular discontent." A bit later, Senator William Frye was even more specific. "We must have the market [of China] or we shall have revolution."

As Frye's remark suggests, politicians responded very promptly to the growing interest in expansion. Some of them, like secretaries of state Gresham and Olney, and Theodore Roosevelt and Senator Lodge, were in some respects actually leading the agitation. "We have a record of conquest, colonization and expansion unequalled by any people in the Nineteenth Century," Lodge boasted in 1895. "We are not to be curbed now. . . . For the sake of our commercial supremacy in the Pacific we should control the Hawaiian islands and maintain our influence in Samoa." And at the other end of the political spectrum, Populist Jerry Simpson cried out in anguish that "we are driven from the markets of the world!" and threw his support behind the campaign for a big battleship Navy.

Senator Nelson Aldrich likewise demanded vigorous action in what he referred to as the "bitter contest" for "industrial supremacy" in the markets of the world. And in Wisconsin, the young Robert M. La Follette (who later became a critic of American expansion) opened his political career by calling in 1897 for a big Navy. He also suggested that Spain's island possessions throughout the world would provide excellent bases for the fleet. Not too surprisingly, La Follette judged that McKinley was headed in the right direction on foreign policy: "No man since Monroe has promised so much for the future wealth, safety and glory of this great republic." Still others, such as Woodrow Wilson, argued in the same years for expansion as a way to strengthen the executive branch of the government and thereby improve the general effectiveness of American politics. All in all, and as symbolized by the Republican Party's platform of 1896, the politicians concluded that "enlarged markets" would produce votes as well as profits.

Even the traditional policy of tariff protection was questioned and modified by Americans who saw reciprocity treaties as a way of penetrating foreign markets. When it was organized in 1895, for example, the National Association of Manufacturers devoted over half its original program to the problems of expanding foreign markets. One of its specific proposals favored reciprocity treaties as a "practical method of extending our international commerce." And within a year the organization had established special commissions to push business expansion in Latin America and Asia. Its leaders also emphasized the role of such expansion in preventing labor unrest and in making it possible to obey the laws on child labor and yet earn a profit.

While he was president of the N.A.M. in 1897, Theodore C. Search summarized the general feeling within the business community. "Many of our manufacturers have outgrown or are outgrowing their home markets," he explained, "and the expansion of our foreign trade is their only promise of relief." Similar organizations, such as the Pan American Society and the American Asiatic Association, concentrated on promoting an expansionist foreign policy in one particular area. As the *Journal of Commerce* observed in 1897, more and more American economic leaders were fixing their eyes on "the industrial supremacy of the world." A growing number of bankers also began to consider overseas economic expansion as an attractive field for investment. Some favored direct loans to foreigners (which often strengthened those who were competing with American firms), while others preferred to finance the operations of companies in the United States. Such differences of opinion over strategy, and the antagonisms developed in competitive struggles, led to conflict within the financial community, and between the bankers and industrialists. Furthermore, the bankers suffered persistent difficulties in the years prior to World War I in raising enough capital to carry through their bigger projects. But the central point is that the financiers did support the general drive for overseas economic expansion.

From the outset, moreover, these economic organizations

enjoyed close ties with leading politicians. The founding convention of the N.A.M. was keynoted, for example, by McKinley. He similarly pushed overseas economic expansion in his address at the opening of the Philadelphia Commercial Museum in 1897. And the N.A.M., no doubt encouraged by McKinley's appointment of Frank A. Vanderlip (Vice President of the National City Bank) as Assistant Secretary of the Treasury, maintained the liaison in its vigorous efforts to win such objectives as reform and enlargement of the consular service. As Theodore Search explained in a letter shortly after McKinley was inaugurated as President, "the manufacturers of the United States never were so deeply concerned in foreign trade as at the present time." And in a similar, and equally vigorous manner, the American Asiatic Association pressed its plans for expansion across the Pacific upon politicians and government bureaucrats.

Such general and active support for economic expansion is often neglected when considering the coming of the Spanish-American War. It is customary to explain the war as a crusade to save the Cubans or to interpret it in psychological terms as a release for national frustrations arising from the depression. But while it may be granted that economic leaders preferred not to go to war as long as they could attain their objectives without it, and although it may be useful to talk about Americans developing a national compulsion to punish Spain for mistreating Cuba, it is equally apparent that such interpretations do not take account of several key aspects of the coming of the war. For one thing, it is clear that various groups saw war with Spain over Cuba as a means to solve other problems. They reached that conclusion, moreover, at the end of a conscious exercise in considering alternatives— not in a blind and irrational outburst of patriotic or ideological fervor. Many agrarians viewed it as a way to monetize silver at home and thus pave the way for a general expansion of their exports to the sterling areas of the world. Some labor groups thought it would ease or resolve immediate economic difficulties. And many important businessmen, as contrasted with the editors of some business publications, came to support war for specific commercial purposes as well as for general economic reasons.

If there is any one key to understanding the coming of the war with Spain, it very probably lies in the growing conviction among top economic and political leaders that American military intervention was necessary in order to clean up the Cuban mess so that domestic *and other foreign policy* issues could be dealt with efficiently and effectively. It should be made clear, however, that in suggesting this explanation of the war there is no direct or implicit argument that other considerations were nonexistent or unimportant. Nor is it being hinted that the whole affair was the product of some conspiracy in high places. Consciousness of purpose is not conspiracy, even if those who are addicted to explaining everything in terms of irrational psychology often seem unable to distinguish between the two. There was consciousness of purpose in high places—as there should be, whatever one's individual judgment on either the goals or the means—but there was no conspiracy.

It likewise seems wise to emphasize the obvious, but nevertheless often overlooked, distinction between explicit economic motives and a more general economic estimate of the situation. Men have on occasion acted in certain ways because their pocketbook nerve prompted them to do so. They still do. Even historians have been known to change jobs (or their points of view) for more money, as well as for their egos, or for better research facilities. And the actions of some influential figures during the period leading up to the war with Spain can only be understood in that light. They wanted intervention to save and extend their property holdings. In a similar way, other men can and do act on the basis of an equally narrow political calculation. Some Americans wanted intervention on the grounds that it would save their personal and party political fortunes.

Yet it is also quite possible, and not at all unusual, for men to act on the basis of a broader, more inclusive organization and integration of information and desires. Sometimes such a conception of the world—or *Weltanschauung*, as it is more formally called—orders data in such a way that political, religious or cultural values are held to be the crucial factors. Thus some Americans undoubtedly supported war against Spain because according to their view of the world it was impossible to have peace or prosperity or good government in Cuba as long as it was ruled by Catholics.

To an extensive degree, however, American leaders of the 1890s entertained a *Weltanschauung* that organized data around economic criteria. They explained difficulties, and likewise advanced solutions and alternatives, by reference to economic phenomena. This did not make them economically motivated in the pocketbook sense, but it did lead them to believe that their objectives in the political and social realms could only be attained through economic means. To somewhat oversimplify the point to gain clarity, it can be summarized in this way.

Men like McKinley and other national leaders thought about America's problems and welfare in an inclusive, systematized way that emphasized economics. Wanting democracy and social peace, they argued that economic depression threatened those objectives, and concluded that overseas economic expansion provided a primary means of ending that danger. They did not want war per se, let alone war in order to increase their own personal fortunes. But their own conception of the world ultimately led them into war in order to solve the problems in the way that they considered necessary and best. These general remarks bearing on historical analysis and interpretation should be kept in mind throughout the book.*

There are three central considerations to be evaluated and connected when explaining and interpreting the war against Spain. The first is that the basic policy of presidents Cleveland and McKinley was to secure the defeat of the revolution in Cuba and what they repeatedly and explicitly called "the pacification of the island" under Spanish rule. Both presidents wanted to get on with other domestic and foreign programs and policies; in particular, both were intensely concerned with vigorous overseas economic expansion into Latin America and Asia.

The outbreak of the Sino-Japanese War in 1894 upset Cleveland considerably, for example, and he formally warned the Congress and the country that the conflict "deserves our gravest consideration by reason of its disturbance of our

---

* See *The Roots of the Modern American Empire* for a more extended discussion of the coming of the war; and the problem of reconstructing a *Weltanschauung*.

growing commercial interests." * Cleveland not only repeated the same general theme in his message of December 2, 1895, but explicitly tied that problem to the outbreak of revolution in Cuba that was "deranging the commercial exchanges of the island, of which our country takes the predominant share." Shortly thereafter, in March and April 1896, Secretary of State Olney told the Spanish that the United States wanted to help "pacify the island."

Speaking with "candor," Olney explained Cleveland's "anxiety," and bluntly repeated the President's "earnest desire for the prompt and permanent pacification of that island." The United States wanted to avoid "a war of races" within the island, and sought "the non-interruption of extensive trade relations [and] . . . the prevention of that wholesale destruction of property on the island which . . . is utterly destroying American investments that should be of immense value, and is utterly impoverishing great numbers of American citizens."

After waiting eight months, Cleveland, on December 7, 1896, personally and publicly reiterated his desire for "the pacification of the island." America's concern, he bluntly pointed out, was "by no means of a wholly sentimental or philanthropic character."—"Our actual pecuniary interest in it is second only to that of the people and government of Spain." In the original draft of his message, Cleveland proposed to conclude with a warning strikingly reminiscent of the *Harper's* magazine remark of 1893 that "if we have fighting to do, it will be fighting to keep the peace." Cleveland originally put it this way: either Spain must end the rebellion promptly or "this government will be compelled to protect its own interests and those of its citizens, which are coincident with those of humanity and civilization generally, by resorting to such measures as will promptly restore to the Island the blessings of peace." He even added, again in the original draft, a deadline specified as "the coming of the New Year." †

The increasing vigor and militance (and even self-righteousness) of Cleveland's approach to Cuban affairs cannot be ex-

* Perhaps it will be helpful to remind the reader that statesmen in general—and those of Cleveland's temperament in particular—do not resort to such phrases as "our gravest consideration" unless they are very serious.

† I am indebted to Professor Walter LeFeber of Cornell University for a copy of this first draft of Cleveland's message.

plained or understood in isolation. The ever more threatening agitation of the agricultural businessmen was a major factor. So was the rising American concern about developments in the Far East. Japan's attack on China had thrown open the lid of Pandora's Box of Imperialistic Rivalries, and American interests such as the American China Development Company (and other firms and banks) were caught and whipsawed in the resulting free-for-all between Japan, Russia, France, England, and Germany.

In the fall of 1896, however, China turned to the United States in an effort to protect its own position by aligning itself with a major power that had not indicated any significant interest in territorial concessions. At the same time they offered a railroad concession to Americans, a delegation of Chinese officials visited the United States. Received and entertained by public and private leaders, the Chinese clearly accomplished their initial objective of intensifying American interest in and concern over economic gains in Asia.

Cleveland's remarks on Cuba in the first draft of his December 1896 message would clearly seem to follow from that anticipated involvement in Asia—particularly since the President had called for the "gravest consideration" of that issue as early as 1894. But Cleveland had just been defeated by McKinley in the election of November 1896, and his position was obviously difficult. As a responsible politician, Cleveland no doubt realized that it would be unfair (and against tradition) to issue an ultimatum that would entrap his successor. He may even have been explicitly advised that McKinley had told Lodge that he "very naturally does not want to be obliged to go to war as soon as he comes in." Nor is it very likely that Cleveland judged it wise on second thought to go out of office as the man who gave the country a war as his farewell gift. In the message as delivered, therefore, he contented himself with the clear warning that "it can not be reasonably assumed that the hitherto expectant attitude of the United States will be indefinitely maintained."

Upon entering the White House, McKinley reiterated Cleveland's demand for prompt "pacification of the island." But in acting on that policy he began very quickly to squeeze Spain (and himself and the United States) into an ever more difficult position. To some extent, this pressure on Spain was prompted by the activity of various groups within the United States which insisted on more vigorous and dramatic action. This has led some historians to conclude that the pro-rebel newspaper campaign against Spain was primarily responsible for the war. Others have reduced the problem to a political issue, arguing that McKinley ultimately accepted war to sustain or save the influence and power of the Republican Party (and his position within it).

These interpretations which stress domestic pressure on the administration do define and raise the second principal consideration in any evaluation of the war. But the wild and irresponsible press campaign initiated and directed by William Randolph Hearst and Joseph Pulitzer never succeeded in whipping up any sustained hysteria for war until early in 1898—*if even then.* The evidence is overwhelming that the psychological Rubicon was not crossed until a few weeks after the sinking of the battleship *Maine* on February 15, 1898. As for the argument that politics was the key to the war, that begs the real point about what provoked the political pressure. The agitation that scared metropolitan (and other) Republicans came from militant agriculturalists who wanted markets—and a symbolic and a real assault on autocratic European power throughout the world.

Several other factors appear far more significant in explaining McKinley's increasing pressure on Spain. One of them is intimately connected with his continuation of Cleveland's policy of demanding prompt pacification. For along with other Americans, McKinley reacted against the very ruthlessness that the thinly veiled warnings from the United States encouraged Spain to employ. In insisting upon certain ends while prohibiting the use of forceful measures, McKinley was more the victim of his own irresponsibility than a puppet jerked about by the yellow press of Pulitzer and Hearst.

Furthermore, McKinley was being increasingly pressured by metropolitan expansionists. Some of those men were economic entrepreneurs acting on narrow interest-conscious motives. They wanted their property protected and their opportunities secured. That outlook was typified by Chauncey M. Depew of the New York Central Railroad, Alonzo B. Hepburn of the National City Bank, Edward F. Cragin of the Union League Club who had ties with the Nicaraguan Canal

Company and Standard Oil, Collis P. Huntington of the Southern Pacific Railroad, financier August Belmont, and John S. McCook of New York who was a railroad lawyer also active in organizing overseas economic ventures. Still another group was made up of broad-gauged expansionists like Roosevelt and Lodge, who saw a war with Spain as a way to bring empire to America by Caesarean section. "I have been hoping and working ardently," Roosevelt candidly admitted, "to bring about our interference in Cuba."

Finally, McKinley himself made it precisely clear in July 1897, that he was determined to finish up the Cuban crisis in order to proceed with other matters. This became apparent in the long instructions given his new minister to Spain (who was also a close friend). The document should also serve to correct once and for all the mistaken impression that McKinley drifted this way and that in response to whatever political winds were blowing. He knew quite well what he desired to accomplish. "The chronic condition of trouble . . . ," it was explained, "causes disturbance in the social and political condition of our own peoples. . . . A continuous irritation within our own borders injuriously affects the normal functions of business, and tends to delay the condition of prosperity to which this country is entitled."

Though it was not unique in the archives of diplomatic history, this assignment of responsibility for domestic welfare to a foreign power was a very striking and unequivocal example of that approach. It revealed beyond any possibility of misunderstanding the inner logic of all expansionist thought *whereby both opportunity and difficulty, good and evil, are externalized.* As Frederick Jackson Turner once acknowledged in a moment of deep insight, the frontier itself was "a gate of escape" from existing responsibilities; and when men began to act on the frontier thesis they merely sustained that pattern of defining issues in such a way that the solutions became progressively dependent upon external factors. Stated as directly as possible, the point is that none of the foreign powers involved—either in Cuba or in Asia—actually threatened the United States, nor did they have any inherent primary responsibility for what McKinley called "the prosperity to which this country is entitled." It was only the definition of American well-being primarily in terms of overseas economic expansion, a definition formulated by Americans, that led to the conclusion that the foreign nations had such obligations.

The related consideration concerning the way that McKinley and other influential Americans envisaged the relationship linking prosperity, social peace, and foreign policy became increasingly clarified during the late summer and early fall of 1897. By August, for example, businessmen were generally convinced that recovery from the depression was being generated and sustained by overseas economic expansion. As a result, many of them began to change their earlier fears that intervention in Cuba would delay prosperity. Instead, they began to feel that it would be wise to remove that distraction so that the new frontier of exports could be given full attention.

In addition, many of those who had sympathized with or actively supported the rebels began to fear that a successful revolution would cause grave difficulties by bringing the lower class to power. McKinley was advised of this very explicitly by a correspondent who reported the growing anxiety that "the troublesome, adventurous, and non-responsible class" would control the island "causing chaos, injury, and loss beyond redemption."

Probably even more important in strengthening the inclination to intervene to pacify Cuba was the renewed outbreak of trouble in the Far East. Germany's seizure of Kiaochow on November 14, 1897, intensified existing fears that Japan and the European powers were going to divide China among themselves. Whether they defined the issue in narrow interest-conscious economic terms, or in a broader analysis that stressed the need of the American economic *system* to expand overseas, American leaders became very disturbed. Most of them looked to Asia, and to China in particular, as the great market which would absorb the surplus. It is beside the point that this did not happen; at issue is the nature of American thought and action at that time.

The influence of these events in the late summer and fall of 1897 was revealed in many striking episodes. In September, for example, Roosevelt discussed personally with McKinley a memorandum in which he advocated war in November, *and specifically recommended that "we take and retain the Philippines."* [Emphasis added.] In November, Senator Orville H.

Platt and a member of the House of Representatives saw McKinley and added their advice that Manila was the key to the entire Asian crisis.* In January 1898, a petition from over 35 leading New York businessmen (many of whom had raised their voices—and pens—as early as May 1897) asked McKinley to intervene with "prompt and efficient measures" in Cuba to put an end to their "tremendous losses" and restore "a most valuable commercial field." And in February other entrepreneurs of the New York State Chamber of Commerce asked for similar action in Asia. Deeply concerned about the crisis in China and its effect upon "the privileges enjoyed under existing treaty rights by Americans," they "respectfully and earnestly" requested "the prompt and energetic defense" of such rights and "the preservation and protection of their important commercial interest in that Empire."

These activities clarify the third central aspect of the coming of the war: the McKinley Administration knew that an important and growing segment of the business community wanted prompt and effective action in Cuba and Asia. Until some time in the latter part of March (or perhaps even the first week in April), McKinley undoubtedly wanted to end the Cuban affair without war. This seems quite clear despite his series of ultimatums to Spain that included a demand for independence (under American guidance) if the United States thought it necessary. But by the last 10 days in March (by which time Germany had secured a 99-year lease to Kiaochow with extensive economic concessions throughout the province of Shantung), the business community was ready to accept war.

A special emissary sent by McKinley to sound out the New York area reported that such key figures as John Jacob Astor, Thomas Fortune Ryan, William Rockefeller, Stuyvesant Fish, and spokesmen for the House of Morgan were "feeling militant." Then Lodge advised McKinley on March 21, 1898, that Boston economic leaders had concluded that "one shock and then an end was better than a succession of spasms such as we must have if this war in Cuba went on." And four days later, the President received by telegram the following intelli-

---

* Here again I am indebted to Professor LeFeber, and to Professor Thomas McCormick of the University of Wisconsin, for sharing documents with me.

gence from a New York correspondent. "Big corporations here now believe we will have war. Believe all would welcome it as relief to suspense. . . . Don't think it necessary now mince matters."

Now the purpose of all this analysis is not to argue or suggest that McKinley went to war because important economic leaders told him to do so.* Neither is it to imply that the public clamor that arose after the sinking of the *Maine* was insignificant. The point is quite different. It is that American leaders went to war with Spain as part of, and as the consequence of, a general outlook which externalized the opportunity and the responsibility for America's domestic welfare; broadly in terms of vigorous overseas economic expansion into Latin America and Asia; and specifically in terms of Spain's inability to pacify Cuba by means (and within time limits) acceptable to the United States, and the separate but nevertheless related necessity of acting in Asia to prevent the exclusion of American interests from China.

This basic *Weltanschauung* underlying American diplomacy led directly to the great debate of 1898–1901 over the proper strategy and tactics of such expansion, a debate that was resolved by the promulgation of the famous Open Door Notes of 1899 and 1900. This national argument is usually interpreted as a battle between imperialists led by Roosevelt and Lodge and anti-imperialists led by William Jennings Bryan, Grover Cleveland, and Carl Schurz. It is far more accurate and illuminating, however, to view it as a three-cornered fight. The third group was a coalition of businessmen, intellectuals, and politicians who opposed traditional colonialism and advocated instead a policy of an open door through which America's preponderant economic strength would enter and dominate all underdeveloped areas of the world. This coalition won the debate, and the Open Door Policy became the strategy of American foreign policy for the next half-century.

Discounted in recent years as a futile and naive gesture in a world of harsh reality, the Open Door Policy was in fact a brilliant strategic stroke which led to the gradual extension

---

* It may be relevant to remind the reader that the United States did in fact start the war by blockading Cuban ports on April 22, 1898; and that the Congress dated its formal declaration of war as of April 21, 1898. Spain declared war on April 24, 1898.

of American economic and political power throughout the
world. If it ultimately failed, it was not because it was foolish
or weak, but because it was so successful. The empire that
was built according to the strategy and tactics of the Open
Door Notes engendered the antagonisms created by all empires, and it is that opposition which posed so many difficulties
for American diplomacy after World War II.

At the outset, it is true, the debate between imperialists and
anti-imperialists revolved around an actual issue—colonialism.
Touched off by the specific question of what to do with Cuba
and the Philippines, the battle raged over whether they should
be kept as traditional colonies or established as quasi-inde-
pendent nations under the benevolent supervision of the
United States. Though the differences were significant at the
beginning of the argument, it is nevertheless clear that they
were never absolute. The Open Door Notes took the fury out
of the fight. And within five years the issue was almost nonexistent. The anti-imperialists who missed that changing nature
of the discussion were ultimately shocked and disillusioned
when Bryan became Secretary of State and began to practice
what they thought he condemned.

Such critics were mistaken in attacking Bryan as a back-
slider or a hypocrite. Bryan's foreign policy was not classical
colonialism, but neither was it anti-imperial. He had never
shirked his share of the white man's burden, though perhaps
he did shoulder a bit more of the ideological baggage than
the economic luggage. He was as eager for overseas markets as
any but the most extreme agrarian and industrial expansionists. As with most other farmers, labor leaders, and businessmen, economic logic accounts for much of Bryan's anticolonialism. Looking anxiously for markets abroad as a way of
improving conditions at home, all such men feared and opposed the competition of native labor. It was that consideration, as much as racism and Christian fundamentalism, that
prompted Bryan to assert that "the Filipinos cannot be citizens
without endangering our civilization."

Bryan's program for the Philippines symbolizes the kind of
imperial anticolonialism that he advocated. Once the Philippine insurrection was crushed, he proposed that the United
States should establish "a stable form of government" in the
islands and then "protect the Philippines from outside inter-

ference while they work out their destiny, just as we have protected the republics of Central and South America, and are, by the Monroe Doctrine, pledged to protect Cuba." Opposition spokesmen gleefully pointed out that this was the substance of their own program.

Bryan also supported the kind of expansion favored by such Democrats as Cleveland. "The best thing of the kind I have ever heard," Cleveland had remarked of Olney's famous assertion that the United States "is practically sovereign on this continent, and its fiat is law upon the subjects to which it confines its interposition." As for Hawaii, Cleveland (and Bryan) wanted to control "the ports of a country so near to Japan and China" without the bother and responsibilities of formal annexation. Informal empire is perhaps the most accurate description of such a program. Both men, along with many other so-called anti-imperialists, favored the overseas expansion of the American economic system and the extension of American authority throughout the world.

So, too, did such men as Roosevelt, Hay and Lodge. At first, however, they stressed the acquisition of colonies, if not in the traditional sense of colonialism, at least in the pattern of administrative colonialism developed by Great Britain after the Indian Mutiny of 1857. Thus the early arguments between Roosevelt and Bryan were to some point. But the Roosevelt imperialists soon modified that initial emphasis in their argument. Part of this was due to their success in pushing through the annexation of Hawaii on July 7, 1898, and to the occupation of Puerto Rico later in the same month.

Even more significant, however, was the way that the rebellion of native Philippine nationalists against American troops forced many anti-imperialists to retreat from their blanket opposition to any territorial acquisitions. To be sure, some of them dwelt upon the obvious: the rebellion symbolized all the evils of empire and should be taken as a clear warning against imperialism. But others interpreted it to mean that the United States would have to take the islands if it was to secure a base for the economic struggle in China, and in their view such a base was absolutely essential. And others, like Bryan, argued that taking the islands was a lesser evil than continuing the war against Spain. Thus the logic of expansionism revealed its strange patterns: just as many had agreed to go to war to pacify Cuba, so in the end did others agree to acquire a colony in order to make peace.

Because it generated so much intense emotion and wild rhetoric, the debate between the Roosevelt and Bryan groups tended in subsequent years to create the mistaken notion that McKinley and his close advisors in the executive branch of the government were largely passive servants waiting patiently for outsiders to decide the issue. Such was not the case. After all, McKinley had discussed the importance of Manila to America's objectives in Asia at least as early as September 1897. And he ordered American troops (already staged in San Francisco) to sail for the Philippines even before he received direct, official confirmation of Dewey's victory at Manila Bay. Subsequent analyses and actions established McKinley and his close associates as vigorous participants in the debate itself, and further suggest that those men did much to work out the strategy of empire that was ultimately accepted by the country at large.

In particular, the long "Review of the World's Commerce," prepared by the State Department's Bureau of Foreign Commerce and dated April 25, 1898, made it apparent that the McKinley Administration understood quite clearly the basic features of the expansionist outlook advocated by Brooks Adams and other unofficial spokesmen. The central and common assumptions as phrased by the Department of State were that "the ability of the United States to compete successfully with the most advanced industrial nations in any part of the world, as well as with those nations in their home markets, can no longer be seriously questioned," and that "every year we shall be confronted with an increasing surplus of manufactured goods for sale in foreign markets if American operatives and artisans are to be kept employed the year around."

This meant very simply that "the enlargement of foreign consumption of the products of our mills and workshops has, therefore, become a serious problem of statesmanship." The "zealous co-operation" of government officials acting under "special instructions" to help private companies was naturally necessary, and had already been undertaken. But the essence of the problem was to devise a strategy that would prevent other industrial powers from pre-empting the underdeveloped areas of the world. "We ourselves have become a competitor in the world-wide struggle for trade," the Department emphasized, and proceeded to define the regions of crucial importance.

China was of course given first attention: it "has, for many years, been one of the most promising fields for American enterprise, industry, and capital." Access to that market, "under conditions which would secure equality of opportunity to the United States, would doubtless result in immense gains to our manufacturers." Thus it was mandatory to prevent Japan and the European powers from excluding the United States: that was an "immediate and most important" objective. But any similar partition of Africa raised "considerations of an economic character of almost equal magnitude," as did any drive by the nations of Europe to enlarge their economic position in Latin America.

Feeling that "nowhere else" were such matters "of more interest" than in China, and very worried about the "large excesses above the demands of home consumption," Secretary of State Day initiated, in June 1898, a special study of the China situation. As such actions indicated, the McKinley Administration was very pointedly and vigorously dealing with the issue of overseas economic expansion without waiting for the end of the debate about imperialism.

All of the elements that went into the making of the Open Door Policy converged within the McKinley Administration as the President appointed his commission to make peace with Spain. Acting individually, and through groups such as the American Asiatic Association and the N.A.M., private economic operators pressured the government with their desires and recommendations. John Hay was appointed Secretary of State in the fall of 1898, and that gave the Adams-Lodge-Roosevelt group an additional lever of influence for their ideas. And McKinley himself made it obvious that the administration already had the central idea of the final policy it was to evolve. For in his instructions to the peace commission of September 16, 1898, he specifically defined the broad issue as "the enlargement of American trade" in the Orient. Then, after discounting the necessity of acquiring "large territorial possessions" in order to win such trade, he explicitly used the phrase "the open door for ourselves" to describe the preferred strategy.

This is of course significant as well as striking, for the first of the Open Door Notes was not written until 1899. It remains so even after recalling that the central idea of obtaining "equality with all competing nations in the conditions of access to the markets" had provided the basis of American policy at the time of the International Conference on the Congo held in Berlin during the winter of 1884–85. For in that situation, as in Asia in 1897–99, the United States confronted rivals who already had spheres of influence or formal colonies. In any event, the point is not to provide some artificial birthday for the policy of the open door, but rather to indicate how the policy emerged from the interplay between private and public leaders.

Perhaps nothing illustrates this as neatly as the way that the arguments inside McKinley's peace commission brought out almost every shade of opinion. Even so, everyone agreed that the United States had at the very least to retain a port and a naval base. Three considerations seem to have convinced the administration to keep all the Philippines. For one thing, the crisis caused by the native rebellion was most easily—though by no means most successfully—resolved in that fashion. In another way, the serious inherent difficulties of keeping the main island of Luzon, or the key city of Manila, without disrupting the political economy of the remainder of the islands soon became apparent even to those who originally favored that kind of solution. And finally, the vigor of German and other expansionism in China exerted considerable influence on the thinking of the administration.

Though many of them felt that they had suffered a terrible defeat in the decision to retain the Philippines, the anti-imperialists actually won their domestic war over fundamental policy with the issuance of the Open Door Notes. Hay's dispatches of 1899 and 1900 distilled the conglomeration of motives, pressures, and theories into a classic strategy of non-colonial imperial expansion. Based on the assumption of what Brooks Adams called "America's economic supremacy," the policy of the open door was designed to clear the way and establish the conditions under which America's preponderant economic power would extend the American system throughout the world without the embarrassment and inefficiency of traditional colonialism. As Hay indicated with obvious anticipation and confidence in September 1899, the expectation was that "we shall bring the sweat to their brows."

Hay's first note of September 6, 1899, asserted the proposition that American entrepreneurs "shall enjoy perfect equality of treatment for their commerce and navigation" within all of China—*including the spheres of interest held by foreign powers.* That principle was soon extended to other underdeveloped areas. His second note of July 3, 1900, was designed to prevent other nations from extending the formal colonial system to China. That axiom was also applied to other regions in later years. Hay also circulated a third dispatch among the powers. Though rarely linked with the first two in discussions of the Open Door Notes, it was nevertheless an integral part of the general policy statement.* In that document, Hay made it plain that the United States considered loans to be an inherent part of commerce. The connection was always implicit, if not rather obvious. "It is impossible to separate these two forms of business activity," as one businessman remarked at the time, "since it is axiomatic that trade follows the loan." The relationship was also and without any question in the minds of American policy-makers when the first notes were written, since such loans were being sought and discussed as early as 1897. Hay's purpose was to close every formal loophole through which America's competitors might seek to counter the strategy of the open door.

The Open Door Notes took the substance out of the debate between the imperialists and the anti-imperialists. The argument trailed on with the inertia characteristic of all such disagreements, but the nation recognized and accepted Hay's policy as a resolution of the original issue. Former Secretary of State John W. Foster summarized this point quite accurately in the *Independent* at the end of 1900. "Whatever difference of opinion may exist among American citizens respecting the policy of territorial expansion, all seem to be agreed upon the desirability of commercial expansion. In fact it has come to be a necessity to find new and enlarged markets for our agricultural and manufactured products. We cannot maintain our present industrial prosperity without them."

It took some years (and agitation) to liquidate the colonial

---

* My own knowledge of this note was extended by the perceptive analysis prepared by Martin J. Sklar of Northern Illinois University.

status of the territory seized during the war against Spain. It also required time to work out and institutionalize a division of authority and labor between economic and political leaders so that the strategy could be put into operation on a routine basis. And it was necessary to open the door into existing colonial empires as well as unclaimed territories. But the strategy that had been set was followed through the Potsdam Conference at the end of World War II, when President Harry S Truman sought with considerable insistence to re-establish the open door for American economic and political influence in Eastern Europe and on the Asian mainland.

The Philadelphia *Press* was correct in its judgment at the time. "This new doctrine established for China is destined to be as important as the Monroe Doctrine has been for the Americas in the past century. It protects the present, it safeguards the future." Quite aware of the grand design, the Boston *Transcript* spelled it out in blunt accents. "We have an infinitely wider scope in the Chinese markets than we should have had with a 'sphere of influence' in competition with half a dozen other spheres." Many European commentators acknowledged that the strategy "hits us in our weak spot." Agreeing with the Boston analysis, a Berlin paper summed it up in one sentence: "The Americans regard, in a certain sense, all China as their sphere of interest."

Americans of that era and their European competitors were basically correct in their estimate of the Open Door Policy. It was neither an alien idea foisted off on America by the British nor a political gesture to disarm domestic dissidents. Latter-day experts who dismissed the policy as irrelevant, misguided, or unsuccessful erred in two respects. They missed its deep roots in the American past and its importance at the time, and they failed to realize that the policy expressed the basic strategy and tactics of America's imperial expansion in the twentieth century. When combined with the ideology of an industrial Manifest Destiny, the history of the Open Door Notes became the history of American foreign relations from 1900 to 1958.

The most dramatic confluence of these currents of ideological and economic expansion did not occur until the eve of American entry into World War I. For this reason, among others, it is often asserted that the United States did not take advantage of the Open Door Policy until after 1917, and some observers argue that the policy never led to the rise of an American empire. In evaluating the extent to which Americans carried through on the strategy of the Open Door Notes, there are two broad questions at issue with regard to statistics of overseas economic expansion, and they cannot be mixed up without confusing the analysis and the interpretation. One concerns the over-all importance of such expansion to the national economy. The answer to that depends less upon gross percentages than upon the role in the American economy of the industries which do depend in significant ways (including raw materials as well as markets) on foreign operations. Measured against total national product, for example, the export of American cars and trucks seems a minor matter. But it is not possible at one and the same time to call the automobile business the key industry in the economy and then dismiss the fact that approximately 15 per cent of its total sales in the 1920s were made in foreign markets.

The other major point concerns the role of such foreign enterprises and markets in the making of American foreign policy. This effect can be direct in terms of domestic political pressure, or indirect through the results of the American overseas economic activity on the foreign policy of other nations. In the broadest sense of gross statistics, moreover, the overseas economic expansion of the United States from 1897 to 1915 is more impressive than many people realize. Loans totaled over a billion dollars. Direct investments amounted to $2,652,-300,000. While it is true that the nation also owed money abroad during the same period, that point is not too important to an understanding of American foreign policy. For the loans and the investments had a bearing on American foreign policy even though balance of payment computations reduce the net figure. Businessmen with interests in Mexico or Manchuria, for example, did not stop trying to influence American policy (or cease having an effect on Mexican or Asian attitudes) just because their investments or loans or sales were arithmetically canceled out by the debt incurred by other Americans in France.

Another misleading approach emphasizes the point that America's overseas economic expansion amounted to no more than 10 or 12 per cent of its national product during those

years. But 10 per cent of any economic operation is a significant proportion; without it the enterprise may slide into
bankruptcy. In that connection, the most recent studies by
economists reveal that exports did indeed spark recovery from
the depression of the 1890s. In any event, the businessmen and
other economic groups *thought* the 10 per cent made a crucial
difference, and many of them concluded that they could not
get it in any way but through overseas expansion.*

Other considerations aside, the conviction of these groups
would make the figure important if it were only one per cent.
Or, to make the point even clearer (and historically accurate),
it would still be significant if all an entrepreneur did was to
pressure the government to support an effort that failed. In
that case the economic indicators would be negative, but the
relevance to foreign policy might be very high. Such was
precisely the case, for example, with the America-China Development Company. It ultimately disappeared from the scene,
but before it died it exerted an extensive influence on American policy in Asia during the first decade of the twentieth
century.

In another way, overseas economic operations which seem
small on paper may mean the difference between survival and
failure to a given firm. Faced by the near-monopoly control
over key raw materials exercised by the United States Steel
Corporation after 1903, Charles Schwab had to go to Chile to
get the ore supplies that were necessary to sustain the Bethle-
hem Steel Company. Schwab's investment was only 35 million dollars, but it played a vital role in his own affairs and
exercised a significant influence on Chilean-American relations. Or, to reverse the example, economic activity which
seems incidental judged by American standards is often fundamental to a weaker economy. This aspect of the problem
can be illustrated by the situation in Manchuria between 1897
and 1904, where approximately one-tenth of one per cent of
America's national product gave the Americans who were
involved a major role in the affairs of that region, and provoked them to agitate vigorously for official American support.

---

* An excellent study of the importance of exports is I. Mintz, *American
Exports During Business Cycles: 1879–1958. Occasional Paper 76* (New
York: National Bureau of Economic Research, 1961).

Their efforts were successful and led to crucial developments in American foreign policy.*

This facet of the Open Door Policy bears directly on the argument that the open door did not actually create an American empire. Leaving aside the question-begging approach which evades the issue by defining empire solely and narrowly in terms of seventeenth- or nineteenth-century colonialism, the problem is not very difficult to resolve. When an advanced industrial nation plays, or tries to play, a controlling and one-sided role in the development of a weaker economy, then the policy of the more powerful country can with accuracy and candor only be described as imperial.

The empire that results may well be informal in the sense that the weaker country is not ruled on a day-to-day basis by resident administrators, or increasingly populated by emigrants from the advanced country, but it is nevertheless an empire. The poorer and weaker nation makes its choices within limits set, either directly or indirectly, by the powerful society, and often does so by choosing between alternatives actually formulated by the outsider. And not only was the Open Door Policy designed to establish the conditions whereby the economic and political power of the United States could be deployed in that manner, it was exercised in that pattern in Asia, Latin America, and Africa. In Canada and Europe, too, for that matter.

Even the implicit dynamic of the policy worked to create the imperial relationship. Let it be assumed, for example, that American policy-makers were not at the time conscious of their superiority or of the expected consequences of that advantage. Then it could be argued that all they wanted was an open marketplace in the tradition of laissez faire; and that such a marketplace would reproduce a relatively pluralistic and balanced political economy in the poorer and weaker societies. But even under the most favorable circumstances, as in the United States during the nineteenth century, the competition

---

* This subject can be explored further in H. Magdoff, *The Age of Imperialism, The Economics of U.S. Foreign Policy* (New York: Monthly Review Press, 1969); and R. W. Tucker, *The Radical Left and American Foreign Policy* (Baltimore: The Johns Hopkins Press, 1971). I am unpersuaded by Tucker's critique.

of laissez faire produced giant entrepreneurs who dominated the little operators or squeezed them out of the marketplace.

In the case of the underdeveloped nations, furthermore, the conditions were anything but ideal for laissez faire, even in the short-run. For not only were the outside operators already giants both absolutely and relatively, but they worked with and through the most powerful elements in the weaker country. This served, as in Asia and Latin America, to create anything but a pluralistic and balanced society. In all respects, therefore, it seems accurate and fair to describe the strategy of the Open Door Notes as imperial in nature, and as leading to the rise of a modern American empire. That the empire had some positive features is not to be denied; its existence is the issue under discussion at this point.

It is impossible, in short, to judge the bearing of overseas economic expansion upon American diplomacy—and thus to judge the importance and efficacy of the Open Door Policy— in terms of gross statistics. The important factors are the relative significance of the activity and the way it is interpreted and acted upon by people and groups who at best are only vaguely symbolized by abstract aggregate statistics. And by these criteria there is no question about the great relevance for diplomacy of America's proposed and actual overseas economic expansion between 1893 and 1915—and throughout the rest of the twentieth century.

Still another interpretation which discounts the significance of the Open Door Policy is based upon America's failure to exercise full control over Japanese and Russian activity in Asia. Though perhaps the strongest argument of its type, it nevertheless fails to establish its basic thesis. Three considerations undermine its conclusions: (1) the Open Door Policy was designed to secure and preserve access to China for American economic power, not to deny access to other nations; (2) America's difficulties with Russia and Japan between 1899 and 1918 stemmed from a failure of judgment concerning the execution of the policy, not from a flaw in the policy itself; and (3) the United States acted with considerable effectiveness between 1915 and 1918 to limit Japan's exploitation of America's earlier error.

In summation, the true nature and full significance of the

Open Door Policy can only be grasped when its four essential features are fully understood.

First: it was neither a military strategy nor a traditional balance-of-power policy. *It was conceived and designed to win the victories without the wars.* In a truly perceptive and even noble sense, the makers of the Open Door Policy understood that war represented the failure of policy. Hence it is irrelevant to criticize the Open Door Policy for not emphasizing, or not producing, extensive military readiness.

Second: it was derived from the proposition that America's overwhelming economic power could cast the economy and the politics of the poorer, weaker, underdeveloped countries in a pro-American mold. American leaders assumed the opposition of one or many industrialized rivals. Over a period of two generations the policy failed because some of those competitors, among them Japan and Germany, chose to resort to force when they concluded (on solid grounds) that the Open Door Policy was working only too well; and because various groups inside the weaker countries such as China and Cuba decided that America's extensive influence in and upon their societies was harmful to their specific and general welfare.

Third (and clearly related to the second point): the policy was neither legalistic nor moralistic in the sense that those criticisms are usually offered. It was extremely hard-headed and practical. In some respects, at any rate, it was the most impressive intellectual achievement in the area of public policy since the generation of the Founding Fathers.

Fourth: unless and until it, and its underlying *Weltanschauung*, were modified to deal with its own consequences, the policy was certain to produce foreign policy crises that would become increasingly severe. The ultimate failures of the Open Door Policy, in short, are the failures generated by its success in guiding Americans in the creation of an empire.

Once these factors are understood, it becomes useful to explore the way that ideological and moralistic elements became integrated with the fundamentally secular and economic nature of the Open Door Policy. The addition of those ingredients served to create a kind of expansionism that aimed at the marketplace of the mind and the polls as well as of the pocketbook.

CHAPTER TWO

*That which is good for communities in America is good for
the Armenians and Greeks and Mohammedans of Turkey.*

THE AMERICAN BOARD OF FOREIGN MISSIONS, 1881

*I would extend the Monroe Doctrine to . . . the assistance of
every people seeking to establish the Republic.*

HENRY DEMAREST LLOYD, 1895

*. . . a republic gradually but surely becoming the supreme
moral factor in the world's progress and the accepted arbiter
of the world's disputes.*

WILLIAM JENNINGS BRYAN, 1900

*If America is not to have free enterprise, then she can have
freedom of no sort whatever.*

WOODROW WILSON, 1912

*Our industries have expanded to such a point that they will
burst their jackets if they cannot find a free outlet to the
markets of the world. . . . Our domestic markets no longer
suffice. We need foreign markets.*

WOODROW WILSON, 1912

The world must be made safe for democracy.

WOODROW WILSON, 1917

THE IMPERIALISM OF IDEALISM

Taken up by President Theodore Roosevelt and his successors, the philosophy and practice of the imperialism that was embodied in the Open Door Notes became the central feature of American foreign policy in the twentieth century. American economic power gushed into some underdeveloped areas within a decade and into many others within a generation. It also seeped, then trickled, and finally flooded into the more developed nations and their colonies until, by 1939, America's economic expansion encompassed the globe. And by that time the regions where America's position was not extensively developed were precisely the areas in which the United States manifested a determination to retain and expand its exploratory operations—or to enter in force for the first time.

Throughout those same years, the rise of a new crusading spirit in American diplomacy contributed to the outward thrust. Such righteous enthusiasm was both secular, emphasizing political and social ideology, and religious, stressing the virtues (and necessities) of Protestant Christianity. In essence, twentieth-century Manifest Destiny was identical with the earlier phenomenon of the same name.

Americans assumed a posture of moral and ideological superiority at an early date. Despite the persistence of the Puritan tradition, however, this assertiveness took predominantly secular forms. Supernatural authority was invoked to explain and account for the steady enlargement of the United States, but the justifications for expansion were generally derived from this world. The phrase "Manifest Destiny," for example, symbolized the assertion that God was on America's side rather than the more modest claim that the country had joined the legions of the Lord. As that logic implied, the argument was that America was the "most progressive" society whose citizens made "proper use of the soil." For these and similar reasons, it was added, the laws of "political gravitation" would bring many minor peoples into the American system.*

Though it had appeared as early as the eve of the American Revolution, the assertion that the expansion of the United States "extended the area of freedom" gained general currency after the War of 1812. President Andrew Jackson seems to have coined the phrase, with his wildcatting intellectual supporters adding many variations. One of the more persuasive and popular, which won many converts during and after the war with Mexico, stressed America's responsibility to extend its authority over "semi-barbarous people." By thus taking up the duty of "regeneration and civilization," America could perform the noble work of teaching inferiors to appreciate the blessings they already enjoyed but were inclined to overlook. In turn, that would prepare them for the better days to follow under America's benevolent leadership.

Near the end of the century, American missionaries and domestic religious leaders began to impart a more theological tone to such crusading fervor. That resulted in part from the effort by the clergy to marry traditional Christianity with the new doctrine of evolution and so adjust their theology to the latest revelations, and also to sustain their influence in the age of science. Josiah Strong was an innovator in that idiom. As a Congregationalist minister in whom the frontier experience and outlook exercised an important influence, Strong concluded that the theory of evolution only substantiated the doctrine of predestination. America had been hand-picked by the Lord to lead the Anglo-Saxons in transforming the world. "It would seem," he explained with reference to the American Indians and other benighted peoples, "as if these inferior tribes

---

* Here consult A. K. Weinberg, *Manifest Destiny* (Baltimore: Johns Hopkins Press, 1935).

were only precursors of a superior race, voices in the wilderness crying: Prepare ye the way of the Lord."

After New England ministers accepted the challenge of saving the heathens of Hawaii, a crusade that began in the eighteenth century, American missionaries were noticeably concerned about Asia—and in particular China. As the Reverend Hudson Taylor explained in 1894, there was "a great Niagara of souls passing into the dark in China." Though they never lost faith, a growing number of missionaries did become discouraged enough to question whether the hell-fire sermon on the dangers of damnation was an approach sufficient unto the need. Some thought fondly of the sword of righteousness, and toyed with the idea of a "Society for the Diffusion of Cannon Balls." That kind of crusade was never organized, but the missionaries did begin in the 1890s to demand formal support and protection from the American Government.

That request, while never acted upon with the same vigor as those from business groups, did receive sympathetic consideration. For one thing, the religious stake in China was significant: America had over 500 missionaries in that country, and their schools claimed a total student body of nearly 17,000 Chinese. Many churches had also supported intervention in Cuba. But the most important factor was the way the missionary movement began to evolve an approach that offered direct support for secular expansion.*

Missionaries had always tended to operate on an assumption quite similar to the frontier thesis. "Missionaries are an absolute necessity," explained the Reverend Henry Van Dyke of Princeton in 1896, "not only for the conversion of the heathen, but also, and much more, for the preservation of the Church. Christianity is a religion that will not keep." Religious leaders began to link the missionary movement with economic expansion in what the Reverend Francis E. Clark of the Christian Endeavor organization called "the widening of our empire." The Board of Foreign Missions also welcomed such expansion as "an ally."

* The best study of this development is P. A. Varg, *Missionaries, Chinese, and Diplomats* (Princeton: Princeton University Press, 1958).

Then, beginning in the mid-1890s, the missionaries began
to change their basic strategy in a way that greatly encouraged a liaison with secular expansionists. Shifting from an
emphasis on the horrors of hell to a concern with practical
reform as the lever of conversion, they increasingly stressed
the need to remake the underdeveloped societies. Naturally
enough, they were to be reformed in the image of the United
States. Such changes would lead to regeneration identified
with Christianity and witnesses for the Lord would accord-
ingly increase.

Not only did this program mesh with the idea of American
secular influence (how else were the reforms to be initiated?),
but it was very similar to the argument that American expansion was justified because it created more progressive
societies. Missionaries came to sound more and more like political leaders, who were themselves submerging their domestic
ideological differences at the water's edge in a general agreement on expansion as a reform movement.

The domestic reformer La Follette offers an excellent example of this convergence of economic and ideological expansion that took place across political lines. He approved taking
the Philippines because it would enable America "to conquer
[its] rightful share of that great market now opening [in
China] for the world's commerce." Expansion was also justified because the United States had a "bounden *duty* to establish
and *maintain* stable government" in the islands. Pointing out
that from the beginning "the policy of this government has
been to expand," La Follette justified it on the grounds that "it
has *made men free.*" Thus, he concluded, "we can legally and
morally reserve unto ourselves perpetual commercial advantages of priceless value to our foreign trade for all time to
come" by taking the Philippines.*

---

* Professor Charles Vevier was probably the first contemporary historian
to explore this imperialism of the reformers. He did so in an unpublished
thesis written at the University of Wisconsin in 1949. Others followed,
e.g.: W. E. Leuchtenburg, "Progressivism and Imperialism . . . 1898–1916,"
Mississippi Valley Historical Review (June, 1952); and P. C. Kennedy,
"La Follette's Imperialist Flirtation," *Pacific Historical Review* (May,
1960). An excellent recent study is J. Israel, *Progressivism and the Open
Door, America and China, 1905–1921* (Pittsburgh: University of Pittsburgh Press, 1971).

Theodore Roosevelt's outlook reveals an even more significant aspect of this progressive integration of secular and ideological expansionism. His concern for economic expansion was complemented by an urge to extend Anglo-Saxon ideas, practices, and virtues throughout the world. Just as his Square Deal program centered on the idea of responsible leaders using the national government to regulate and moderate industrial society at home, so did his international outlook revolve around the idea of American supremacy being used to define and promote the interests of "collective civilization."

Thus it was necessary, he warned in his Presidential Message of December 1901, to exercise restraint in dealing with the large corporations. "Business concerns which have the largest means at their disposal . . . take the lead in the strife for commercial supremacy among the nations of the world. America has only just begun to assume the commanding position in the international business world which we believe will more and more be hers. It is of the utmost importance that this position be not jeopardized, especially at a time when the overflowing abundance of our own natural resources and the skill, business energy, and mechanical aptitude of our people make foreign markets essential."

Roosevelt integrated that kind of expansion with ideological considerations and imperatives to create an all-inclusive logic and set of responsibilities which made peace itself the consequence of empire. In his mind, at any rate, it was America's "duty toward the people living in barbarism to see that they are freed from their chains, and we can free them only by destroying barbarism itself." Thus, he concluded, "peace cannot be had until the civilized nations have expanded in some shape over the barbarous nations."

The inherent requirements of economic expansion coincided with such religious, racist, and reformist drives to remake the world. The reason for this is not difficult to perceive. As they existed, the underdeveloped countries were poor, particularistic, and bound by traditions which handicapped business enterprise. They were not organized to mesh with modern industrial systems in a practical and efficient manner. It was economically necessary to change them *in certain ways and to a limited degree* if the fruits of expansion were to be harvested. As with the missionaries, therefore, the economic and political leaders of the country decided that what was good for Americans was also good for foreigners. Humanitarian concern was thus reinforced by hard-headed economic requirements.

The administrations of Theodore Roosevelt understood this relationship between economic expansion and overseas reform, and explicitly integrated it into the strategy of the Open Door Policy. It was often commented upon in dispatches and policy statements concerning China and Latin America. In his famous Corollary to the Monroe Doctrine, for example, Roosevelt (who thought of the Open Door Policy as the Monroe Doctrine for Asia) stressed the need for reforms and asserted the right and the obligation of the United States to see that they were made—and honored.

It was in connection with the Algeciras Conference of 1905–06, however, that the relationship was most fully (and even brilliantly) explained and formally made a part of the Open Door Policy. Growing out of the imperial rivalry in Africa between Britain, France, and Germany, the Algeciras (or Moroccan) Conference proceeded on two levels. The dramatic battle involved limiting German penetration to a minimum while giving it superficial concessions. In that skirmish the United States sided with England and France. But the conference also offered the United States a chance to renew and reinforce its old drive of the 1880s to secure equal commercial rights in Africa. Roosevelt and Secretary of State Elihu Root used the strategy of the open door to wage both campaigns. Their policy instructions on the specific problems of organizing an international Moroccan police force, and on instituting financial reforms, revealed their full understanding of the nature and the extent of the interrelationship between reform and economic expansion.

After discussions with Roosevelt, Root summarized the issue beautifully. Police reform was essential: it was "vital" to American "interests and no less so to the advantage of Morocco that the door, being open, should lead to something; that the outside world shall benefit by assured opportunities, and that the Moroccan people shall be made in a measure fit and able to profit by the advantages of the proposed reform." Fruitful economic intercourse depended upon "the existence of internal conditions favorable thereto." Those prerequisites included not only the "security of life and property," but establishing "equality of opportunities for trade with all natives." *

The need to enlarge the domestic market within Morocco, so that the open door would "lead to something," called for both negative and positive kinds of reform. Root defined the first as actions designed to remove conditions "which impair the freedom of salutary foreign intercourse with the native population." It was thus necessary to modify religious discrimination against non-Muslims; to establish the "orderly and certain administration of impartial justice" which guaranteed "vigorous punishment of crimes against persons and property;" to insure "exemption from erratic taxes and [similar] burdens" upon business enterprise; and to maintain an internal police force strong and efficient enough "to repress subversive disorder and preserve the public peace."

Root was equally blunt about the positive kind of reform. In the fundamental sense, Moroccan poverty and stagnation had to be ended. Economic development had to be initiated. There had to be enough of the kind of "improvement of the condition of the people that will enable them to profit by the opportunities of foreign trade." Loans had to lead to development: poor people cannot buy the goods and services exported by the richer industrial countries. No income, no purchases; no purchases, no trade; no trade, no prosperity in America and no "salutary" effects in the poorer country. Or so, at any rate, ran the logic and the fears of the open door strategy.

Root went on, in his handling of American policy during the conference, to stress the importance of securing access for American capital to the competition for public works construction. That was not only desirable as an economic opportunity in and of itself, but also represented one of the ways in which a minimum level of general development could be facilitated. Transportation and sanitation systems were as important as large loans or legal reforms in establishing the

---

* Unlike many important documents, this remarkable and extremely significant dispatch has been published. The citation is: Root to White, November 28, 1905; *Papers Relating to the Foreign Relations of the United States, 1905*, pp. 678–79.

conditions for successful enterprise. Root was unequivocal
about the crucial element in arranging such financial reform:
"the 'open door' seems to be the sound policy to advocate."

At the end of the conference, the American representative
reported that the principle of "the open door in matters of
commerce" had been acknowledged, and thus the way had
been prepared for American participation in "the execution of
public works, or the future development of the great mineral
wealth of Africa." In the narrow sense, the Algeciras episode
offers an illuminating perspective on newspaper stories about
the present-day activities in Africa of the Rockefeller and
Kaiser corporations (to name but two), and other reports on
American governmental loans for public works such as high-
ways and power installations.

The broader aspects of the analysis and policy statement
prepared by Roosevelt and Root are even more significant.
That document establishes once and for all the connection
between, and the convergence of, the drive for overseas economic expansion and the urge to reform other societies according to American and industrial standards. It likewise
removes any doubt about whether or not American leaders
were conscious of the relationship. And finally, it helps clarify
the nature and the dimensions of the tragedy and the terror
of American foreign policy that evolved out of the Open Door
Policy.

On the one hand, of course, the positive features of the
reforms, including the general concern to initiate a minimum
of economic development, emerge very clearly. On the other
hand, it becomes apparent that the United States was opening
the door to serious and extensive unrest, as well as to potential economic development and political reform. Perhaps the
failure to understand this, or a not unrelated kind of persistent
wishful thinking that such unrest could somehow be avoided,
provides the final, irreducible explanation of America's difficulties in foreign affairs during the twentieth century. For
America's integrated reformist and economic expansion provoked trouble. And the reaction to the trouble ultimately took
the form of terror.

First: it undertook to initiate and sustain drastic, fundamental changes in other societies. The process of wrenching

Morocco, or China, or Nicaragua out of their neo-feudal, primarily agrarian condition into the industrial era involved harsh, painful alterations in an established way of life. Even under the best of circumstances, those consequences can only be mitigated. They cannot be entirely avoided.

Second: the United States identified itself as a primary cause of such changes. It thereby also defined itself as a principal source of the related pain and unhappiness. This is true, not only in connection with those groups in power which oppose the changes as they begin, but also for those who suffer from the consequences without means to oppose or moderate them, and even for others who generally approve of the new ways but despair of the costs and question the morality of outsiders interfering in such fundamental and extensive respects.

Third: the United States wanted to stop or stabilize such changes at a point favorable to American interests. This was at best naive. Even a modest familiarity with history reveals that such alterations have wide and continuing consequences. It was at worst a knowing effort to slap a lid on dynamic development. That attempt can only be described as a selfish violation of the idea and ideal of self-determination, and even as an evasion of the moral obligation to accept the consequences of one's own actions.

Fourth: the effort to control and limit changes according to American preferences served only to intensify opposition within the developing countries. The extent to which Algerian revolutionaries of the 1940s and 1950s revealed and illustrated all these points in their attitudes toward the United States offers a particularly relevant example of the tragic consequences of American reformist and economic expansion as it emerged during the Roosevelt administrations.

The integration of these elements was carried forward, and given classic expression in the rhetoric, style, and substance of the diplomacy of President Woodrow Wilson and Secretary of State Bryan. Both men were leaders of the American reform movement, and they brought to their conduct of foreign affairs a religious intensity and righteousness that was not apparent in earlier administrations and which may not have been matched since their time. As Protestants imbued with a strong sense of Anglo-Saxon self-consciousness, they personified the assertive idealism that complemented and reinforced the economic drive for markets.

Bryan was a Fundamentalist in religious matters. Typified by the famous "Cross of Gold" speech which climaxed his nomination for the presidency in 1896, his sense of calling and mission infused all his political actions with a kind of hell-fire enthusiasm and determination. Those characteristics could be misleading, and in the Crisis of the 1890s prompted a good many Americans to view Bryan as a threat to social order. But as revealed even in the "Cross of Gold" speech (where he defined everybody as a businessman), as well as in his actions, he was wholly a reform capitalist. Bryan himself joked about the misconception. Upon at least one occasion, when he visited the White House after his defeat in the election of 1904, he did so with considerable charm. President Roosevelt was one of those who had hurled all kinds of invective and wild charges at Bryan at one time or another during their political rivalry. As he arrived to make an invited call on the victor, Bryan revealed a kind of pleasant fatalism about such things. "Some people think I'm a terrible radical, but really I'm not so very dangerous after all."

As far as foreign affairs were concerned, Bryan's outlook was that of the Christian leader who concluded that his society needed overseas markets and was determined to find them. He fully intended, however, to do so in such a way that order and stability would be assured, a protestant peace secured and preserved, and the backward nations protected from rapacious foreigners while being led along the path of progress by the United States. Confident that Wilson was a man with the same goals, Bryan could without any reservations praise the President, in May 1914, as one who had "opened the doors of all the weaker countries to an invasion of American capital and American enterprise."

Candidly asserting America's "paramount influence in the Western Hemisphere," Bryan's objective was to "make absolutely sure our domination of the situation." Such moral and economic expansion, he explained in 1913, would "give our country such increased influence . . . that we could prevent revolutions, promote education, and advance stable and just government . . . we would in the end profit, negatively, by not having to incur expense in guarding our own and foreign interests there, and, positively, by the increase of trade."

While no less determined—his will won him more than one defeat—Wilson's idealism was that of the high church Presbyterian Calvinist who viewed himself and the United States as trustees of the world's welfare. The destiny of America was to be "the justest, the most progressive, the most honorable, the most enlightened Nation in the world." Small wonder, then, that Wilson led the country into World War I with the argument that "the world must be made safe for democracy." Or that he considered his own postwar program to be "the only possible" plan for peace which therefore "must prevail."

Wilson was both responsible and candid enough to admit that all was not perfect either in America or the rest of the world. But since he considered the philosophy of revolution to be "in fact radically evil and corrupting," he insisted that the only recourse was "a slow process of reform" led by trustees such as himself. At least, that is to say, *within* the United States. But America, just because it was the elect among the trustees of the world, had both a right and an obligation to use force "to do justice and assert the rights of mankind."

Wilson's imperialism of the spirit was well defined by his attitude toward the Philippines. The United States should grant independence to the Filipinos just as soon as American leadership had instructed them in the proper standards of national life, instilled in them the proper character, and established for them a stable and constitutional government. Such noble objectives justified—even demanded—the use of force. "When men take up arms to set other men free," he declared, "there is something sacred and holy in the warfare. I will not cry 'peace' as long as there is sin and wrong in the world."

But since Wilson's fundamental assumption about the nature of man was that he "lives not by what he does, but by what he thinks and hopes," this type of imperialism was, by the President's own standards, the most persuasive and extensive of any that could be devised. For in effect—and in practice —it subverted Wilson's support for the principle of self-determination. He asserted that other peoples were at liberty, and had a right to be free; but he judged whether or not they chose freedom by his own standards. Or, as he put it during the Mexican crisis, he would approve and recognize none but "those who act in the interest of peace and honor, who protect private rights, and respect the restraints of constitutional provisions."

Both then and later, Wilson used American power to go behind the forms of government to see if the substance squared with his criteria and, if it did not, he deployed American power in an attempt to force reality into correspondence with his imagery and ideals. The policy was the broadest kind of imperialism. Thus his refusal to go along with American corporations that wanted to recognize and sustain the regime of Victoriano Huerta during the early phases of the Mexican Revolution is at most only half the story. Wilson was perfectly willing to intervene vigorously, even to the brink of war, in order to force the Mexicans to behave according to his standards. "I am going to teach the South American republics," he explained to a British diplomat, "to elect good men."

These features of Wilson's foreign policy have understandably led many historians, including some of his admirers, to characterize his diplomacy as "moral imperialism," "imperialism of the spirit," or "missionary diplomacy." While accurate as far as it goes, that approach is seriously misleading because it ignores or neglects the extensive degree to which Wilson advocated and supported overseas economic expansion. It also does Wilson an injustice. For he brought the two themes together in a manner that surpassed even the similar achievement of Roosevelt and Root.

The single most important insight into Wilson's propensity and ability to fuse those two traditions very probably lies in his Calvinistic *Weltanschauung*. Two of Calvin's central assumptions concerned the complementary nature of economics and morality, and the responsibility of the trustee for combining them to produce the welfare of the community. He emphasized these very clearly and forcefully in his writings, and tried to carry them out in actual practice. It is of course true that Wilson was not Calvin (though upon occasion the President's actions provoked some of his critics to remark that there seemed to be some confusion in his own mind on that issue).

Nor was he a disciple in the rigid and narrow theological or clerical sense. But he did make sense out of reality from the basic vantage point offered by Calvinism, and his consolidation of economics and ideas stemmed from that conception of the world.

Granted this combination (contradictory as it may have been) of Calvinism and capitalism, the consideration most directly pertinent in comprehending Wilson's handling of foreign policy is his commitment to the frontier thesis of Frederick Jackson Turner. They enjoyed a close personal and intellectual friendship while Turner was developing his thesis about American expansion and its prosperity and democracy as an advanced student at Johns Hopkins University. Wilson accepted the argument as the central explanation of American history. "All I ever wrote on the subject," he later remarked of Turner, "came from him." That was true, even though it was an exaggeration. Wilson shaped and used the intellectual tool of interpreting American politics from the perspective of the British parliamentary system on his own (and it was a stimulating approach). Even so, the frontier thesis was a crucial element in his thinking about the past and the present.

Wilson put it very directly as early as 1896 in explaining the Crisis of the 1890s. "The days of glad expansion are gone, our life grows tense and difficult." He read George Washington's Farewell Address in the same light. Wilson argued that Washington "would seem to have meant, 'I want you to discipline yourselves and . . . be good boys until you . . . are big enough to stand the competition . . . until you are big enough to go abroad in the world.'" Wilson clearly thought that by 1901 the United States had become a big boy: expansion was a "natural and wholesome impulse." And in a speech on "The Ideals of America" of December 26, 1901, which was remarkable for its close following of the frontier thesis, he projected the process indefinitely: "Who shall say," he asked rhetorically, "where it will end?"

With the publication the next year of his five-volume *History of the American People*, it became apparent that Wilson saw overseas economic expansion as the frontier to replace the continent that had been occupied. A section in Volume V (which reads like a close paraphrase of some essays written by Brooks Adams) recommended increased efficiency in government so that the United States "might command the economic fortunes of the world." Referring a bit later to the Philippines as "new frontiers," he concluded his analysis by stressing the need for markets—markets "to which diplomacy, and if need be power, must make an open way." In a series of lectures at Columbia University in April 1907, he was even more forthright. "Since trade ignores national boundaries and the manufacturer insists on having the world as a market, the flag of his nation must follow him, and the doors of the nations which are closed must be battered down." "Concessions obtained by financiers must be safeguarded," he continued, "by ministers of state, even if the sovereignty of unwilling nations be outraged in the process. Colonies must be obtained or planted, in order that no useful corner of the world may be overlooked or left unused. Peace itself becomes a matter of conference and international combinations." It was something of an anti-climax to learn that Wilson expected "many sharp struggles for foreign trade."

His persistent repetition of that warning serves to symbolize the extent to which Wilson's campaign for the presidential nomination and election in 1912 stressed overseas economic expansion. During January and February he reviewed the importance of a merchant marine, and bewailed the weaknesses of the banking system which handicapped American financiers in overseas competition. By August, when he won the nomination, he was ready with a general interpretation. The United States was an "expanding" nation. "Our industries have expanded to such a point that they will burst their jackets if they cannot find a free outlet to the markets of the world. . . . Our domestic markets no longer suffice. We need foreign markets." And also, he added, a major effort to educate the general public on the problem and its solution. Wilson was even more specific about the reason behind his sense of urgency at a campaign dinner for his supporters among the working class. (Not many day laborers could afford the prices, but their leaders attended.) "We have reached, in short, a critical point in the process of our prosperity. It has now become a question with us," he warned, "whether it shall continue or shall not continue." "We need foreign markets," he reiterated, because "our domestic market is too small." And as McKinley and Root before him, Wilson in 1912 unequivocally pointed to Germany as the most dangerous rival of the United States in that economic struggle.

Wilson's dramatic language about American prosperity seemed within a year to have been justified. The nation entered a recession at the end of 1913, and the downswing continued in 1914. Even before that unhappy development, or before he had to cope with the Mexican and Russian Revolutions, Wilson revealed the keen and sophisticated way in which he integrated crusading idealism and hard-headed economics. The situation in which he displayed such leadership was almost literally waiting for him as he moved into the White House in March 1913. Giant American bankers wanted a prompt if not immediate policy statement on their efforts (in conjunction with the Japanese and European financiers) to push through a large loan to China. Wilson's response has usually been interpreted as an abrupt and significant break with the whole tradition and practice of overseas economic expansion. That conclusion has been reached by an intellectual broad jump of prodigious proportions, taking off from the fact that Wilson did refuse to support the bankers in that one operation. But historical interpretation is not broad jumping. The fact is indisputable. The conclusion is wrong. In order to understand the apparent contradiction in Wilson's action, however, it is necessary to consider several factors that are seldom integrated into the analysis.*

It is essential first of all to review the difficulties that arose in putting the open door strategy into operation in Asia. Given the objective of winning the economic and political victory without the war (or wars), American leaders faced a difficult task. There was no easy answer to their problems, and most certainly no handbook of operations for them to follow. They had to make difficult choices in innovating tactics, and to cope

---

* Martin J. Sklar has analyzed this episode in great detail; he has published a summary of his findings as "Woodrow Wilson and the Political Economy of Modern United States Liberalism," *Studies on the Left* (1960). While he reached similar conclusions quite independently, I have benefited since the first edition of this book appeared in 1959 from conversations with him and from reading the first draft of his Master's Thesis.

with limitations and other troubles imposed by events at home and in China. To avoid confusion in outlining such considerations (all of them cannot be summarized in one neat paragraph), they will be numbered.

First: the natural and obvious tactic was to go it alone, plunging ahead in China with the hope of rapidly establishing extensive American influence. President William Howard Taft tested this approach. "I regard the position at Peking as the most important diplomatic position that I have to fill," he explained in April 1909, "and it is necessary to send there a man of business, force and perception." He followed through by applying direct and personal pressure on the head of the Chinese Government to secure participation by American financiers (and industrialists) in a railroad development project in Hukuang Province. His objective was "a practical and real application of the open door policy."

The United States never abandoned this ideal of direct action. It remained the preferred method of exploiting the Open Door Policy in Asia. Other techniques were seen as means to establish the preconditions for handling the problem in that manner. But as Taft and other American leaders discovered, there were two major difficulties involved in pursuing that course of action. One was defined by the simple (though perhaps to many surprising) fact that American entrepreneurs were unable *on their own as capitalists* to accumulate sufficient private capital to do the job alone.* The other reason was more obvious. Such a blunt, bold move by the United States was sure to provoke, and did provoke, sharp and increasing opposition from Japan and other industrial nations. If persisted in, that confrontation would lead to war. Yet the policy itself was designed to avoid war. For both

---

* Historians have almost wholly neglected this extremely important problem of capital shortage in twentieth century America. It is handled indirectly in the studies of the Federal Reserve System, but its part in private and official policy—and the relationship between them—has not been explored in any significant or substantial investigations. Yet it provides, as will appear below, a very important insight into American diplomacy after the 1890s. For that matter, it can be shown that the underlying solution evolved between 1913 and 1939—that of having the government help directly and indirectly in accumulating capital for the private sector—appeared very early (if not literally first) in connection with overseas economic expansion.

reasons, therefore, American policy-makers had to consider other tactics.

Second: it was possible to work with the Russians, and thereby strengthen them against the Japanese. China (and probably Siberia as well) would then be developed in concert with the Tsar. The approach was not only conceivable, it was actually discussed. The Russians proposed the idea as early as the 1890s. They persistently repeated their overtures during the subsequent 15 years, but the McKinley, Roosevelt, and Taft administrations never explored them seriously. Secretary of State Hay did indicate some early interest, but Roosevelt (who supported the plan when first outlined) squashed the idea. The most promising exploration of it was undertaken by the financier-railroad magnate Edward Averell Harriman at the close of the Russo-Japanese War. Though plagued by many difficulties, he was making important progress toward a broad agreement with the Russians when he was stopped by the American Panic of 1907, and then by death in 1909. Harriman's close associate, Willard Straight, tried unsuccessfully to sustain the project at that time. The development of American-Russian economic relations did not affect foreign policy in a significant way until the end of the 1920s.*

Third: another approach, based on traditional balance-of-power maneuvers, was actually tried by President Roosevelt on the eve of, and during, the Russo-Japanese War. By encouraging and supporting Japan, which he took to be the weaker as well as the more reliable power, he hoped to wear down and cancel out both countries as opponents of American predominance. It was expected that the result would be an open field for American economic and political influence. Several advisors warned Roosevelt that, even if the tactic was

* On this matter see: E. H. Zabriskie, *American-Russian Rivalry in the Far East* (Philadelphia: University of Pennsylvania Press, 1946); W. A. Williams, *American-Russian Relations, 1781–1947* (New York: Rinehart and Co., 1952); and C. Vevier, *The United States and China, 1906–1913* (New Brunswick: Rutgers University Press, 1955). A convenient indication of business interest is provided by McKinley's Assistant Secretary of the Treasury, Frank A. Vanderlip, in his essay: *The American "Commercial Invasion" of Europe* (New York: Scribner's Magazine, 1902). Also see W. C. Askew, "Efforts to Improve Russo-American Relations Before The First World War: the John Hays Hammond Mission," *Slavic and East European Review* (December, 1952).

sound, he should support Russia.* Appearances notwithstanding, they cautioned the President, Japan was likely to be the stronger power in a short war, and Russia the more likely to co-operate. They were correct, and Japan proceeded to defeat Russia and push American interests out of Manchuria.

Fourth: that failure prompted Washington to make a virtue out of necessity and work with Japan. Policy-makers offered two variations on that theme.

One group maintained that Washington should join Tokyo in order to control and develop China as partners. Those men argued from many motives. They had prejudices in favor of Japan or against China, and took a somewhat fatalistic view of Japan's power. Some were even willing, in the final showdown, to acquiesce in a broad measure of Japanese control of China. Though they influenced policy, they faced several handicaps in persuading other leaders to accept that tactic. Japan provided increasing evidence that it would never be satisfied with an equal relationship. And that only intensified another difficulty: the majority of American policy-makers did not really want a partnership—as indicated by their refusal to consider working with Russia. The Open Door Policy, even as originally conceived, anticipated a China strong enough to resist partition by Japan and European powers and strong enough to handle its responsibilities in connection with being developed by American entrepreneurs, but not strong enough to evict the foreign devils. Giving Japan a free hand under the name of partnership meant abandoning the very policy that was designed to assure American supremacy.

These factors strengthened the second group, whose plan for working with Tokyo was considerably more sophisticated. Their plan was based on the idea of exploiting developing economic ties with Japan in order to win both a short-term and a long-term objective: in the short-run, to secure Japanese markets and also an indirect share of Japan's expansion on the Asian mainland; but, in the long-run, to use that economic involvement in Japan as a fulcrum upon which to rest America's political lever, which could then be used to control the

---

* One such figure, Horace N. Allen, is the subject of an excellent biography by F. H. Harrington, *God, Mammon and the Japanese* (Madison: University of Wisconsin Press, 1944).

extent of Japan's expansion. The essence of this plan was outlined by an American representative in China to Secretary of State Bryan in 1915, when Japan confronted Peking with its extensive Twenty-One Demands. "Our present commercial interests in Japan are greater than those in China, but the look ahead shows our interest to be a strong and independent China rather than one held in subjection by Japan." After a good many false starts and temporary setbacks, this approach was adopted by the United States and followed down to 1939, when the Administration of Franklin Delano Roosevelt made a strong effort to coerce Japan into retreating from China by using American economic influence over Japan's economy.

Fifth: Japan enjoyed many geographical advantages, and others of an economic and military nature that stemmed from its hierarchical social and political structure, which bedeviled and frustrated American efforts to put the Open Door Policy into action. In many respects, at any rate, it was not until the mid-1920s that the United States began to compete effectively in Asia.

The result of that handicap, and of the difficulty American entrepreneurs encountered in accumulating sufficient capital of their own, was to turn American policy-makers—both private economic leaders and elected or appointed officials—toward the idea and practice of joining international financial combines or consortia.* These organizations were similar to

---

* Since this subsequently raised a question of historical interpretation that claimed far more intellectual energy and time than it warranted, it may be useful to examine the issue. The great majority of American historians during the last 50 years has operated from the basis of the *Weltanschauung* of humanitarian laissez faire. Quite naturally (and, given their understanding of the assumptions of that outlook, quite logically), they have defined economics and politics as separate entities that operate or impinge upon each other in much the same fashion as two billiard balls. As a result, they have forever been engaged in vehement, and sometimes bitter, arguments over which billiard ball— the red economic one or the white political one—caused the other one to move. They have sustained a long dispute over the question of whether it was the bankers who made foreign policy, or whether it was the politicians who made banking policy.

Yet the issue is itself a pseudo-problem. For, even by the axioms of laissez faire, economic actions were held to produce the general—including the political—welfare. Given conditions of representative government, the political leaders who won office would be those who acted on an internalized understanding of that fundamental truth. Hence they would

the pools or gentlemen's agreements that developed in domestic economic affairs. Banking firms from several countries combined to share an opportunity in China (or another underdeveloped nation) on an agreed-upon percentage basis. Less capital was thereby required from each unit and, since deadly competition was avoided, the risk was decreased. That more than balanced the chance that any one unit could monopolize the field and the profit.

It should not be imagined, however, that American leaders abandoned their basic assumption when they shifted to the tactic of implementing the open door strategy through consortium agreements. Some were more patient than others, but all of them fully expected the economic power of the United States to dominate such arrangements, and thereby establish the nation's predominant economic and political position. Indeed, Secretary of State Knox was so confident of his proposal of 1909 to neutralize the Manchurian railways (a maneuver he expected to reestablish American power in the region) that he did little to camouflage its rather obvious purpose. Not unexpectedly, America's rivals turned it down out of hand.

Sixth: It soon became apparent, moreover, that the consortium tactic was in general less than successful from the American point of view. This harsh and disappointing reality was the product of a combination of factors which were not

---

not separate politics and economics in the way that later historians have done: they would instead hold that good economics was good policy.

Even during the heyday of laissez faire, in the nineteenth century, American politicians and entrepreneurs took for granted the interrelationship between, and the interpenetration of, business and politics. The most perceptive among them realized at the turn of the twentieth century, moreover, that the marketplace of laissez faire had to be managed in foreign affairs just as in domestic affairs if the free enterprise or capitalist system was itself to survive.

Thus both economic and political leaders viewed the tactic of consortia as natural and legitimate. Who acted first is beside the point. This is so, not only because individuals from both groups responded to the need in a similar way at the same time, but also because both groups acted in a reciprocal fashion. The consortium tactic represented a true consensus, not the result of the bankers controlling the White House—or vice versa.

One of the best introductions to such matters, now happily available in translation, is G. Lukacs, *History and Class Consciousness* (Cambridge: The M.I.T. Press, 1971).

only interrelated, but whose effect on American participants in the consortia soon began to snowball into a serious crisis. Since there were a good many such elements in the situation, it may help to avoid confusion if they are enumerated formally.

A: the competitors of the United States feared its power. They broadly shared the American belief that over the long-run they were doomed to an inferior position.

B: thus they worked, both as private entrepreneurs and as governments, to combine inside the consortia against the United States. In the narrow, illustrative sense they used their power to outvote American participants.

C: these rivals soon realized, moreover, that American operators were having trouble accumulating capital. They responded in a natural way: they refused to facilitate the sale of American securities on their own exchanges.

D: Americans did not of course accept such opposition passively, and the result was a growing stagnation of the consortia.

E: this accelerated and intensified existing opposition to the consortia inside China. On the one hand, the Chinese Government became increasingly dissatisfied. On the other hand, Chinese critics of the consortia, who came to view them as symbols of outside domination, increased their agitation against the foreigners and also against their own government for negotiating such agreements.

F: as a result, independent economic entrepreneurs in several industrial nations began to compete with the consortia. The Chinese Government turned to them in exasperation with the consortia, and out of its fear that continued inaction would lead to revolution. They hoped that independent entrepreneurs could act effectively enough to dull the edge of the antiforeign unrest. In the United States, moreover, the independents began to argue that the consortium approach was the equivalent in overseas economic affairs of unfair competition at home.

G: finally, the consortium members had reluctantly concluded that it was necessary to help China organize its own government affairs before they could make any significant profit on economic development projects. Such reorganization loans, as they were called, were viewed unfavorably for three main reasons. First: they involved less profit per se. Second: they required some clear assurance from their own governments that China would be made to meet its obligations. And third: that factor raised in turn the specter of more unrest in China.

This long and admittedly rather complicated review of the circumstances and conditions incident to implementing the strategy of the Open Door Policy at the time of President Wilson's inauguration in March 1913, has had one main purpose: to clarify the basic situation in order to grasp the great significance of two crucial aspects of Wilson's action. President Wilson, Secretary of State Bryan, and other top government and private leaders understood the situation very accurately and clearly. They were not wandering in the dark alleys of ignorance and confusion. Wilson's decision not to support the bankers (and the consortium) in pushing through the long-pending reorganization loan was made on the basis of his integration of reform and economic expansionism, and was very consciously designed to cut free of the limitations and dangers of the consortium tactic in order to reassert American power and influence in China and Manchuria. When they asked Wilson for a statement of policy, the American bankers were edgy and anxious. For one thing, they wanted to know where they stood with the new President. He was a Democrat coming in after 16 years of Republican rule, and his periodic vivid and righteous rhetoric about reform worried some businessmen. The bankers also felt that time was running out on the specific reorganization loan. They wanted either to push it through or get out of the affair.*

This tone of fish-or-cut-bait, which is apparent in the documents pertaining to the attitude of the bankers, can be misleading if it is interpreted too literally or narrowly. Wall Street was *not* on the verge of abandoning overseas economic expansion, either in general or in China per se. If their request

---

* It might be argued that the bankers were determined in any event to leave the consortium, and in a clever maneuver used the President to accomplish that objective. After careful evaluation, however, the evidence does not persuade me that the bankers were absolutely set on withdrawal.

on the reorganization loan was not met, they planned to (and did) turn to smaller industrial and developmental loans. The bankers needed and asked for two kinds of help, both of which were relevant to the reorganization loan. They wanted firm and formal government support in their dealings with China and other consortium members. And they sought the same kind of backing from the government in order to solve their problem of accumulating capital.

The turn to the government for help in corralling capital was known, explained, and documented by a good many people at the time. One State Department official, for example, admitted ruefully that it was impossible "for us alone to float any very large international loan." The clearest public exposition of this factor was provided, however, by Willard Straight. After his long tenure as advisor to Harriman, during which time Straight also served periodically in the Far Eastern Division of the Department of State, he went to work for the House of Morgan (which took the lead in consortium affairs). In a series of articles and speeches during 1912, 1913, and 1914, he candidly described the problem in great detail. His point of departure was the proposition that firms engaged in overseas economic expansion were "national assets;" "representatives of our country, trustees for its trade and of its reputation."

He usually began by explaining the difference between borrowing from the public, by selling bonds and other securities, and obtaining the funds from other banks through commercial loans. Commercial loans could not provide enough money. After all, the banks participating in the consortium were the giants of the American financial community. Hence the bankers had to go to "the public." "It is not the bankers who provide the money to finance a foreign loan," Straight remarked bluntly, it comes instead from bonds "sold to the public." As the bankers had learned through experience, "the American investor is not willing to buy Chinese bonds unless he believes that the American Government will protect him by all possible diplomatic means."

Thus the issue was "whether our Government will back us up." "If the American public," Straight summarized, "is to be educated to the point of financing the sale of our materials abroad—and that is the question of foreign trade and foreign loans—the American Government must make some statement which will reassure the public and give them the thought and the belief that in case of default or in case of difficulty . . . the Government will act as the advocate of the public . . . and see that the American investor gets what is his due."

Beginning with the Wilson Administration, and continuing to a steadily increasing extent, the Government of the United States proceeded to provide what Straight and the bankers asked—and considerably more. Tax monies collected from individual citizens came to be used to provide private corporations with loans and other subsidies for overseas expansion, to create the power to protect those activities, and even to create reserve funds with which to make cash guarantees against losses. The bankers lost in their effort to secure that line of policy by one hard push in March 1913, but the final program as it existed in 1972 far exceeded their original objectives.

Wilson was quite willing, even eager, to help the bankers and other entrepreneurs engaged in overseas economic expansion. But he was perceptive enough to realize that the Open Door Policy had to be reasserted and upheld outside the framework of the consortia, and in a way that would strengthen America's position in the underdeveloped countries. That meant in the narrow sense, as Secretary of State Bryan phrased it, that Wilson refused to back the bankers in the reorganization loan because "the American group . . . could not have a controlling voice" in the operation.

For that matter, Bryan provided the best general explanation of Wilson's decision. Significantly, it was offered as a public statement. "The President believed that a different policy was more consistent with the American position, and that it would in the long run be more advantageous to our commerce . . . I may say that American interests will be protected everywhere. . . . The President in his policies as thus far announced has laid even a broader foundation for the extension of our trade throughout the Orient. He is cultivating the friendship of the people across the Pacific. . . . The President's policy contemplates the formulation of an environment which will encourage the growth of all that is good. . . . So, the government, while it cannot trade, can give to trade an environment in which it can develop, and that is the duty of our government to do."

Or, as Wilson said in a memorandum to Bryan, the basic objective was "the maintenance of the policy of an open door to the world." This explicit and heavy emphasis on long-run objectives explains why it is so misleading to interpret the President's refusal to support the bankers in the reorganization loan as a change in basic policy. Even the published documents leave no doubt about Wilson's vigorous support for economic expansion. Bryan reported, for example, that the cabinet expressed full agreement on "a strong declaration favorable to the extension of our commerce in the Orient." And Wilson's own dispatch explaining his action is even more explicit. He was "earnestly desirous of promoting the most extended and intimate trade relationship" with China. Americans "certainly wish to participate, and participate very generously, in the opening to the Chinese and to the use of the world the almost untouched and perhaps unrivaled resources of China." He closed with a sober promise to "urge and support" such expansion, and to provide American entrepreneurs with "the banking and other financial facilities which they now lack and without which they are at a serious disadvantage."

Finally, Wilson's critical words to and about the bankers in his public reply to their request must be evaluated in the context of these other factors. The verbal wrist-slapping was a gesture quite in keeping with Wilson's reformist outlook, and also an obvious maneuver to win favor with the progressives in both parties. It also served to enhance America's image in the eyes of the Chinese. Here was the President of the United States accepting a point made by foreign critics. The criticism was not insincere, but it did not mean the end of official support for the bankers, or for general overseas economic expansion. It merely symbolized a more sophisticated approach to those objectives. The reformer as expansionist would be more successful than the conservative as expansionist.

Any doubts concerning Wilson's basic position were removed by subsequent events. After "very satisfactory" conversations with Bryan, Straight reported to a meeting of bankers and other entrepreneurs that the Secretary of State was most co-operative. "No one could have been more ready to support [us] and to telegraph Peking, and urge measures on the part of the Chinese Government." Even more revealing, perhaps, was the relationship between the Wilson Administration and the National Council of Foreign Trade. Secretary Bryan and Secretary of Commerce William Redfield were the major speakers during the first day of the council's national convention in May, 1914.

This date is significant, for it specifies the policy of the Wilson Administration at a time when it was clear that America was suffering a serious economic downturn, yet at an hour prior to the outbreak of World War I. Secretary Redfield, who had been president of the American Manufacturers Export Association and a vigorous advocate of overseas economic expansion before Wilson called him to the crusade for the New Freedom, led off with a broad outline of government policy. He assured the corporation leaders that "because we are strong, we are going out, you and I, into the markets of the world to get our share." A bit later, in 1915, Redfield revealed even more clearly why he was so vehement about overseas economic expansion. Speaking again to businessmen, he emphasized that "it is a noble work that we are engaged in. It carries with it so much of hope, so much of growth, so much of power, such a promise of prosperity ... [It is] the pendulum ... [that] controls the whole movement of the mechanism."

Secretary Bryan spoke next. First he reminded the audience that President Wilson had already made it clear that it was official policy to "open the doors of all the weaker countries to an invasion of American capital and enterprise." Having made that point, Bryan referred to an engaging custom of one such country as a way of convincing the businessmen of his deep concern for their welfare. "In Spanish-speaking countries," he reminded them, "hospitality is expressed by a phrase, 'My house is your house.' ... I can say, not merely in courtesy —but as a fact—my Department is your department; the ambassadors, the ministers, and the consuls are all yours. It is their business to look after your interests and to guard your rights."

On the next day the convention left its downtown quarters for a special meeting in the East Room of the White House. President Wilson had seen fit to take time from his more official duties to address the delegates. His purpose was to assure them that he gave full and active support to a mutual campaign to effect "the righteous conquest of foreign markets." Perhaps it was because some in his audience seemed startled by that candid statement of policy, but in any event Wilson went on to emphasize the point by remarking that such an objective was "one of the things we hold nearest to our heart."

As in earlier periods, the question of whether or not American leaders acted from personal economic motives is beside the point. Indeed, such an approach raises false questions. Without any doubt, the businessmen acted on an economic calculus, and it is sophistry to camouflage the obvious as the complex. It is far more important that many of the businessmen and politicians were thinking about American foreign policy in terms of the functioning of the economic *system*, and that they saw overseas economic expansion as the key element in such security and welfare.

In most respects, furthermore, the Wilson Administration agreed with the businessmen about the best means to facilitate overseas economic expansion. One section of the Federal Reserve Act, for example, had just that purpose. Wilson's tariff commission also concentrated on enlarging and securing markets for surplus production. An even more dramatic step was taken with the passage of the Webb-Pomerene Act. This law developed out of the consensus on the need to improve America's weapons in the battle for supremacy in world markets, a concern heightened by the realization that the postwar struggle would be even tougher. It repealed the antitrust laws for overseas operations, thus providing a bipartisan American answer to foreign cartels. Another law, the Edge Act, extended the provisions of the Federal Reserve Act which encouraged American financial operations overseas. Wilson also reactivated the old American banking consortium as the chosen instrument of American open door expansion in the Far East. These moves took on added significance in the context of the Bolshevik Revolution in Russia in November 1917 (after which event Wilson undertook to extend the open door to Russia), but it is vital to realize that these acts represented a consensus between the Wilson Administration and the business community which had been apparent as early as 1912.

An understanding of this consensus, and of the related convergence of the reformist and economic drives for expansion, offers a key insight into America's entry into World War I. Most Americans shared Wilson's nationalistic outlook. None but a handful of citizens quarreled with his assertion that it was the destiny of the United States to become the "justest, the most progressive, the most honorable, the most enlightened Nation in the world." Indeed, a sizable plurality thought, if they did not assume, that the destiny was being realized in their own time. In the early months of the war, therefore, it was quite natural for them to feel, along with Wilson, that America had neither reason nor necessity to enter the conflict.

But, and again in agreement with Wilson, most Americans wanted the Allies to win, and they were willing to help bring about that result. Whatever the faults and sins of England and France, they were better than autocratic Germany. America could work with them toward a peaceful, prosperous, and moral world, whereas such would be impossible if Germany won. This attitude, and the actions which it prompted, led Wilson and America into a position where they had either to abandon their determination and destiny to lead the world or go to war.

The early economic decisions made by businessmen and the Wilson Administration committed the American economic system to the Allied war effort. That did not, in itself, make it inevitable that America's nonbelligerent alignment with the Allies would involve America in the war on their side; but it did make it extremely difficult for Wilson to achieve his objectives in any other way.

The American economy was in a depression when the war erupted. Financier J. Pierpont Morgan described the situation in an accurate and straightforward manner. "The war opened during a period of hard times that had continued in America for over a year. Business throughout the country was depressed, farm prices were deflated, unemployment was serious, the heavy industries were working far below capacity [and] bank clearings were off." Vanderlip's comment was more elliptical: "The country was not in a prosperous situation."

The first economic shocks of the conflict subjected the system to even more difficulties. The stock market and the cotton exchange were closed on July 31, 1914, and did not reopen for public trading for many, many months. "We were looking after our own troubles," Vanderlip later explained, and "bankers in general were not considering technical matters of neutrality." Instead, Vanderlip went on, "we had the idea very much of keeping up our foreign trade throughout the world." In making that effort, it was not very surprising that American entrepreneurs concentrated on reopening their connections with the Allies, who together with their colonies had purchased 77 per cent of American exports in 1913—and with whom the majority of American bankers had their closest connections.

But in restoring America's foreign trade by tying it to England and France (and by expanding old connections with such nations as Russia), rather than by insisting upon economic neutrality, Wilson and American businessmen tied themselves to a prosperity based on the Allied war program. Wilson developed no other plan to end the depression, and hence this way of dealing with the problem exerted a subtle but persuasive influence on later decisions.

Economic ties to the Allies also reinforced the bias of Wilson's ideology and morality toward defining German naval warfare as the most important diplomatic issue of the war. Wilson denounced submarine warfare on moral and humanitarian grounds, whereas he opposed British trade restrictions on legal and historical precedents. And the fact that Wilson launched no crusade against the Allied food blockade of Germany, which had equally devastating moral and humanitarian consequences, dramatized this double standard.

This ability to make such fine moral discriminations forced Wilson into an extremely difficult situation. He hoped to remain a nonbelligerent until a stalemate developed and then step in as the arbiter of the settlement and as the architect of a world organization to establish and maintain peace. But by seeming to foreshadow the defeat of England and France, the success of submarine warfare also threatened his ability to lead the world to permanent peace. Wilson resolved his difficulties (and apparently eased his troubled conscience) by defining the situation as similar to the case of the Philippines. America was justified in using force "to do justice and assert the rights of

mankind." To that end, war against Germany would be prose-
cuted until it established "a government we can trust."

By the time of World War I, therefore, the basic dilemma
of American foreign policy was clearly defined. Its generous
humanitarianism prompted it to improve the lot of less fortunate peoples, but that side of its diplomacy was undercut
by two other aspects of its policy. On the one hand, it defined
helping people in terms of making them more like Americans.
This subverted its ideal of self-determination. On the other
hand, it asserted and acted upon the necessity of overseas
economic expansion for its own material prosperity. But by
defining such expansion in terms of markets for American
exports, and control of raw materials for American industry,
the ability of other peoples to develop and act upon their own
patterns of development was further undercut.

Those unfortunate aspects of American foreign policy were
summarized rather well by an American reformer who at one
time had shared the attitude of Roosevelt and Wilson. He even
agreed that entry into World War I was necessary. But he
broke with Roosevelt and Wilson over the very points which
undercut the ideal, and the practice, of self-determination.
Perhaps his judgment is too harsh, yet it offers an important
insight into Wilson's failure and into America's difficulties at
mid-century. For that reason, but not as a final verdict either
on Wilson or the United States, it deserves consideration.

Looking back across the years, Raymond Robins reflected on
the origins of the crisis in American diplomacy in these words:
"Wilson was a great man but he had one basic fault. He was
willing to do anything for people except get off their backs
and let them live their own lives. He would never let go until
they forced him to and then it was too late. He never seemed
to understand there's a big difference between trying to save
people and trying to help them. With luck you can help 'em—
but they always save themselves."

One of the most helpful aspects of that estimate of Wilson
and his diplomacy lies in the suggestion that it offers about
American entry into the war and America's response to the
revolutions which occurred during and at the end of that conflict. For given entry into the war on the grounds that "the
world must be made safe for democracy," the crucial questions

become those about the definition of democracy and the means to insure its security. Having answered those questions, it may then be possible to determine and understand the reasons why the effort did not succeed.

CHAPTER THREE

I am proposing, as it were, that the nations should with one accord adopt the doctrine of President Monroe as the doctrine of the world. . . .

I am proposing that all nations henceforth avoid entangling alliances. . . .

I am proposing government by the consent of the governed . . . freedom of the seas . . . and that moderation of armaments which makes of armies and navies a power for order. . . .

These are American principles, American policies. We could stand for no others. And they are also the principles and policies of forward-looking men and women everywhere, of every modern nation, of every enlightened community. They are the principles of mankind and must prevail.

WOODROW WILSON, JANUARY, 1917

The Peace which we propose must be a people's peace . . . guaranteeing to each nation freedom for economic and cultural development. Such a peace can only be concluded by the direct and courageous struggle of the revolutionary masses against all imperialist plans and aggressive designs.

Overthrow those robbers and enslavers of your country. . . . Let them no longer violate your hearths! You must yourselves

THE RISING TIDE OF REVOLUTION

*be masters in your own land! You yourselves must arrange
your life as you see fit! You have the right to do this, for your
fate is in your own hands!*

THE COUNCIL OF PEOPLE'S COMMISSARS, TO THE WORKERS
OF THE WORLD, NOVEMBER–DECEMBER, 1917

PRESIDENT WILSON [*remarked that*]. . . . *There was certainly
a latent force behind Bolshevism which attracted as much
sympathy as its more brutal aspects caused general disgust.
There was throughout the world a feeling of revolt against
the large vested interests which influenced the world both in
the economic and in the political sphere. The way to cure
this domination was, in his opinion, constant discussion and
a slow process of reform; but the world at large had grown
impatient of delay.*

FROM THE MINUTES OF A MEETING OF THE BIG FIVE
AT THE PARIS PEACE CONFERENCE, JANUARY, 1919

*The question now arose whether we ought to include in the
new terms of the armistice other problems, such as that of
Poland.*

PRESIDENT WILSON *suggested it might be unwise to discuss a
proposal of this sort on its individual merits, since it formed*

part of the much larger question of . . . how to meet the so-cial danger of Bolshevism.

FROM THE MINUTES OF THE MEETING OF THE SUPREME
WAR COUNCIL IN PARIS, JANUARY, 1919

Woodrow Wilson's attempt to use America's great power to make the world safe for democracy, and to establish an international order to maintain that security, was an essentially conservative effort. His definition of democracy, his emphasis on preserving that particular society, and the means he proposed to accomplish the task were rooted in the nineteenth-century liberal conception of the world. And his view of human nature, his political theory and action, and his idea that the United States would take over the international role that Great Britain had played between 1815 and 1915 further characterized him as a man of that outlook and tradition. Wilson was confident that the principles and procedures of nineteenth-century liberalism were just and sound; he felt, therefore, that the basic problem was to establish a framework in which they could produce the well-being of all concerned.

Wilson's reservations about the existing state of affairs did not include any doubts concerning the fundamental structure of society. He did, however, realize that the rise of the large corporation, and similar organized groups in the political economy, called for some changes in the *Weltanschauung* of nineteenth-century liberalism. There were three broad approaches that could be followed. One answer was to evolve a new philosophy and program to fit the facts of advanced industrial society. Another involved extensive and probably somewhat ruthless government intervention to recreate the political economy of the individual entrepreneur.

But both of those proposals involved drastic action, and Wilson had no intention of embarking upon such a course. "We shall deal with an economic system as it is and as it may be modified," he announced as he entered the White House in 1913, "not as it might be if we had a clean sheet of paper to write on." That strong antipathy to fundamental change limited Wilson to the third alternative. He accepted the corporation and similar groups and tried to modify and adapt, and thereby sustain, his nineteenth-century liberalism in a situation in which the individual had actually lost much of his power to initiate, or even control, affairs that affected him immediately and fundamentally.

Despite the series of specific and general revolutions that occurred throughout the world between his election in 1912 and his death in 1924, Wilson never seriously altered his conception of the world. As indicated in an article in the *Atlantic Monthly*, he was still looking at the end of his life for "The Road Away From Revolution." But the impact of these revolutions provoked many Americans formerly in agreement with him to modify their outlook. A majority of those who left Wilson's position emphasized the need for America to oppose the revolutions with more determination, and to continue its independent expansion with greater vigor. Only a few argued that it was wiser to accept the revolutions and to modify or change America's traditional conception of the world. Taken together, however, those who disagreed with Wilson were more numerous than those who continued to support him. In the end, therefore, Wilson's crusade was defeated by revolutions overseas and by the domestic American response to these upheavals.

At the hour of its entry into the war, however, America broadly shared the assumptions of Wilson's liberalism and responded to his definition of America's war aims. Though it admitted that there were exceptions in reality, American liberalism was a philosophy derived from the axiom and belief that a harmony of interests actually existed and could be secured. Such an underlying community of interest was held to eventuate in community well-being if it was not distorted or thwarted. As a consequence of their ideological childhood within the tradition of natural law, their enormous natural resources, and the absence of any serious opponents in the New World, Americans had followed the line of least resistance in developing their political economy. Founded on a simple (if not crude) concept of natural law, its theory was as neat a circle as ever was drawn freehand. Conflicts of interest were asserted to be mere appearances, or the result of misguided action by others, because the doctrine of a harmony of interests defined them in that fashion. Hence intervention in the social process was necessary and justified only to remove the obstacles placed there by others who did not understand or honor the truth.

Though negative in form, such intervention became very positive in practice, for the theory defined every opponent of the United States as being misadvised about the nature of the world. In a way that John Locke had tended to do in his own philosophical writings which provided the master text for liberalism, Americans became very prone to define their rivals as unnatural men. They were thus beyond the pale and almost, if not wholly, beyond redemption. Reinforced by an expansionist, or frontier, interpretation of history that explained nationalistic expansion as a necessary and justified part of natural law, the theory was further supported by ethnic and religious prejudices. The final result was that domestic problems became international problems, for it was necessary to remove the restrictions upon America's natural right to resolve its domestic difficulties by natural expansion.

This outlook was literally an all-encompassing conception of the world. Americans could not only conquer nature, but they could put their self-interest to work to produce the well-being and the harmony of the world. Their theory not only held that they could do these things; it asserted the natural necessity of action. Any other course violated natural law and thus subverted the harmony of interests. Throughout the twentieth century, and particularly after World War I, the thesis was advanced with great force by various American experts in casuistry. But the logic of the theory itself led most Americans to the conclusions in complete innocence. They were neither hypocrites nor sophists; they simply accepted and believed the idea that American expansion naturally improved the world—as well as being necessary for their own democracy and prosperity.

Turning from these general characteristics of American liberalism, it is helpful to outline the more specific nature of the society which Wilson and other Americans had in mind when they asserted that the world must be made safe for democracy. Supported by an examination of the means proposed to accomplish that task, such a review will provide considerable insight into the international and domestic opposition which developed between 1917 and 1920. There are several ways to approach this task of definition, but one of the most fruitful is to consider American liberalism from the vantage point of its outlook on key issues: economics, politics, social questions such as race, color, and religion, and the international phenomena of nationalism, colonialism, and imperialism.

As defined by Wilson and other Americans, the economic aspect of democracy was based on the classical liberal assumption of a society composed of free, independent, and enlightened individuals who acted in their own self-interest as producers and consumers. For the consumer, price was the criterion of self-interest. For the producer, it was profit—or the wage contract that the worker negotiated with the owner. Since all of these indicators could be measured in money, the interplay of the various self-interests in the market place produced an automatic and perpetual functioning of the system. Hence the profit motive, if allowed to operate freely through the individual, produced the maximum benefit for the community as well as the welfare of the individual.

Given a natural system of this character, the government had neither cause nor justification to intervene in economic affairs except for a few well-defined purposes. Almost all were negative in nature: protecting the validity of the money, or measuring, system; maintaining order; enforcing the definition of economic malpractices; and clearing out any remnants of mercantilism. Its one positive responsibility was nevertheless vitally important to the functioning of the system: the protection and extension of the market in which the principle of free competition could operate. As with mercantilism, classical liberal economics led to an expansionist foreign policy.*

---

* Liberalism's intervention in domestic affairs should not, however, be misconceived as another similarity with mercantilism. Mercantilists intervened on the assumption that there was *not* any natural harmony of interests, and that men had therefore to create such harmony as there was by conscious, rational effort. The liberal, in contrast, intervened to establish conditions under which competition would—through the power of Adam Smith's famous Hidden Hand—allow the natural harmony of interests to assert itself. The distinction is crucial.

In most cases, therefore, the liberal state maintained and extended the practice of colonialism. In others, it modified the pattern of expansion into what British historians have called "informal empire" or "free-trade imperialism," where the liberal state relied upon its industrial and general economic power to structure and control weaker or less developed nations.* Local or native peoples often ruled, but they did so within limits (and rules) defined by their economic ties with the imperial power. As far as the weaker country was concerned, this meant in practice that one segment of society ruled. When this pattern of events was called democracy, as it often was, the rest of the population tended to conclude that democracy was not what it wanted. For this reason, as well as in consequence of the more obvious economic results of the policy, such peoples were inclined to respond to radical leadership that offered them a greater share in running affairs, as well as a more general distribution of wealth.

Wilson's original program was designed to perform the domestic and international functions of the liberal state. As with Theodore Roosevelt before him, however, Wilson was confronted by the fact that free competition worked to restrict free competition. As implied by its very name, the system of natural law tended to establish a balance among the powerful or cunning survivors of competition. It was impractical, if not impossible, to destroy the successful competitors. And neither Wilson nor the majority of Americans even considered substituting a different system. To cope with the domestic side of the dilemma, Wilson moved toward a modification of the classical liberal position. He accepted the existence of certain large groups, particularly the corporation and the labor union, and attempted to fit them into traditional liberal economic and social theory.

While at first glance this may seem to offer a rational and perceptive solution, even a modest amount of reflection reveals at least two fundamental weaknesses. In the first place, the result of equating the organized and institutionalized group with the individual is to create a kind of syndicalism or corpo-

---

* Here see: H. S. Ferns, "Britain's Informal Empire in Argentina, 1806–1914," *Past and Present* (1953); and J. Gallagher and R. Robinson, "The Imperialism of Free Trade," *The Economic History Review* (1953).

ratism in which the groups (or blocs) compete with each other. The individual, unless he is one of the very few to attain a position of great power or high authority within such blocs, has almost no role in the formulation of alternatives, and only moderate and occasional influence in choosing between programs or policies developed by the top leaders. The second weakness concerns the way in which this ostensible solution promotes discouragement, disillusionment, and finally apathy or a particularly narrow and selfish kind of cynicism, as the discrepancy between the theory and the reality becomes increasingly apparent.*

Despite such weaknesses in that outlook, of which he was not totally unaware, Wilson nevertheless transferred his approach to domestic affairs to the problems of foreign policy. His conception of the League of Nations, for example, was clearly evolved in that fashion. And for Wilson, as for his predecessors and successors, the Open Door Policy was America's version of the liberal policy of informal empire or free-trade imperialism. None of them had the slightest idea of organizing the co-operative, planned, balanced economic development of world resources. Wilson aimed to use American power, inside and outside the League of Nations, merely to order the world so that such classical competition could proceed in peace. If this could be done, he was confident that American economic power could take care of the United States —and of the world.

Wilson's political ideas and objectives were equally traditional. Based on the same principle of natural law which underwrote liberal economic theory, liberal political theory asserted that each individual participated in the process of decision-making on the basis of his own self-interest. Given the existence of natural political freedoms, such as those of speech and association, the individual's exercise of his positive freedom to participate in the political process would lead to democratic decisions. The theory asserted, in short, that the

* For further discussion of this development see, *The Contours of American History* (New York: World Publishing Co., 1961). The best known (but nevertheless unsuccessful) attempt to squeeze such syndicalism into the framework of liberalism is J. K. Galbraith, *American Capitalism. The Theory of Countervailing Power* (Boston: Harper & Bros., 1952).

enjoyment and exercise of natural political rights assured the individual of his share of power.

More than was the case in economic matters, however, Americans were aware of the discrepancy between this theory of political liberalism and the reality of their political experience. For a generation before entering World War I they had grappled, through the instrument of the bipartisan Progressive movement, with the imbalance created by the impact of consolidated economic power on the political process. They grew ever more aware that such economic power exercised disproportionate political influence—directly by organized pressure on elected representatives and indirectly by the broad political and social consequences of economic decisions. As one American of the time expressed it, "the dollar votes more times than the man." Some Americans, probably Wilson among them, ultimately sensed that the Mexican Revolution was in part a violent protest against a similar discrepancy between theory and reality. This experience helped them understand a bit more the general revolt against political liberalism and was a restraining factor in their response to the challenge, but it did not lead them to formulate and act upon a new conception of democracy.

This reluctance to embark upon a thoroughgoing re-examination of the existing order was the result of many factors. Some of them were negative. By comparison with the depression years of the 1890s, for example, the period after 1900 seemed bright and rosy. In addition, the war intensified the general psychological propensity to go along with the existing order despite its weaknesses and failures. A more important consideration, and one that was positive in character, was the renewed confidence that came with recovery from the depression.

Reforms such as the initiative and the referendum, the direct election of senators, and numerous antitrust prosecutions encouraged the belief that classical liberalism could be modified to work under new conditions. And the convergence of the reformist and economic expansionism generated enthusiasm for America's mission in the world. The frontier interpretation of American history, having been modernized to fit an industrial society, was once again becoming an article of faith—just as its agrarian version had become in the 1830s and 1840s. Americans increasingly considered themselves once more on the move to "extend the area of freedom."

But this new enthusiasm in the United States developed at a time when classical liberalism was coming under heavy criticism in much of the world. Thus there were many doubts about the *kind* of freedom that America was extending, as well as about the morality of doing so. In addition to questions about the economic effects of such overseas expansion, there was also skepticism about some of its political and social characteristics. An increasing number of foreigners was aware, for example, that political and social democracy in the United States were largely limited to white Anglo-Saxons.

When transferred to the world scene, those color and ethnic restrictions became even more apparent. Democracy tended in practice to be replaced by an outlook summarized in the familiar phrase about the white man's burden. That approach was based on the quite different thesis that colored people were somehow never ready for democracy and self-government. It was possible, of course, to defend various limitations on democracy and representative government on logical as well as historical and practical grounds. Indeed, a very great deal of intellectual and emotional energy was invested in that effort by Americans, as well as by Europeans with colonial empires to defend.

Such arguments were not very strong, however, because political democracy had begun, even in the white Western countries, as a process in which only a small segment of the adult population participated. Colored peoples pointed out, quite plausibly, that their societies were already structured for such a form of democracy. And when, as was the case with American liberalism, it was further implied, if not vehemently asserted, that democracy *really* worked only for white, Anglo-Saxon, Protestant Christians, the appeal of democracy suffered even more. For this argument led rather rapidly to the conclusion that even at best democracy meant little more than the modification of colonialism in the direction of less harsh protectorates or open-door imperialism.

For these reasons, American liberalism's definition of democracy as it pertained to self-determination and colonialism lost much of its democratic content once it moved beyond Western Europe. Colonial societies began to realize that America's anticolonialism neither implied nor offered freedom from extensive and intensive foreign influence. Whatever the evidence that Wilson ever entertained any idea of actually trying to limit such absentee authority to its absolute minimum of voluntary respect and emulation, and the data is neither extensive nor convincing, it is clear that he never developed or pushed such a program.

At best, Wilson's actions were in keeping with the principles of a moralistic and paternalistic open-door imperialism. At worst, he intervened with force in the affairs of other nations. America's verbal support for the principle of self-determination became in practice the reordering of national boundaries in Europe on the basis of ethnic and linguistic criteria. Though it had considerable relevance for Western Europe, this principle and practice of nationality had less meaning in Eastern Europe—and still less throughout the rest of the world. But it was not even applied to many areas. Japan was treated as an inferior, for example, and the colonial empires were hardly touched. They were most certainly not broken up into independent states according to the principle of self-determination. And even though some improvements did result from the mandate system where it was applied, that approach was characterized by minimum changes in the existing pattern of colonialism.

Taken seriously, a commitment to the principle of self-determination means a policy of standing aside for peoples to make their own choices, economic as well as political and cultural. It is based on a willingness to live and let live—a broad tolerance for other peoples' preferences and a willingness, if the opportunity is offered, to help them achieve their own goals in their own fashion. It is the philosophy of an integrated personality, and it might be defined as the foreign policy of a mature society.* Though it avowed this principle, the actions of America in the realm of foreign affairs did not follow this

---

* It could of course be maintained with considerable power that the philosophy of self-determination actually leads, if followed rigorously, to pacifism, and to anarchism practiced within small communities. Both Wilson and the Bolsheviks declined to pursue the logic that far.

pattern. Hence it was not surprising, as Wilson's actions became apparent, that many peoples of the world felt misled by Wilson's slogans about self-determination. It was one thing to shape one's own culture, but quite another to be pushed aside while others haggled over ethnic statistics and then drew lines on a map.

As suggested by many of his actions in Mexico, and by his call for war without quarter until Germany erected a government that "we can trust," Wilson's liberal practice was not in keeping with his liberal principles. This became even more apparent as he began to reveal his ideals about a League of Nations. That program amounted to a direct and almost literal application of the principles of America's domestic liberalism to the world at large. The League of Nations became the state, and its function was to maintain order and enforce the rules of the game at the international level. Given such security, the national pursuit of self-interest would, according to the doctrine of a harmony of interests, produce peace and prosperity throughout the world.

Beyond that point, however, the attempt to formulate an international system on the principles of such liberalism encountered a difficult issue. It was simple to say that the League corresponded to the state, but it was not at all easy to specify the power structure of the international state. The logical answer defined it as a Parliament of Man, but that did not answer the question; it only asked it in a different way. It was still necessary to specify such mundane but vital things as the nature of the franchise and the institutional structure of the government. Wilson answered these questions by combining his concept of America's supremacy with the political theory of classical liberalism. Every nation could vote, but nothing could be done without the prior existence of a concert of power (or harmony of interests) among the big nations. That was as weighted a franchise as ever proposed under the name of liberalism, particularly since Wilson assumed that America (in association with Great Britain) would lead the concert of major powers.

Considered on its own merits, the idea of a concert of power among the strongest nations had much to recommend it on the grounds that it assigned responsibility to those with the ability to make basic decisions. But when judged against the rhetoric and principles of classical liberalism it was quite clearly a contradiction in terms. For by the key tenet of liberalism, namely the existence of a harmony of interests, it was possible to produce the general welfare only under conditions of free competition. Yet by establishing an oligopoly of power, and formalizing it in an unconditional guarantee of "the territorial integrity and existing political independence" of the nations admitted to the League (on criteria prescribed by the oligopoly itself), Wilson's proposal destroyed the possibility of free competition. And it was precisely on this point that the League of Nations was attacked by some American liberals themselves, as well as by radicals and conservatives in the United States and throughout the world.

Both at home and abroad, the radicals made the most fundamental criticism because they challenged all of Wilson's definitions of liberal democracy. Their assault was supported, particularly in the early years of the revolutionary upsurge throughout the world, by a heretical movement within liberalism itself which strengthened the radicals by weakening Wilson's position. Left-wing liberalism developed from the same philosophy of natural law which classical liberalism cited as the sanction for its own program. But while they accepted the doctrine of a natural harmony of interests, the heretical liberals went on to raise the question as to why the existing society did not correspond to the ideal society. In reply, they argued that certain institutions, particularly that of private property in its large, concentrated, and consolidated forms, prevented the natural harmony from emerging from the free interplay of individuals pursuing their self-interest. That analysis led the heretics to the conclusion that it was necessary to make structural changes in the existing society before the workings of natural law could produce the general welfare. In sharp contrast, Wilson (and the conservatives) would support nothing more than a "slow process of reform" in which they saw no need, and most certainly had no intention, of shaking the foundations of the status quo. Hence the heretics proposed many measures, particularly in economic, social, and international matters, which approximated some of those advanced by the radicals. But the heretic liberals were drastic reformers, not revolutionaries. This was a vital distinction, for in time it led the heretics to oppose the radicals as vigorously as did the classical liberals or even the conservatives.

For their part, the radicals started from a fundamentally different premise. They denied the existence—save perhaps in some mythical past—of a natural harmony of interests. They held that conflict was the essence of life and that it would never end short of death. Yet they also argued that each broad conflict within society was resolved on a higher level and thus produced a better life in the new society. And, in some of their most free-wheeling arguments and prophecies, they asserted that later conflicts would be nonviolent and would concern ideas and broad cultural issues. Men would dispute the best means of becoming more human, not the distribution of wealth and power. In its own way, therefore, the radical theory promised a society not too different from the one prophesied by the heretical liberals on the quite different basis of a harmony of interests inherent in natural law. But the radicals not only thought it necessary to go further in changing society, they also accepted revolution as a justifiable and honorable method.

In economic matters, for example, they denied the validity of the liberals' market economy. They judged it neither fair nor truly efficient. They advocated instead the idea of planned production for use and welfare. To accomplish this, they proposed that the government should take title to resources and direct the production of goods and services for all the society on an equitable basis. Such economic decisions would not only facilitate development in other areas of life, they would also become the stuff of politics, and in that fashion politics would once again become relevant and meaningful to each citizen. This mode of production and distribution would not only make work itself meaningful to the individual and the group, but would end the struggle for raw existence and hence free men for personal and cultural development.

Radicals made no discrimination as to which men would enjoy the fruits of the revolution, except that they excluded those who fought to retain their privileges of the past. They handled the question of religion in two ways. In the broadest sense they secularized it, converting it into a faith in the ability of man to realize his full potential in this world. More immediately, either they attacked it as a façade for privilege and power or interpreted its idealism as support for their program. As for color or ethnic origins, they denied the validity of such criteria as the basis of any decision, an attitude that enabled them to avoid Wilson's contradiction between self-determination and nationality and the exclusiveness of his Protestant Christianity and Anglo-Saxonism. In this way, radicals appealed to all men across all existing—or proposed— boundaries.

Their approach to self-determination gave the radicals a double-edged weapon against colonialism and the less overt forms of imperial expansion such as the Open Door Policy. For by asserting the right of self-determination, they identified themselves with anticolonialism, which was the lowest common denominator of nationalism, yet also aligned themselves with the more developed and specific expressions of nationalism. Thus they offered leadership to those who wished to end formal colonialism, as well as to others who sought to assert their full sovereignty against spheres of influence and similar restrictions established under the Open Door Policy.

In the broadest sense, therefore, the radicals offered the peoples of the world an explanation of their existing hardships, a program to end such difficulties and build a better world, and leadership in that common effort. This radical assault on classical liberalism and conservatism was a direct challenge to Wilson and to the United States. And through the communist victory of November 1917, in Russia, all those separate revolutions—in economics, politics, social values, and international affairs—seemed to become institutionalized in a nation of tremendous potential.

Though obviously of great importance to an understanding of American diplomacy in the twentieth century, the Bolshevik Revolution and the subsequent rise of the Soviet Union as a thermonuclear power can nevertheless be overemphasized to the point of creating serious errors of analysis and interpretation. Indeed, that very preoccupation (and the warped perspective that it created) does a great deal to explain many otherwise perplexing actions by American leaders. It helps tremendously, for example, to account for the near-panic manifested by otherwise perceptive, intelligent, and sober men when

Castro sustained his power in Cuba.* And in a broader sense, it offers considerable insight into the reasons why American leaders persistently interpreted political and social unrest throughout the world as a consequence of the Bolshevik Revolution, and why they steadily expanded the nation's overseas commitments beyond any rational calculation (even by the axioms of their expansionist *Weltanschauung*) of the country's resources. This myopic and self-defeating preoccupation with the Bolshevik Revolution existed long before the Soviet Union orbited a man in space. Fundamentally, and from the outset, American leaders were for many, many years more afraid of the implicit and indirect challenge of the revolution than they were of the actual power of the Soviet Union.

The great majority of American leaders were so deeply

---

* Perhaps the most striking example of this is provided by Adolf A. Berle, Jr. Berle, prior to the Cuban Revolution, was one of the most astute and rigorous minds seeking to resolve the tragedy of American diplomacy in a creative manner. For that matter, his analyses of the domestic political economy continue to exhibit those exceptional characteristics. But Castro so provoked and frightened Berle that he was unable (along with others) even to interpret the Cuban crisis within the limits of his formerly sophisticated expansionism.

Before the Cuban Revolution, for example, I had the good fortune to hear Berle expound for two hours in an exceedingly brilliant manner on the dangerous consequences of America's expansion within the strategy of the Open Door Policy. He spoke knowingly and candidly about the way that the expansion of corporations into Latin America influenced the politics of those countries, and of the manner in which they returned an unfair share of their gross profits to the United States—and thereby intensified tensions even further. He concluded his analysis with a remark so simple and eloquent, as well as true, that it visibly and deeply affected the twenty-odd men and women who heard it: "Either we build a true and brilliant community in the Western Hemisphere—or we go under."

Now the central point of all this should not be misunderstood. Let the whole issue of expansionism stand moot. What remains, and what cannot be rationalized away, is the inability of Berle to act on his own aphorism. For the Cuban Revolution offered the United States an almost unique opportunity to get on with the work of building a community in the Western Hemisphere. Yet Berle very soon interpreted that revolution as part of a conspiracy by the Soviet Union to spread communism. Neither Berle nor the others of the large group he symbolizes made any serious or sustained effort to jump in, *even within the assumptions of their expansionist outlook*, and help the moderate elements begin that work—which would in turn have given them a very strong position within the revolutionary coalition. A more saddening example of the unhappy consequences of reading world history since 1917 in terms of the Bolshevik Revolution would be very difficult to find.

concerned with the Bolshevik Revolution because they were so uneasy about what President Wilson called the "general feeling of revolt" against the existing order, and about the increasing intensity of that dissatisfaction. The Bolshevik Revolution became in their minds the symbol of all the revolutions that grew out of that discontent. And that is perhaps the crucial insight into the tragedy of American diplomacy.

Those other specific and general revolutions would have continued and reached their climaxes even if the Bolsheviks had never seized power in Russia. They were revolutions that had been fed and sustained by the policies of the West itself for more than a century. American policy was fundamentally no more than a sophisticated version of those same policies.

The underlying nature of the tragedy is defined by the confrontation between those two elements, not just or primarily by the conflict between the United States and the Soviet Union. The tragedy was of course dramatized, and unquestionably made more intense, by the way that American leaders reduced all such revolutions to the Bolshevik Revolution. Indeed, their behavior could be offered as a textbook example of the reductionist fallacy. Or, to use a metaphor from daily life, they blinded themselves at the outset of their search for an answer to the "general feeling of revolt" that disturbed them so much.

It is vital to realize, therefore, that the radical and revolutionary impact was not limited—even between 1917 and 1921—to events in Russia. On the European scene, communists came to power in Hungary and showed strength in Germany; * and the heretical liberals attacked the status quo in England and other countries. The Arab Revolution in the Middle East, while it was predominantly anticolonial and nationalistic and was led by liberals and conservatives, nevertheless represented the international elements of the broad radical movement. A similar pattern emerged in the Far East. Chinese revolutionaries, some of whom did look to Russia for advice and leadership, asserted their rapport with the radical challenge—on

---

* The reader should remember that the army of the Soviet Union had nothing to do with this communist revolution in Hungary at the end of World War I. As will be seen, it was the West, under the leadership of President Wilson and Herbert Hoover, which intervened to overturn the earlier communist revolution.

domestic as well as international issues. And Japanese conservatives (and liberals), who asserted their nationalistic and ethnic equality with the West, pre-empted certain radical policies as weapons for their own purposes. All of these developments, considered individually and en masse, posed serious problems for American leadership at the end of World War I.

Confronted directly by the opposition overseas, Wilson faced still other difficulties. His original hope to establish a concert of power with Great Britain and France was weakened by their initial opposition to certain of his proposals. The revolutionary ferment in Europe, Asia, and the Middle East only intensified the determination of the imperial powers to retain and strengthen their existing empires. A similar reaction occurred in America, and Wilson's coalition for the crusade to make the world safe for democracy disintegrated into a great internal struggle over what policy would enable America to assert its power most effectively in dealing with Japanese and European competitors and the wave of revolutions engulfing the world.

Wilson's personal dilemma symbolized the broader difficulties faced by classical liberalism. According to the basic principles of natural law, he should have accepted the revolutions as competing units which would contribute their share to a broader and deeper harmony of interests. But his expansionist philosophy of history, his crusading zeal and his nationalism—which also were integral parts of his liberalism—prompted him to oppose the revolutions as barricades on America's road to domestic well-being and world leadership. The tragedy was defined by his attempt to resolve the dilemma by preserving and extending democracy through a policy of open-door expansion.

His approach satisfied neither his own followers nor the foreigners who looked to America (and to Wilson in particular) for a creative alternative to the revolutionaries. Instead, it left the battleground to the conservatives and the radicals. By attempting to achieve security through the traditional policy of the open door, America's conservatives emphasized the weakest aspects of Wilson's own program. And the liberals, having failed to offer a positive and effective alternative of their own, had in the end no place to go but into a bipartisan alignment with the conservatives.

CHAPTER FOUR

I. A GREAT DEBATE OVER THE TACTICS OF EMPIRE

It is wrong, perhaps, to say that Hughes stole Wilson's thunder, for Wilson himself had stolen Hay's.

A. WHITNEY GRISWOLD, 1938

I want for my part to go in and accept what is offered us, the leadership of the world. A leadership of what sort, my fellow citizens? . . . a liberating power . . .

Article X is the heart of the enterprise. . . . [It] says that every member of the League, and that means every great fighting power in the world, . . . solemnly engages to respect and preserve as against external aggression the territorial integrity and existing political independence of the other members of the League. If you do that, you have absolutely stopped ambitious and aggressive war.

WOODROW WILSON, 1919

If perpetual, [Article X] would be an attempt to preserve for all time unchanged the distribution of power and territory made in accordance with the views and exigencies of the Allies in this present juncture of affairs. It would necessarily be futile. . . . It would not only be futile; it would be mischievous.

THE LEGEND OF ISOLATIONISM

Change and growth are the law of life, and no generation can impose its will in regard to the growth of nations and the distribution of power, upon succeeding generations.

ELIHU ROOT, 1919

We are a great moral asset of Christian civilization. . . . How did we get there? By our own efforts. Nobody led us, nobody guided us, nobody controlled us. . . .

I would keep America as she has been—not isolated, not prevent her from joining other nations for these great purposes—but I wish her to be master of her own fate. . . .

HENRY CABOT LODGE, 1919

You must either give them independence, recognize their rights as nations to live their own lives and to set up their own form of government, or you must deny them these things by force. . . . You must respect not territorial boundaries, not territorial integrity, but you must respect and preserve the sentiments and passions for justice and for freedom which God in his infinite wisdom has planted so deep in the human heart that no form of tyranny however brutal, no persecution however prolonged can wholly uproot and kill. Respect nationality, respect justice, respect freedom, and you may have some hope of peace. . . .

But your treaty does not mean peace—far, very far from it.
If we are to judge the future by the past it means war.

WILLIAM E. BORAH, 1919

Though they did not do so at the time, Americans have come
to think of the 1920s as the nation's Lost Weekend in international affairs, as a period when the United States disregarded its world responsibilities by getting inebriated on the
homemade gin of isolationism. Natural though it may be to
take that view, looking back at the era through the smoke
and debris of World War II with a vision distorted by decades
of cold war, such an outlook nevertheless produces serious
misconceptions about American diplomacy. It not only de-
forms the history of the decade from 1919 to 1930, but it
also twists the story of American entry into World War II
and warps the record of the cold war.

Reconsidered, the postwar era appears as a crucial period
during which American leaders debated, formulated, and put
into operation their basic policy in response to the broad
revolutionary movements that erupted between 1910 and
1919. Approached in that fashion, the great debate over the
League of Nations appears less as a fight over accepting or
rejecting one document and one organization, or as a personal
struggle between Senator Henry Cabot Lodge and President
Wilson, and more as a broad argument over how America
should sustain and extend its power and authority in a world
of revolutions.

Though often defined and interpreted as an argument over
strategy for achieving basic objectives, the fight over the
League of Nations was in reality a conflict over tactics, or the
means of implementing the strategic program. The vast majority of American leaders, both private and official (and of
both parties), accepted the Open Door Policy as the strategy
of the United States in foreign affairs. That was not at issue.

Wilson and his supporters advocated joining the League of
Nations on the grounds that its system of collective security
to preserve the fundamental features of the status quo offered

the best method of keeping the world safe for the Open Door Policy. Given that framework, American power consolidated behind the integrated program of reformist and economic expansion would produce the perpetual welfare of the United States and the world. The bulk of Wilson's opponents accepted every essential point in that argument except the unequivocal involvement in a system of collective security which was in their view charged and committed by Article X of the League Covenant to a course of action that was—in Root's words—both futile and mischievous. They argued, in short, that Wilson's tactics would subvert the strategy.

Only a small, even tiny, minority maintained that the strategy itself was either inherently wrong, or that it had been rendered obsolete by the upsurge of revolutions throughout the world. Such men automatically opposed the tactics proposed by Wilson and his other critics. They disagreed among themselves over the kind of strategy that should be adopted to insure the security and welfare of the United States. Some wanted to align America more openly and actively with the revolutionary ferment in the world. Others were more conservative, but thought that the best strategy was to concentrate on affairs at home and let the example of a successful America win international influence and authority for the nation.* Whatever those differences, the minority as a group nevertheless insisted that the nation had to re-evaluate its role in the world and develop policies relevant to the new circumstances. And they had enough votes in the Senate to insure Wilson's defeat on the League of Nations.

Thus the end result of the great debate was neither a bold new strategy nor approval for Wilson's tactical proposal for implementing the existing one. The consensus that emerged was based on an agreement to push American overseas political and economic expansion, and on a further decision to avoid the policy of collective security on the grounds that it might easily weaken the United States, both defensively and

---

* These conservatives—a minority within a minority—are the only men to whom the term *isolationist* can be applied with any relevance or accuracy. The term is thus extremely misleading when generalized even to all those who voted against the League Treaty, let alone the policy-makers of the interwar years. Its use has thus crippled American thought about foreign policy for 50 years.

offensively, by tying it to various features of the status quo that were sure to disappear—and others that ought to be altered by America itself. The key to understanding American diplomacy of the 1920s is the realization that it was based on this coming of age of the Open Door Policy. It represented, indeed, a synthesis of the Open Door Notes, the Monroe Doctrine, and Washington's Farewell Address. By preserving and using its independence of action, America would employ its great economic power and ideological attractiveness through the means of the Open Door Policy to apply the principles of the Monroe Doctrine to the entire world. Woodrow Wilson and Herbert Hoover agreed that this was the "road away from revolution."

Often presented as classic antagonists, Wilson and Hoover actually complemented each other in their common effort to preserve the world of classical liberalism.* Wilson's greater human appeal made him a more successful politician and gave him more insight into certain aspects of the revolutionary ferment throughout the world. But Hoover thought more incisively about the basic problems of saving liberalism in an age of corporations and labor unions (even if he did not solve those issues), and also understood the dangers of an a priori commitment to the principle and practice of collective security.

Hoover unquestionably grasped the central weakness of Article X. It was seldom necessary for dealing with small conflicts; and, where the case was marginal, the collective security approach initiated a momentum that could easily turn it into a major crisis. When applied to one of two major powers involved in a conflict over vital national interests it would not resolve fundamental issues. Either the nation judged the aggressor would retreat only to emerge more antagonistic and dangerous or it would fight. To this extent, at least, and despite his personal aloofness, Hoover understood the principle and the psychology of self-determination better than Wilson.

For such reasons, coupled with his far better understanding

---

* Readers who find this so unusual an interpretation as to be dismissed at the outset are referred to Hoover's recent volume, *The Ordeal of Woodrow Wilson* (now in McGraw-Hill paperback edition). It is a moving tribute to Wilson, and also an illuminating review of American foreign policy at the end of World War I. See also the forthcoming study by Joan Hoff Wilson.

of the American economy, and its interrelationships with the world, Hoover placed less emphasis than Wilson on the political aspects of foreign policy. He felt that the right kind of politics would evolve from sound economics, and that it was more important to avoid serious political mistakes than to strive for brilliant political victories.* Hoover therefore concentrated, both while he was Secretary of Commerce (1921–1929) and President (1929–1933), on the more prosaic—but no less vital—job of building the kind of a *system* of overseas economic expansion envisaged by the strategy of the Open Door Policy. He wanted working agreements with the advanced industrial nations: they were to accommodate their differences peacefully so that they could stand together in the face of the revolutionary challenges of the age. On the other hand, and while he most certainly wanted to limit and control that ferment throughout the world, Hoover viewed the poor and underdeveloped societies as "the crippled countries" that should be helped by the United States.

During the crisis defined by communist triumphs in Russia and Hungary, and the revolutionary activity elsewhere in the world, Wilson and Hoover worked together very effectively. Both men grasped the fundamentals of America's dilemma. They realized, in different but overlapping ways, the broad challenge of the revolutions against the liberal world. They saw that the assault had grown out of the failure of liberalism to realize its theory and ideals, and hence understood the need to make it work in the United States as well as elsewhere. They agreed, moreover, that peace was a necessary prerequisite for this to be accomplished. At that point, however, the problem became very difficult. Policies had to be formulated to deal with each aspect of the crisis, yet all such policies had to be co-ordinated in one general outlook and program. Otherwise, American diplomacy would ultimately fail and leave the United States in a negative and weakened position.

Naturally enough, the issue of what to do about the communist victories in Russia and Hungary was of immediate importance. Hoover has provided a classic statement of this fact: "Communist Russia was a specter which wandered into

---

* Even if this propensity be called conservative, the conservatism involved is temperamental and not ideological.

the Peace Conference almost daily." The crisis completely disrupted Wilson's original peace program, making it necessary to delay the work of reforming the world under American leadership as part of sustaining America's own democracy and prosperity. First priority had to be given, at least temporarily, to the problem of checking the revolutions. That specific phase of the crisis was generalized, though not in communist form, by similar upheavals in the Middle East and Asia, where anticolonialism and nationalism challenged the existing order. But the noncommunist revolutions served to intensify rather than mitigate the differences among the victorious Allies. England and France, for example, opposed some of Wilson's suggestions concerning Germany and colonial territories. And Japan, though formally allied with the Western powers in Europe, was busy in Asia trying to exploit the anticolonial and nationalist revolutions for its own imperialist purposes. Yet all three powers shared Wilson's opposition to the communist revolutions, and their help was necessary if the liberal coalition was to be effective.

Though it sometimes appeared vague, even irresolute and contradictory, Wilson did develop a general program to cope with the complex crisis. His objective was to structure the peace settlement so that America could provide the intellectual, moral, economic, and military power and leadership to reinvigorate and sustain the liberal way of life throughout the world. So strengthened, liberalism would effectively undercut, and ultimately defeat, its revolutionary and radical antagonists.

True to the logic of his frontier-expansionist outlook, Wilson concluded that the victory abroad would insure domestic American welfare. That would make it possible to embark upon his desired "slow process of reform," which was to be based upon "some sort of partnership" between capital and labor, with the government playing the multiple roles of agent for each broad group within society and mediator between all of them. American diplomacy was thus the instrument of domestic well-being, and to this end Wilson proposed and acted upon two key ideas. He insisted upon Article X of the League of Nations Covenant, which secured the "territorial integrity and existing political independence" of member states

(Russia was excluded), and he sought to halt further revolutionary gains.

Wilson actively opposed the communist revolutions in Russia and Hungary. To do so he resorted to force, the manipulation of food supplies, and economic and military aid to counter-revolutionary groups. In Hungary, for example, Wilson collaborated closely with Hoover in employing the American Food Relief Mission to unseat the radical government of Bela Kun by denying needed supplies to that country as long as the communists stayed in power. This American intervention to overthrow a locally established communist government in Hungary offers more than just an illuminating parallel with the Russian intervention in Hungary in 1956. Of course, the Russians were directly ruthless. Yet it is self-righteous to argue that the American use of food to accomplish the same kind of objective was somehow more moral or civilized. Furthermore, the American action in 1919 may well have influenced the vigorous and very serious debate among Russian leaders before their decision to intervene with the Red Army in 1956.

In Russia, moreover, the United States used guns as well as the control of food and other economic supplies in its support of anti-Bolshevik forces. A great many efforts have been made, particularly during the years of the cold war, to prove that the United States did not intervene in Russia to overthrow the Bolshevik Revolution. Only a few of them have been based on extensive research and argued with any degree of sophistication. And even those have not been convincing because the evidence does not bear out the contention.*

The key to understanding and interpreting American intervention in Russia was supplied by Wilson himself. He did so while arguing against Winston Churchill, who advocated ruthless armed assault on the Bolsheviks, in a meeting of the Big Five at the Paris Peace Conference on February 14, 1919.

* The best efforts to establish this view are by B. M. Unterberger, *America's Siberian Expedition, 1918–1920* (Durham: Duke University Press, 1956); and G. F. Kennan, *Soviet-American Relations, 1917–1920* (Princeton: Princeton University Press, 2 vols., 1956, 1958). For a contrary view see: R. D. Warth, *The Allies and the Russian Revolution* (Durham: Duke University Press, 1954); and this writer's *American-Russian Relations, 1781–1947.*

In reply to Churchill's powerful rhetoric, the President put it all in two sentences: "*President Wilson . . .* himself felt guilty in that the United States had in Russia insufficient forces, but it was not possible to increase them. It was certainly a cruel dilemma."

Since it was Wilson himself who said in January 1918, that policy toward Russia was "the acid test" of Allied and American intentions, it does not seem unreasonable to suggest that the President knew he was failing his own examination question. Wilson and his advisors first attempted from November 1917 through the spring of 1918 to resolve the "cruel dilemma" by aiding anti-Bolshevik forces short of committing American troops. They realized that open armed intervention would very probably strengthen the Bolsheviks by enabling them to play upon the normal patriotic feelings of all Russians. As should be obvious, that policy did *not* mean that the Wilson Administration approved of the Bolsheviks, and it did *not* mean that the United States refrained from intervention.

Two developments changed the situation, and that early strategy, by the early summer of 1918. First, the Bolsheviks were still in power, and Wilson was clearly interested in seeing them overthrown. He had by that time ignored several overtures from Moscow. Second, Japan was intervening in Siberia, and that was viewed by Wilson as a danger to the Open Door Policy throughout Asia, *including Siberia.* Wilson considered it "essential" to maintain the open door strategy by checking the Japanese maneuver. The resulting policy was a bit complex, perhaps, but by no means so complicated or shrouded in mystery as to be impervious to research and analysis. The United States intervened against the Bolsheviks with troops and aid to anti-Bolshevik Russians, and it did so in a fashion designed to thwart Japan's ambitions in Siberia, Manchuria, and Northern China. Those who try to defend American action by denying the anti-Bolshevik side of it might be more effective in their general purpose, as well as more accurate, if they would defend the policy as a rather sophisticated attempt to accomplish an extremely difficult task.

Several factors combined to limit the extent and the effectiveness of American intervention. At first, the war against Germany claimed priority. Then, after the armistice, opponents of intervention in Russia (such as Senators William E. Borah and Hiram S. Johnson) blocked more vigorous action by threatening a Congressional investigation. Wilson told his subordinates to overcome that opposition by "the utmost frankness" in describing the situation and the objectives to Senate leaders. His assistants replied that the critics were holding the high ground: "Senator Johnson is demanding that troops be withdrawn from Archangel, and there is considerable support of his position on the ground that our men are being killed and no one knows why they are still there." In addition, American troops in Russia made it clear that they were against the policy. Some of them refused to fight. And finally, the anti-Bolshevik forces offered poor and uninspiring leadership in Russia. The cruel dilemma was finally resolved by the Bolsheviks who won the Russian civil war.*

While Wilson handicapped himself in his efforts to block Japan by refusing to work directly and vigorously either with China or the Russians, he did stabilize the situation after Japan's first penetration into Manchuria and Siberia. His persistent opposition, manifested by the American forces and his efforts to reorganize and use the banking consortium to keep the Japanese from taking over the Chinese Eastern Railway, did prevent Tokyo from consolidating its initial gains.

Finally, Wilson opposed both traditional colonialism and revolutionary nationalism, seeking a compromise in the mandate system, under which the Open Door Policy would be used to reform the political and economic life of the areas according to American interests. And in all of this program, he vigorously asserted (though he was not always able to maintain) the predominance of American power and leadership. Granted its essentially conservative character, for it was a program designed to preserve the existing order in the face of broad revolutionary challenges, Wilson's program was about as comprehensive an approach as anyone could have devised.

Along with Herbert Hoover, who helped Wilson formulate

---

* Wilson was more successful in Poland. As in Hungary, Hoover and the President collaborated to use American control of food supplies to bring conservatives to power. The conservatives were then given arms and money during their efforts to extend Poland's boundaries eastward into Russia, and into the Baltic States.

and put it into operation, such men as Elihu Root, Charles
Evans Hughes, and Henry L. Stimson initially supported the
program and its policies. Had they continued to do so, the
League of Nations Treaty would have passed the Senate, for
the influence of these men would have been sufficient to over-
ride the opposition. Hence it is vital to understand the reasons
that led these key leaders to leave Wilson and join other opponents of the treaty.

Political and personal motives no doubt influenced all of
Wilson's opponents, but the basic sources of their opposition
can be found in their conception of America and its role in
the world. For the group led by Hoover, Hughes, and Stimson,
one factor seems crucial. They had more insight into the structure and functioning of industrial society and thus grasped
the weaknesses of classical liberalism more thoroughly than
Wilson. As men who knew the market as well as the library,
they were aware that the liberal system in practice did not
function according to its theory. That knowledge led them
to propose a more concrete program for the future.

With Wilson, they accepted the principles of natural law,
but they knew from experience that the individual was no
longer free to act in accordance with this theory. The individual had become part of a larger group. Realizing that, they
had more specific ideas about how to define and structure what
Wilson vaguely referred to as "some sort of partnership" between capital and labor.

Hoover provided the most advanced intellectual leadership
within this group. He analyzed America's mature industrial
system as an intrinsically corporate society composed of, and
organized on the basis of, three primary units—capital (including agriculture), labor, and the government. The objective
was to establish a pattern in which, despite their differences
and short-run conflicts, those groups would work together to
create the conditions under which the natural harmony of
interests would manifest itself. Hoover even predicted four
ways in which the effort to create such a corporate society
might fail: large business interests could take over and produce fascism; labor could win out and turn to socialism; the
government bureaucracy could itself become dominant and
create a kind of ad hoc and aimless tyranny; or the govern-

ment would become in practice the market place in which the
other units scrambled for power and profit, an alternative that
Hoover quite accurately called capitalistic syndicalism.*

Transferred to the international scene, Hoover's analysis
pointed to the necessity of defining and establishing a similar
community with Germany, Japan, and Italy, as well as with
England and France. Secretary of State Hughes explicitly
called for such a "community of ideals, interests, and purposes." That kind of community would not only strengthen
each country individually, but would, being led by the United
States, be capable of controlling the revolutionary challenge
to the existing order. While Hoover was the central figure in
this group opposing Wilson over Article X, the others understood the approach, accepted its central features, and worked
in their own ways to put it into operation.

These men recognized that the American economy was an
interrelated and interdependent *system*, rather than a random
conglomeration of individual operations mysteriously unified
by the abstract functioning of the market place. This knowledge, which most of them had gained as practicing entrepreneurs or as corporation lawyers before they entered politics,
was the source of their differences with Wilson and the basis
of their own foreign policy. Since they thought about economic and political affairs as an interlocking system, they had
far more in common with mercantilists than with the advocates
and philosophers of laissez faire. They were not mercantilists:
mercantilism was a *Weltanschauung* of the seventeenth and
eighteenth centuries. The term is used for the purpose of

* Perhaps the most striking evidence of Hoover's long thought about
these problems comes from his early books on mining engineering. See,
for example, the discussion of the injustices of corporations and other
capitalists, and of the rights and legitimate expectations of labor, in these
items: *Principles of Mining Valuation, Organization, and Administration*
(1909); "The Training of the Mining Engineer," *Science* (November,
1904); "Economics of a Boom," *The Mining Magazine* (May, 1912).
Also consult, where available (it is unfortunately something of a rare
item), his *American Individualism* (New York: Doubleday, Page, and
Co., 1923). This approach to Hoover is developed in more detail in this
writer's *Contours of American History*. One of the nicest introductory
essays to Hoover was prepared by a graduate student at the University
of Wisconsin, Robert E. Treacy, as a seminar paper entitled "Herbert
Hoover to 1920."

offering an analogy that may help clarify their efforts to transform the existing private enterprise syndicalism into a truly
corporate capitalism.

Two similarities to mercantilism are important for understanding the outlook and activities of such men as Hoover and
Hughes. One concerns the active role of government in promoting the internal organization and stability of the economic
system. Hoover and others such as Bernard Baruch and Owen
D. Young gave considerable attention to the problem of rationalizing the domestic economy through such institutions as trade
associations and by establishing the practice and habit of close
co-operation between government and business. Of itself, this
was nothing new. Theodore Roosevelt and Herbert Croly of
the Progressive movement favored it, and Woodrow Wilson
practiced the same kind of collaboration during World War I.
But Hoover and Baruch did a great deal to develop, extend,
and popularize the idea through the 1920s.

The second aspect of their political economy that bore similarities to mercantilism affected foreign policy even more directly. For in thinking of economic activity in terms of the
system, while at the same time keeping their basic capitalistic
concept of economic life, such men as Hoover, Hughes, and
Stimson emphasized that the overseas economic expansion of
the system was *necessary* for continued prosperity. Corporation and banking leaders agreed. The result was a vitally important integration of thought: political and economic leaders
came to share the same idea about the relationship between
domestic and foreign policy. Overseas economic expansion became an integral part of the domestic expansion of the system
itself, rather than the interest or concern merely of certain
segments of the system. This did not conflict with the average
citizen's understanding of America's greatness and prosperity,
for the frontier thesis explained the nation's democracy and
well-being in terms of just such expansion.

For these reasons, and because most of them had less of the
crusading temperament than Wilson, men such as Hoover and
Hughes stressed the importance of extending America's economic empire. So, too, did most businessmen. Many economic
leaders, such as Thomas Lamont of the House of Morgan,
originally favored Wilson's program for peace, thinking it a

good plan to stabilize world conditions and prepare the way for American expansion. But the majority of corporation leaders and bankers lost their early enthusiasm for Wilson's approach, some because they came to agree with Hoover's criticism of the League Covenant and others because they were anxious to get to work "in the frontier countries" and hence wanted to stop wasting time in an apparently endless, and profitless, argument.

Frank Vanderlip caught the spirit of that growing impatience in his remark (and concern) about what he called "the war after the war." He had organized the American International Corporation in 1914 for the specific purpose of opening up the poor, underdeveloped countries. In similar rhetoric, the *Wall Street Journal* emphasized its concern with the "stupendous trade battle" then developing. Another man with the same ideas—and fears—was Silas H. Strawn of Montgomery, Ward & Co. He flatly asserted that the United States "must expand"; a failure to do so "would result in such intense competition as to precipitate an economic panic in this country the like of which has never been seen." And John Hays Hammond warned the N.A.M. of the same danger. "It is obvious . . . that we must either curtail the capacity of our factories . . . or we must depend upon the exploitation of foreign countries for the relief of our congested home markets." All such economic spokesmen, as well as the majority of the political figures who opposed Wilson, stressed expansion of the American economic system, as well as the enlargement of their own particular operations. But they were less immediately concerned with the political and ideological aspects of that imperial growth. They generally assumed that those features of the American system would develop more or less automatically as a consequence of economic progress; or, if not, that such affairs were the concern and responsibility of the politicians.

Two other groups also opposed Wilson over the issue of Article X. Each did so, however, for different reasons. The vigorous empire men, led by Senator Henry Cabot Lodge and Theodore Roosevelt, defined America's role as the new—and better—British Empire. At home, they called for an aristocratic elite to control labor and capital within the framework of an industrialized concept of *noblesse oblige*. Overseas, they proposed to use America's power to implement the Open Door Policy and build a modern industrial empire. "Let us make it our policy," advised Lodge, "that what we shall do and when we shall do it shall be determined by us." Some businessmen shared his view. Edward A. Filene, who was at one time national director of the Chamber of Commerce, thought that the United States was "in the exact position of a man of peace in a frontier community. It is our duty to advocate and to stand ready to join an International Vigilance Committee." He assured America that it could, "*in no way, write a better insurance policy for its future material prosperity.*" In their own way, such politicians and businessmen agreed with Bismarck's classic phrase: "If there is to be a revolution, we would rather make it than suffer it." This outlook led them to support the Hoover group once Wilson was defeated on the League issue.

At the other extreme was an even smaller group of men who were almost doctrinaire laissez-faire liberals in domestic affairs and antiempire men in foreign policy. Led by Senator William E. Borah, they made many perceptive criticisms of existing policy, but their specific policy suggestions did not appeal to many Americans. Their domestic proposals, based as they were on an almost pure theory of competition, had but little relevance to a mature and complex industrial society. Hence they attracted little support from urban or rural businessmen and almost none from organized labor. Each of those groups wanted to regulate or control competition in its particular behalf. The men around Borah suffered from similar weaknesses in foreign affairs, for in criticizing America's imperial expansion they opposed the general feeling that this expansion was economically necessary as well as ideologically and morally just.

In an ironic way, moreover, the Borah group undercut its own position by aligning itself with the Lodge and Hoover groups to defeat Wilson's League treaty. For in this fashion they inadvertently strengthened the impression that America was not (and need not become) involved politically by such economic expansion. Hence it was difficult for Borah and similar critics to attract much organized and effective support for their own program. They were often misunderstood, furthermore, as a result of their opposition to Wilson. These weaknesses and misimpressions tend to obscure the fact that their criticism was insightful and fundamental, that they were by no means as naive about international politics as their critics charge, and that they had a strangely "modern" attitude toward aid to underdeveloped nations.

The argument advanced by Borah and other antiempire spokesmen was based on the proposition that America neither could nor should undertake to make or keep the world safe for democracy. They maintained that the idea was unrealistic because it neglected the different cultural traditions of most of the rest of the world and because of the power that some or all of those nations could bring to bear against the United States. And even if it were possible to build such an empire, they concluded, the effort violated the spirit of democracy itself. Borah provided a classic summary of these two arguments in one of his speeches attacking the proposal to clamp a lid on the revolutionary ferment in China after 1917. "Four hundred million people imbued with the spirit of independence and of national integrity are in the end invincible. There is no power which can master them or hold them in subjection. Warships and Gatling guns and dead students may mislead some but the forces which determine the action of empires and great nations lie deeper."

Borah and others also relied on this assumption in making their assessment of events in Europe, Latin America, and Asia, and in proposing modifications of American policy. Johnson, for example, concluded that the story of American loans to Latin American countries was "a sordid tale, at once grotesque and tragic." Concluding that his investigation of the facts had "stripped some of the hypocrisy" away from the usual accounts of the policy, he pointed out that American money was used to "maintain dictators in power," and that it was "party to the suppression of every natural right of citizens of South American Republics." Johnson quickly added that citizens at home also suffered. Some were subject to "shameful, and even infamous, exploitation" by the bankers who sold the securities. And everyone lost because of the bitter reaction against the United States.

Representative Fiorello La Guardia and Senators La Follette

and Borah joined Johnson's attack. Borah condemned the "drumhead diplomacy" of Wilson and Bryan in Central America, and denied that the Monroe Doctrine gave the United States any right to intervene throughout the hemisphere in that manner. Just as he opposed the narrow policy of many business interests in China, Borah also used his influence to block the oil companies and other groups that wanted vigorous intervention against the government of the Mexican Revolution. He played a significant role in the appointment of Dwight Morrow as Ambassador to Mexico, and supported Morrow's ultimately successful efforts to halt the deterioration of relations and to negotiate an interim settlement of the oil and other property issues.

As that action suggests, Borah and the other anti-imperialists were more than critics. They offered many positive suggestions. Borah was particularly active, for example, in urging the government to take the lead in the economic reconstruction of Europe, and in reaching some agreement on limiting armaments in the Pacific. La Guardia, Johnson, and La Follette all supported the recognition of Russia for economic reasons as well as on the grounds that such action was in keeping with the principle of self-determination. Borah agreed with those arguments and added others that were even more perceptive. He concluded that a rapprochement with the Soviet Union was "the key to a restored Europe, to a peaceful Europe." In addition, he thought that the United States could play a crucial role in creating the circumstances in which there could "emerge a freer, a more relaxed, a more democratic Russia." Finally, and perhaps most striking of all, Borah offered a keen analysis of the importance of Russia to America's general security. His estimate of the strategic and power factors was considerably more astute than the supposed realism of most of the critics who dismissed him as an isolationist.

Borah warned in 1923 that American policy—"a narrow-visioned, intolerant policy"—was helping to push Russia and Germany together. That was "not at all desirable," and he urged the government to recognize the Soviets as a move to weaken that relationship. A bit later, after Japan had again indicated its determination to expand on the mainland of Asia, Borah offered a very direct warning: unless the United States moved to prevent it, Russia would be forced to come to terms with Japan. "I feel more strongly than ever," Borah wrote Secretary of State Stimson in 1932, "that our relationship with Russia ought to undergo a change. I am satisfied that by proper steps taken upon the part of our government any close relationship between Russia and Japan could be avoided." * Dramatic as they are, Borah's observations on the interaction between the United States, Russia, Germany, and Japan were only conclusions drawn from his basic insight into the broader issue. His remark of 1925 on the consequences of American policy toward Russia was indeed prophetic: "So long as you have a hundred and fifty million people outlawed in a sense, it necessarily follows that you cannot have peace."

Toward underdeveloped and poor countries, Borah and others like him manifested a complex and somewhat contradictory attitude. Men like La Follette and Borah were of course concerned and sympathetic with the problems of poverty and independence. But they did not in the last analysis believe that a nation or a people could be given freedom and prosperity by outsiders. They were very skeptical of the argument that democracy could be exported along with surplus commodities and manufactured goods or created by foreign loans. That conclusion was an integral part of their knowledge of, and judgment on, European colonialism and America's own imperial expansion. They were all opposed, as La Follette put it, "to the dollar diplomacy which has reduced our State Department from its high place as a kindly intermediary of defenseless nations, into a trading outpost for Wall Street interests, aiming to exploit those who should be our friends."

As a result, Borah and the others preferred to deal with other nations on a strict, even narrow, economic basis, leaving them alone and free to use their wealth as they saw fit. Clearly enough, they underestimated the importance per se of a minimum, and improving, level of economic welfare, and of the relationship between that foundation and the development of

---

* Borah's analysis was borne out, not only by Russia's open bid for a nonaggression treaty with China and the United States, but also by its decision, after that overture was declined, to sign with the Japanese. American policy of the years 1904–1912 was thus repeated with the identical results.

political and cultural maturity. And they discounted—no doubt because they generalized American experience to other nations—the great difficulties that underdeveloped countries faced in starting and sustaining such improvement on their own. Yet they were willing to help nations weakened by war or catastrophe or nations just getting started in their own development. Perhaps this explains their preference, when pushed to the wall (as in the case of Liberia in the 1920s), for outright grants of assistance over government loans or private investment.

Of all Americans, the group around Borah most clearly understood the principle and practice of self-determination in foreign affairs. For that reason, as well as other aspects of Borah's criticism, President Wilson singled out Borah as his most important critic—as the man who might turn out to be right. In his own time, however, Borah enjoyed little praise and almost no support. He served as spokesman for various small groups which sought to change policy toward Russia, China, and Latin America, but at most—with the possible exception of Russia—these groups exercised a minor influence on American foreign policy. Borah himself became stereotyped as a naive, irresponsible, and wrong-headed gadfly. But a generation later, in the midst of a cold war, those who like their history with a twist of irony might find it illuminating to compare his speeches and letters between 1917 and 1935 with the most recent policy proposals advanced by later "realists" who had ignored or deplored his earlier actions.*

Opposed by the powerful coalition of Hoover, Root, Lodge, and Borah, and unwilling to compromise over Article X, President Wilson lost his battle for the League of Nations Covenant. But most of his opponents shared Wilson's conception of America as the leader of the world, and they turned quickly from the tactical skirmish with him to the work of putting

---

* The orthodox view of Borah can be reviewed in R. Ferrell, *Peace in Their Time* (New Haven: Yale University Press, 1952). The most recent biography is M. C. McKenna, *Borah* (Ann Arbor: University of Michigan Press, 1961). A stimulating article is O. S. Pinckney, "William E. Borah: Critic of American Foreign Policy," *Studies on The Left* (1960). The best volume of Borah's own remarks is *American Problems. A Selection of Speeches and Prophecies by William E. Borah* (New York: Duffield & Co., 1924); but it is unfortunately rather hard to find.

the strategy into operation through the policy of the open door.

II. THE INTERNATIONALIZATION OF BUSINESS

We are seeking to establish a Pax Americana *maintained not by arms but by mutual respect and good will and the tranquilizing processes of reason. . . .*

When we have a clear sense of our own interests, we are just as inflexible as others.

CHARLES EVANS HUGHES, 1924

We must finance our exports by loaning foreigners the wherewith-all to pay for them. . . . Without such loans we would have the spectacle of our neighbors famishing for goods which were rotting in our warehouses as unusable surplus.

JOHN FOSTER DULLES, 1928

We must find a profitable market for our surpluses.

HERBERT HOOVER, 1928

Our investments and trade relations are such that it is almost impossible to conceive of any conflict anywhere on earth which would not affect us injuriously.

CALVIN COOLIDGE, 1928

The present is a time of great unrest and disquiet throughout the world, and it is to the interest of all governments to try to maintain order and stability.

HENRY L. STIMSON, 1932

Confronted by revolutionary opposition throughout much of the world, plagued by conflicts with and among their recent Allies, and disturbed by the continued antagonism between the victors and the defeated, American policy-makers con-

cluded that peace was the *sine qua non* of any effort to implement the strategy of the Open Door Policy. Without stability
and peace, there could be no economic expansion, which all of
them considered the dynamic element in producing America's
well-being. In the view of these men, at any rate, most of the
troubles they faced in the 1920s had either been caused by
World War I or had been intensified by that disruption of law
and order. It later became fashionable among historians and
other commentators to criticize leaders like Hoover and
Hughes (as well as Borah) on the grounds that they were
naive, or that they trusted Germany and Japan too much on
too little evidence. Much of that criticism resulted from interpreting the 1920s in a very narrow, relativistic manner. Men
who had to fight Germany and Japan (and who thought they
might well have to fight Russia) concluded that anyone must
have been blind or misguided not to see what would happen
if those countries were not blocked by the threat—or the use
—of force. That judgment was further strengthened by the
effect of World War II on attitudes toward force: having
come to use force without limit in international affairs, and in
many respects to take that approach for granted, such critics
tended to define realism in foreign affairs largely in terms of
such an acceptance of force.

Whatever its merits as a general approach to foreign policy,
that point of view produces serious misconceptions about
American policy-makers of the 1920s. In the first place, those
men were not naive about power. All of them had broad experience in economic and legal affairs, which are hardly unrelated to conflicts of power, and had also participated in the
American war effort. None of them were pacifists. It is true
that they preferred not to employ force. Neither did they take
its use casually or cynically. But those characteristics may be
signs of their maturity instead of symptoms of their naiveté.

In the broader sense, men like Hoover and Hughes understood the crucial point about the strategy of the Open Door
Policy that their critics overlooked: *it was designed to win
the objectives without recourse to war*. These critics might
with more relevance (and perhaps even profit) examine the
objectives instead of continuing to condemn the reluctance to
resort to force. It is one thing to say that the objectives of

American foreign policy in the twentieth century could not have been achieved without resorting to force. That is a straightforward, cogent line of argument. But contrary to the apparent belief of many people who follow that interpretation overtly or implicitly, it does not prove two other things. It does not prove that any nation which resisted (or resists) those objectives was (or is) evil, and therefore to blame for subsequent conflict or violence. And it most certainly does not prove that men were naive because they were inclined either to abandon or modify those objectives, or postpone the victory, rather than use force. Finally, the leaders of the 1920s were hardly naive in seeing a correlation between war and social unrest culminating in revolutions, or between war and the restriction of democracy even in the United States.

American leaders concluded that the best way to reconcile the necessary expansion of the American economic system with the necessity of peace was by working out a general concert of policy among the United States, Great Britain, France, Germany, and Japan based on the acceptance of the Open Door Policy by all those powers. Such a de facto entente in behalf of a "community of ideals, interests, and purposes" was designed to operate on three levels. The nations would compromise their differences and stand firm against the Soviet Union and other revolutionary movements. Thus aligned, they would direct and set limits on the development of colonial, mandated, and other nonindustrialized areas. Finally, America's economic predominance would enable it to guide the operation while at the same time strengthening and extending its own open-door empire.

In this fashion, economic expansion became both a means and an end for American policy-makers. Defined as a goal because of its vital importance to the continued success of the domestic economic system, it was also considered a means to build the empire of peace and prosperity which would secure the world for continued expansion in the years to come. One of the most striking features of American diplomacy of the 1920s was the extent to which all policy-makers expressed this in their public, as well as private, remarks. President Harding urged Americans to "operate aggressively" and "*go on to the peaceful commercial conquest of the world*" in order to avoid social conflict at home. Though by no means gregarious, President Coolidge was not backward about expressing his similar view of America's role in the world. Feeling it was "perfectly obvious" that if any action was "wrong . . . within the confines of the United States, it is equally wrong outside our borders," Coolidge asserted that "the one great duty that stands out requires us to use our enormous powers to trim the balance of the world." It was in keeping with that outlook, moreover, that Secretary of State Hughes explained that "the preponderant thought among us undoubtedly is that our influence would not be increased by pooling it" in an organization such as the League of Nations.

Less traditional in their conceptions of empire than Coolidge, Hughes and Hoover explicitly sought to eliminate "the old imperialistic trappings." In a crisis, they agreed with Coolidge: interventions undertaken "to discourage revolutions" were not war "any more than a policeman on the street is making war on passers-by." But Hoover and Hughes concentrated on *preventing* revolutions by the expansion of American economic power. Anxious to locate "the antidote to Bolshevism," Hughes understandably viewed "the tendency to have revolutions" as a "regrettable condition" of world affairs. He also emphasized the importance of controlling key raw materials. And he reacted promptly to a warning from his departmental advisors that "the vast increase in the surpluses of manufactured goods . . . must find a market, if at all, outside the United States." Hence he gave first priority to the problem of establishing and maintaining peace in order to "deal with the economic verities."

Striving for an American-led community of interests with other industrial nations, it was natural for him to conclude that "it is self-determination which makes for wars and places obstacles in the way of all plans for keeping the peace." That sentence provides one of the neatest, if also most unnerving, clues to the tragedy and the terror of American diplomacy. For, committed in principle to self-determination, Hughes was turning away from that axiom in order to insure the expansion and consolidation of the status quo.

Stimson shared this concern with "peace and order." At home, he thought that the "richer and more intelligent" citizens should manage affairs. Extending that hypothesis to the world, he defined America as the elite of international society. As for the white man's burden, he believed "in assuming it." His basic strategy called for the expansion of "big, high-class American business" throughout the world and for political intervention of the subtle and behind-the-scenes variety that would not arouse the antagonism of the natives or the American public. According to Stimson, such a foreign policy would ultimately bring inferior peoples into step with America's standards and practices. His vigorous and extensive conception of America's role in the world led Stimson to feel more at home with Franklin Delano Roosevelt than with Herbert Hoover, but during the 1920s he shared with Hughes and Hoover a broad area of agreement.

Though officially no more than Secretary of Commerce from 1921 to 1928, Hoover demanded, and received, a quasi-official veto over foreign policy as a condition of entering the cabinet. Armed with this authority, he exercised great influence on foreign affairs. Highly disturbed by the "spread of revolution over one-third of the world," he developed a program designed to halt the "drift toward socialism." Hoover's basic proposition was simple: the American system was "the *only* safe avenue of human progress." Concluding that the world was "passing from a period of extreme individualistic action into a period of associational activities," he sought to organize the new system within a capitalistic framework that protected political democracy. He approached the problem by defining labor and capital as "both producers . . . not classes." As such, they had "great areas of mutual interest," the most important of which was the continued existence of corporate capitalism itself. Hoover was aware that American labor was not radical, and he wanted to keep it from moving in that direction.

In formulating his ideas concerning such a co-operative, or corporate, capitalistic political economy, Hoover understood that the corporation had asserted its fundamental supremacy over the banker. Between 1900 and 1916, the corporation had been forced to rely temporarily on the financier for capital. But soon after the war the corporation began producing enough surplus capital to finance and thereby control most of its own decisions. The bankers were still important, and struggled bitterly for a time to regain their earlier power, but they were on the defensive.*

Some of their battles had an important bearing on foreign policy. In Latin America and Asia, for example, the financiers fought hard for policies that would help them reap profits they could use at home. Those efforts delayed or blocked some of the more sophisticated programs advocated by Hoover, such as his desire to limit investments to productive enterprises. The bankers often disregarded such rational, equitable, and long-range considerations. They operated far more as narrow, interest-conscious entrepreneurs. Partly as a result of that nature of their dealings, and also because of the general impact of their expansion, the financiers antagonized many foreigners. That only complicated and increased their difficulties. Along with the Great Depression, those considerations ultimately convinced the bankers of two things: they needed to evolve a new and more equal relationship with the corporations; and both economic groups had to increase, regularize, and institutionalize the kind of government assistance that Willard Straight had helped initiate before World War I. Such an approach finally brought the bankers, the corporations, and the government into a very intimate working arrangement concerning domestic and foreign affairs during the years of the New Deal and World War II, but it did not change the underlying primacy of the corporations.

Based on his understanding of the central role of the corporation, Hoover developed his conception of associational capitalism around two themes. First, all economic co-operation would center on the corporation; and second, the government, representing the populace at large, would co-operate with the corporation to insure national prosperity and democratic procedure. Hoover first announced his approach at the national

---

* R. Finch and M. Oppenheimer have argued, in a three-part article in *Socialist Revolution*, Vol. I, Nos. 4, 5, and 6 (July–December, 1970), that the bankers-as-institutional-investors reasserted a significant degree of control after World War II. Some of their evidence indicates that this happened in connection with specific corporations. But their examples do not undercut the analysis offered here about the *outlook* of American leadership. Foreign policy has not been redefined as a short-term profit-taking operation.

economic conference of 1921, which was originally called by President Wilson to implement his own idea of "some sort of partnership" between capital and labor. The problems were dangerous and difficult, Hoover admitted, but "a large degree of solution could be expected through the mobilization of co-operative action of our manufacturers and employers, of our public bodies and local authorities. . . . While our industry and commerce must be based upon incentive to the individual, yet the national interest requires a certain degree of co-operation . . . in order that we may reduce and eliminate industrial waste, lay the foundation for constant decrease in production and distribution costs, and thereby obtain the fundamental increases in wages and standards of living" that would guarantee "increased social stability" and world peace.

Hoover understood that labor had to participate in this co-operation, and upon many occasions voiced public support for unionization and for collective bargaining. It is of course true that Hoover feared and opposed socialism; and in the years after the Bolshevik Revolution and the end-of-the-war labor unrest in the United States he was concerned that the unions might through their practice if not their intent push the emerging corporate capitalism ever further to the left. But most of the usual criticism of Hoover on the labor issue is misleading because it is based upon such a narrow conception of the general question.

Hoover was not prolabor in the sense of giving it first priority in his policies or in taking its side in any situation. Yet several elementary truths are always overlooked in judging Hoover by that elementary standard. The American labor movement of the 1920s was not very large, for example, and it accepted the basic features of the existing capitalist system. Furthermore, its few leaders who concerned themselves with the underlying problems of the relationship with management, and of markets, revealed broad areas of agreement with Hoover.

This was particularly significant in connection with foreign affairs. The labor movement did have two primary reservations about the policy of overseas economic expansion. It worried that jobs lost to foreign workers when an American corporation established a branch factory in another country were not balanced out by new investment at home or by the increased trade. And a few leaders fretted about the possibility that such expansion would lead to wars involving the United States. In general, however, the labor movement in the 1920s supported America's overseas economic expansion because it provided more sales and because it was interested in expanding its influence over the labor movements in foreign countries. The latter consideration was nothing new, for labor had backed the Spanish-American War and President Wilson's intervention in Mexico for the same reason.

In his approach to the problem of stabilizing agriculture at the level of prosperity created by the war, Hoover stressed co-operation between individual farmers. They should work together to control production and marketing, which would in turn maintain and even enlarge their foreign markets as well as helping them at home. Though it may seem unrelated to foreign affairs, the issue of agricultural surpluses actually offers in many respects the neatest overview of how overseas economic expansion was the central theme of American foreign policy in the 1920s. It is also worth exploring because it provides a clear picture of the more general problems facing Hoover and other American leaders.*

While one would expect the farmers to be concerned about their markets, it may be surprising to realize the extent to which bankers and industrialists shared that concern. Hoover described the problem very clearly. Farmers were in "great difficulties," he explained in 1921, because of their "position of inequality in purchasing power as compared with other industries." That imbalance was "already digging a grave of unemployment" for the nonagricultural sectors of the economy. Part of Hoover's understanding very probably came from his experience in handling war relief, and from his close friendship with Julius Barnes, who was a major grain exporter. But the most important point concerns the way he analyzed the farm problem as an integral aspect of the whole political economy. "We must have," he concluded, "the co-operation of our bankers and our industry." They "must be brought together"

---

* Mrs. Brady Hughes and James McHale have written illuminating master's theses on the post-World War II aspects of this relationship of agriculture to foreign policy.

with the farmers by the government—and specifically by Hoover's Department of Commerce—to work out a solution for the problem. It is not unusual, of course, that George N. Peek, a manufacturer of agricultural implements, shared that view. He thought it was a question of exporting the surpluses or else "we are going to have state socialism." But Baruch and other eastern urban leaders like Otto Kahn had the same idea. So did Charles G. Dawes, a midwestern financier who had economic and political connections with eastern bankers.

The trouble arose over how to underwrite the exports. Farmers generally wanted the government to sell their surpluses abroad, paying them the difference between the world price and the American price from government funds, or from money collected from the processor and the consumer at home. Senator Peter Norbeck provided a blunt summary of the basic approach at the end of 1922. "Slowly but surely, the idea is getting home that it [the issue] is the surplus, and that the way to stimulate the market is to find some way to dispose of the surplus. Sell it at a good price, if we can; sell it at a poor price if we must; give it away if we cannot do better. . . . In other words, let agricultural products have the same benefit of a similar control that big business gives its products."

Acting through their representatives in the Congress, the farmers pushed their program into law in 1927 and again in 1928. It was vetoed both times. The key to understanding those vetoes lies in the negative and positive sides of Hoover's broad outlook as applied to the agricultural crisis. On the negative side, he militantly opposed the plan advocated by the farm bloc. First: it put the government into business. That not only threatened to accelerate the movement toward socialism or bureaucratic tyranny, *but it also increased the risk of serious international conflict by formally tying the government to economic activities. Conflicts in the market place would automatically become political conflicts.* Second: the two-price system proposed by the farmers was unfair to the consumer because it forced him, either through increased taxes or higher retail prices, to pay twice for a loaf of bread.

On the positive side, Hoover and others like Baruch, Kahn, and Dawes had their own solution which tied agricultural prosperity to industrial and financial well-being. Their approach was to loan money abroad, particularly to European industrial countries. That would not only provide funds for buying American farm surpluses (directly, and as a result of general prosperity), but it would also facilitate the building of that broader convergence of interest which Hoover and Hughes were so eager to establish. They also anticipated at least four other benefits: (1) such loans would give the United States influence on foreign countries creating lines of direct and formal responsibility to Washington; (2) the loans would help solve the broader problem of post-war recovery throughout the world; (3) by giving strong if unofficial approval to the loans, the government would help the bankers obtain the kind of assistance they needed in accumulating capital from the average citizen; and (4) the plan would satisfy the agricultural bloc and thereby strengthen the Republican Party at a time when it was again in danger of losing the farm vote.

For that matter, the easiest way to fix all such considerations in one's mind is to remember that Dawes won the Republican nomination for vice president in 1924. He got the call because of his role in negotiating the huge, inclusive international economic arrangement known as the Dawes Plan, and more directly because he was a midwesterner who could plausibly argue that the program would solve the farm problem. The plan itself was much more than a device to sell agricultural surpluses. It was based on American loans to Germany, which would enable that nation to start reconstruction while also paying reparations to England and France. That triple play would abet economic development among the defeated as well as the victors and thus increase the demand for all kinds of American exports.

Clearly, then, Hoover, Hughes, and other American policymakers of the 1920s viewed overseas economic expansion as the crucial element in establishing a secure foundation for peace, and in guaranteeing the successful functioning of the American political economy. Secretary of State Hughes explained the point in a particularly direct manner: "All political questions . . . broadly, have some economic aspect or some economic force lying back of them." It was only natural, therefore, that the "businessman has the most direct interest in the conduct of foreign relations." And to the Secretary, at any rate, it was obvious that one of his main responsibilities concerned "the enlarging of the opportunities for industry and commerce by the recognition and extension of the policy of the 'Open Door'." A good example of the way this strategy guided all foreign policy actions is provided by the tariff legislation of 1922. For the central importance of that law lies not so much in the rates that it established on various goods, but rather in Section 317, which specified that the principle of the open door was to be written into all enabling agreements negotiated with foreign countries.

Hoover's view of the relationship between domestic welfare and overseas economic expansion was even more explicit. The "export market becomes of peculiar importance to us," he noted in 1924, "in maintaining a stable and even operation of our domestic industries. It has an importance in that regard far beyond the percentage of our exports to our total production." It was a crucial "part of our domestic progress, both socially and economically." Hence it was essential for the government to provide "protection and support to Americans interested in the development of American enterprise abroad."

One of Hoover's most significant acts of assistance involved a thorough reorganization and beefing-up of the Department of Commerce in order to push such economic expansion. The importance of that work is suggested by the way that later Secretaries of Commerce, including Democrats Harry Hopkins, Henry A. Wallace, and Luther Hodges, identified their own programs with both the ideas and the policies stressed by Hoover. Hoover picked his assistants with extreme care, and hence it is illuminating to review their basic ideas. Some of the most revealing statements of their outlook were provided by Julius Klein, who served as Hoover's top aide during the time he was Secretary of Commerce. Klein described the general objective as "the internationalization of business" under the leadership (and the predominant influence) of the American corporation. As one who accepted the frontier-expansionist explanation of American history, he offered in 1927 a brilliant two-paragraph statement of the thesis advanced by Brooks Adams, Frederick Jackson Turner, and other philosophers of the frontier, presenting it as a major policy statement under the title, "The Tendency of the Frontier is to Move Westward."

Klein's essay opened with the unequivocal assertion that "the economic history of the world has been a history of frontiers." "This movement started from China," he explained, and then "swept through central Asia," Greece, and Rome on its way to establishing Europe "as the center of world commerce." Then America "became the great frontier [and in turn]. . . . The history of the United States itself has been a history of frontiers." The result was in Klein's view the final example of the way that the last frontier became in turn the newest center of expansion. "Now the circle is complete, the last great frontier has been conquered, and we come to a new era of world history. America, with an economic and industrial organization which is the fruit of centuries of world progress, is facing across the Pacific what is at the same time the oldest and the newest trade area." The Chinese Empire had become America's economic frontier.

Another document of similar interest was an analysis of the branch factory movement prepared by Louis Domeratzky, Chief of the Commerce Department's Division of Regional Information. He interpreted what he called "the aggressive expansion policy" of American corporations as the final proof of America's economic predominance. It had developed as a balance wheel to offset domestic fluctuations and as a way of evading tariff restrictions thrown up by foreign countries against American exports. He also emphasized the newer significance of the overseas investment program in "the exploitation of foreign natural resources" to provide raw materials for American production. Given the ability to provide their own capital, Domeratzky saw the process as one which the corporations would continue indefinitely. Hoover not only agreed with that analysis, but sought after the crash in 1929 to generate the recovery of the entire economy by stressing such overseas expansion of American corporations.

The Great Depression is always offered as proof of the limitations and the failure of Hoover's ideas and policies. That judgment is neither very accurate nor particularly helpful. Hoover did not cause the depression. It was brought on by the general malfunctioning of American and world capitalism. His after-the-fact critics offered no significant preventatives before the crisis, and in large measure derived their own programs from the general ideas already put forward by Hoover.

For the most part, such critics merely compare Hoover's efforts to end the depression with the state of the economy after the start of World War II, credit the New Deal with the improvement, and offer harsh and unfavorable conclusions about Hoover. Their verdict conveniently ignores the failure of the New Deal to generate sustained recovery until armament orders began to roll in during the latter part of 1940; it slides over the social and psychological, as well as many of the political and economic, costs of the prosperity achieved; and in general neglects to mention that President Franklin Delano Roosevelt and Secretary of State Cordell Hull relied ever more extensively on overseas economic expansion to counter the economy's propensity to stagnate.

Some partisans of the New Deal assert that a double standard of judgment is involved in pointing out such aspects of the Roosevelt record. The reverse is more nearly true, for the weaknesses of the New Deal are certainly as relevant as the failures of Hoover in reaching any general conclusions about recent American history. Beyond the question of explaining Hoover's approach to the depression, the real issues involve the objectives sought by Hoover and the New Deal, the consequences of their actions, and the extent to which they were aware of—and concerned about—those consequences.

Both Hoover and Roosevelt wanted freedom, prosperity, and peace for the United States. Neither of them approached the problems facing twentieth-century America with the attitude and outlook of a narrow nineteenth-century entrepreneur. Hence there is little relevance in shooting down Hoover as a Simon Legree of industrialism. That target is a straw man. The difficulty is to explain why Hoover was unwilling to plunge into the crisis of the depression with the attitude of "do something, anything" manifested by Roosevelt during his first term.

Hoover was not cautious because he was callous or ignorant. He hesitated because of what seemed to him the serious dangers inherent in all the easy or obvious remedies. In contrast, Roosevelt charged forward with little regard for the rather obvious, as well as the more subtle or latent, consequences of his actions. What is so revealing in this connection is the way the critics of Hoover admit—at least when pressed —to many reservations about the effects of the New Deal. They are often very perceptive in their evaluation of those results, but they seem never to realize that their criticisms were offered in advance—as premonitions—by Hoover.

A good example of this irony is provided by President Dwight David Eisenhower's famous warning in 1962 about the dangers to democracy posed by the growth of a military-industrial complex with great influence inside the government. That blunt admonition found favor with most of those who criticize Hoover. Yet Hoover was intensely concerned in 1930–1932 that fascism would begin to develop if big business was allowed to gain great influence in combating the depression. Thus he flatly rejected several versions of the program ultimately adopted as the N.R.A. by the Roosevelt Administration, an approach that did delegate extensive power to business. Hoover also feared the consequences of giving the government primary and formal responsibility for saving capitalism through overseas economic expansion. He argued with great force and insight that such a policy would turn every economic clash into an international political incident and thereby continually increase world tensions.

In a different way, Hoover feared that socialism would result from giving labor a predominant role in the fight against the depression. That was probably Hoover's main mistake. American labor was not inclined toward socialism. It sought no more than a position of parity with the farmer and the corporation. Even so, Hoover's analysis was not demolished by that error. For his most general fear about precipitate action in the depression was based on an astute analysis of the kind of syndicalist capitalism that would emerge from trying to balance the major elements of the political economy through ad hoc government intervention. He thought that approach would produce a nameless but nevertheless insidious kind of bureaucratic and presidential tyranny that would deaden public interest and participation in government, and that would fail to produce either peace or prosperity.

It may be that Hoover is one of the few tragic figures in American history. Each of his analyses of the main alternatives in 1930–1932 contained a significant amount of truth. And it seems quite likely that his failure to commit himself and the nation to any of those possibilities was the result of a temporary psychological bloc in the face of such unhappy choices that prevented him from taking any vigorous action. Be that as it may, the irony of all the liberal and New Deal criticism of Hoover lies in the way that the New Deal and subsequent administrations carried certain essential aspects of Hoover's basic foreign policies to their logical and extreme conclusions.

While it is certainly true that many of those later developments were inherent in Hoover's program, just as his were implicit in the Open Door Notes, it is vital to realize that his successors went far beyond Hoover's actions. Perhaps the most effective way to dramatize this point is by comparing Hoover's assumption in 1920 that the Soviet Union would collapse if confronted by a hostile world with the thesis advanced by George Frost Kennan in 1947 that the policy of containment would "force" such a result. The similarity is obvious and significant. But Hoover's program was characterized by a moderation and ambivalence that had been lost by the time Kennan made his proposal.

Hoover did not like socialism or communism, and he opposed the Soviet Union. But he also understood the great danger inherent in externalizing evil in the form of one country, in resting American security and welfare exclusively on the outcome of a trial of strength with one other nation. Hence he did not define American foreign policy so narrowly in terms of putting direct pressure on the Russians. He thought that the inherent difficulties of realizing the ideals of socialism or communism in a backward country would, when combined with the successful example of the United States, ultimately turn the Russians away from doctrinaire communism toward the American model. And that, in turn, would create the conditions for steady American improvement.

Hoover did not enjoy Borah's empathy with revolutions in general, or the Senator's specific insight into the Soviet upheaval. But neither did he make the reductionist error of simplifying the problem to the point of thinking that the challenge of the Bolshevik Revolution could be dealt with through policy toward Russia. He understood very clearly that the only effective answer would be in avoiding war between the advanced industrial nations, and in making capitalism produce results in the poor countries as well as in the rich nations. That analysis brought Hoover back to the importance of a program of overseas economic expansion that would actually develop the poor societies. An understanding of this broad outlook makes it possible to resolve the contradictions of his specific approach to Russia.

Hoover was candid and insistent about the proper way to handle the Russian problem. His remarks at the end of 1921 in a letter to Secretary Hughes about American food shipments to the Soviet Union were not only revealing of the specific subject, but were similar to Secretary of State Root's explanation in 1906 of the role of reform in furthering American influence in Morocco. "The relief measures already initiated are greatly increasing the status and kindness of relations and their continuation will build a situation which, combined with other factors, will enable the Americans to undertake the leadership in the reconstruction of Russia when the proper moment arrives." By the proper moment he meant the end of Soviet rule. Hoover continued his analysis with a blunt explanation of why the United States could not allow other nations—and in particular Germany—to function as middlemen in shipping American exports to Russia. "The hope of our commerce lies in the establishment of American firms abroad, distributing American goods under American direction; in the building of direct American financing and, above all, in the installation of American technology in Russian industries. We must, of necessity, in the future finance our own raw materials * into Russia and if our manufactured goods are distributed through German hands it simply means that when Germany has established trade of sufficient distribution to warrant her own manufacture we shall lose the market."

Because they wanted the immediate economic market and the longer-range political influence, Hoover and Hughes unofficially encouraged Americans to embark upon the economic penetration of Russia even though they refused to recognize the Soviet Government or to allow it to negotiate loans in

* By "raw materials," Hoover meant food stuffs.

the United States. Perhaps the history of American-Russian relations reveals no greater irony than the fact that this covert approval of certain specified economic relations, designed to speed the collapse of the Soviets and strengthen American influence in the following government, led Americans to contribute significantly to the recovery and development of the Soviet economic system. At the end of the 1920s, indeed, it was the depression-racked American economy which looked to Russian markets as a crutch for its own recovery. And by that time more Americans, including some among the Hoover, Hughes, and Stimson group, were thinking of Russia as a potential ally against Japan and Germany.

Such thoughts were far from the minds of Hoover and Hughes as they undertook to integrate Germany and Japan into their American-led community of industrial powers. Concerned with making Germany safe against internal revolution and strong as a bulwark against world communism, Hoover and Hughes gave high priority to its recovery. Their main lever to overcome the opposition of France and England was the astute and forceful use of American economic power. Hughes finally backed France and England into the entente by controlling the relationship between the debts they owed to the United States and the reparations they demanded from Germany.

Hughes accomplished this by tying the reduction of Allied debts to the United States to a similar cut in German reparations to Britain and France. This move, formalized in the Dawes and Young plans (1924 and 1929), enabled the United States to speed the end of military occupation of Germany and to open the way for its re-entry into the Western community. In line with this objective, they supported the Locarno Pact of 1925, by which Germany, France and Britain underwrote the boundaries of western Europe but left the frontiers facing Russia unguaranteed. More than one American leader viewed the Locarno Pact as the first political result of the nation's economic policy. It was in the context of this general settlement in Europe that the American Government encouraged private loans to Germany as a further move to speed that nation's recovery.

All of this was done quietly, much of it "unofficially," and all of it without American entry into the League of Nations. None of these considerations alters the fact that the effort was part of a broad program of conscious involvement in world affairs for well-defined objectives. As Senator Borah remarked at the time, "It does not rise even to the level of sophistry" to assert that such actions are described accurately by the term "isolationism."

But neither is it true, as others have maintained, that American policy was designed to make Germany dominant in Europe. American leaders wanted peace, and to that end they sought the reintegration of Germany into a Western community led by the United States. They were willing to go—and did go—a long way to facilitate German recovery and to accept or acquiesce in the assertion of German strength. It was the failure of American policy, not a mistake, which contributed to the coming of World War II.

American policy in Asia after World War I was characterized by similar features, though the problem itself was more complex. China was not only considered important as an area which would absorb large quantities of American surpluses, but it had been a region of American interest, activity, and influence for more than a century. It was impossible to ignore developments there, even had the policy-makers wished to do so. But neither was it possible to step in and run the show. On the one hand, Americans did not want a formal empire and, on the other, Japan blocked that kind of action. Japan's position was further strengthened by its color and ethnic affinities with the rest of Asia. Its occupations of parts of Manchuria and Siberia and its old alliance of 1902 with Great Britain also increased its bargaining power.

Working from the basic premise that wars and revolutions had to be prevented in the Far East, and concluding that the best way to accomplish that was to bring Japan into the American-led "community of ideals, interests, and purposes," Hughes offered Tokyo two commitments: a generous and unquestioned share in the development of China and an understanding that the United States would help check China's revolutionary nationalism. In return, he asked Japan's agreement to the Open Door Policy and to a program of balanced naval power in the western Pacific. Given that *quid pro quo*,

Hughes was confident that the United States—as represented by the banking consortium and other businessmen—could control the situation over the long haul. Concerned with future markets for the American economic system, not formal empire, he was willing to sacrifice immediate and marginal goals. Here, as elsewhere, Hughes was following Wilson, who had revitalized the consortium in 1917, acknowledged Japan's special position in Manchuria the same year, and specified in 1919 that it was "essential" to assert and maintain the open door in Siberia and elsewhere throughout Asia.

Hughes overcame Japan's reluctance to commit itself to such a program by a combination of three kinds of diplomacy. First, he made astute use of pressures and attitudes which reinforced his hand. These included the general postwar desire for disarmament, America's traditional support for the Open Door Policy, the agitation in Canada and Australia (as well as in England itself) against Britain's alliance with Japan, economic and social unrest in Japan, the growing strength of the Bolsheviks in Siberia (which worked to push Japan out but also to encourage other nations to compromise their differences), and the general opposition to China's attempt to assert its economic and political sovereignty. Second, his tactic of opening the discussions at the Washington Conference with a concrete plan for disarmament, under which America would take the lead, kept Japan and other opponents off balance. Most important of all, however, was his willingness to give Japan "an extraordinary favorable position" in northeastern Asia in order to establish "co-operation in the Far East."

Japan accepted the offer (though with some skepticism and private reservations), and the agreement was formalized in the Four- and Nine-Power Treaties signed in Washington in 1922. Those documents defined the coalition of industrial powers in the Pacific, just as the Dawes and Young plans and the Locarno Pact did in the Atlantic. The United States, Japan, France, and Great Britain agreed to respect each other's rights in various island possessions, to uphold the status quo in Asia, and to proceed with the development of China and other areas within the framework of the Open Door Policy. Answering some of his critics at home, who feared that the treaties weakened America's position, Hughes justifiably asserted that the negotiations and settlement "were conducted within limitations defined by the American Government."

American leaders honored their understanding of those commitments throughout the ensuing decade. China's protest against the limitations imposed upon it by the Washington treaties was brushed aside with the cryptic reply that "various American expressions of sympathy with an academic position may have misled the Chinese," and that the "matter had been decided at Washington adverse to the Chinese view." Entertaining that attitude toward conservative Chinese nationalists, it was natural for Hughes to ignore the appeals for sympathy and help made to the United States by Sun Yat-sen, leader of the revolutionary nationalist movement in China. He did not even open Sun's letter.*

Russia was more responsive to Chinese requests. It offered Lenin's theory of imperialism, which gave Chinese nationalists an explanation of their country's weakness; Marxian economic theory, which outlined a way to gain strength rapidly; the example of a successful revolution; and advisors in the art of such revolution. Thus armed with ideas and encouragement, and goaded by Western policy and actions, the revolutionary nationalist movement in China gathered momentum and acquired a stronger sense of direction and purpose.

Leaders in the United States replied with the assertion that America had "a responsibility for effort directed toward saving the Chinese from their own folly." This remark, a somewhat astringent and blunt synthesis of all the themes implicit in open-door imperialism, characterized an attitude which limited America to a very few alternatives. Since they ignored, or disapproved of, the possibility of working either with Russia to check Japan or with liberal Chinese nationalists, American leaders had one basic choice. They could join four-power action against the left-wing revolutionary movement in China, but simultaneously effect a broad understand-

---

* While some of the quotations in this section come from unpublished documents, American policy toward China between 1917 and 1923 can be followed in its basic outlines in the appropriate volumes of *Papers Relating to the Foreign Relations of the United States.* Also see: D. Borg, *American Policy and the Chinese Revolution, 1925–1928* (New York: Macmillan, 1947); and A. W. Griswold, *The Far Eastern Policy of the United States* (New York: Harcourt, Brace & Co., 1938).

ing with conservative nationalists in China. Within that context, they could then undertake a vigorous program of economic development in China. Or they could work with and through Japan, considering that nation as an agent of American policy and a channel through which American economic power would develop China.

The difficulty in resolving the issue stemmed from several considerations. Either proposal could be defended as a continuation of the Open Door Policy designed to establish American predominance in Asia without recourse to war. The idea of working with and through Chinese conservative nationalists who were dependent upon American aid was the ideal way of putting the policy into operation. The central drawback of the approach was the probability that it would, if undertaken with vigor and determination, lead to war with Japan. That was undesirable per se, and doubly so because after 1917 American leaders feared war as the hothouse of revolution.

The other proposal involved working with and through Japan until American economic power asserted itself in that country as well as in China. This argument took into account the dangers of war and revolution, considerations which tended to compensate for the fact that it again postponed the day of American pre-eminence in Asia. Despite its short-run disadvantages and frustrations, however, it was a persuasive answer to the question of how best to implement the open door in Asia. Though continually challenged by different groups for conflicting reasons, this developed as the basic outlook of American policy-makers from the Bolshevik Revolution until the strong American note delivered to the Japanese Government in November 1941. Neither Wilson, Hughes, nor Hoover considered going to war against Japan; and later leaders argued that American economic power could confine Japanese action within limits defined by the United States.

Beyond the broad considerations of preventing wars and revolutions, policy in Asia was strongly influenced by the last phase of the struggle between the bankers (supported for the time by certain traders and exporters) and the corporations to define the basic character and set the tone of American foreign policy. Though they reasserted their power during and immediately after World War I, the corporations did not have enough surplus capital to embark immediately on further expansion everywhere in the world. For one thing, the severe depression of 1920–1921 caused some temporary loss of influence to the bankers. Then, after recovery began in 1922, the corporate leaders emphasized domestic investments as well as direct overseas investments in factories, service installations, and the development of raw material supplies.

Such companies as Ford, General Motors, International Business Machines, and American Telephone and Telegraph concentrated their activities in European and other industrialized countries. Others, including oil and mining corporations and such raw material processing firms as the Aluminum Corporation of America, centered their attention on the Middle East, Latin America, and parts of Asia. This activity led to a great expansion of direct overseas investments during the 1920s. In 1919 they totalled 94 million. By 1925, they had jumped to 268 million. Up again to 351 in 1926, they ballooned to 602 million in 1929.

For their part, the bankers were caught in a more difficult situation and their actions were more complex and contradictory. On the one hand, they agreed with corporation executives and government leaders that expanded exports were "essential to industrial prosperity." They accepted the analysis prepared by William B. Fleming, the State Department's adviser on commercial treaties: "A number of our big manufacturers . . . in normal times can produce enough to supply the home market in seven months." As the editors of the *Acceptance Bulletin,* one of the key journals of the financial community, pointed out in January 1922, "it is useless to attempt to further develop our own country until a satisfactory market is created for our surplus products." Thus the bankers supported Secretary of State Hughes in his drive for "effective recognition of the Open Door Policy."

On the other hand, the bankers admitted that they lacked the capital for an all-out loan campaign. Fred I. Kent of the Bankers Trust Co., George H. Kretz of the National Park Bank, and George Woodruff of the First National Bank of Joliet, Illinois, offered typical testimony on that crucial point. Perhaps the most dramatic and impressive evidence was provided by the failure of the National City Bank to establish and sustain a world-wide chain of branch banks to finance such expansion. This fundamental weakness forced the financiers to follow less perfect alternatives. Some, like the House of Morgan, continued to pursue their broad strategy of working with and through the British and French while expanding their connections in Germany. Others decided that Europe should be given priority for the capital that was available. Some of that group argued that there would be no possibility of expanding into the underdeveloped countries if Europe collapsed. The rest of them thought that they would be able to move into the poor nations through the European door. In general, therefore, the capital that was directly available for the underdeveloped countries was relatively small in amount and was further limited to short-term loans. The result, as in Latin America, was a scramble for investments that were neither very sound nor very productive.

This drive for accounts did, however, intensify two existing features of banking policy. Financiers continued their maneuvers to obtain government assistance in accumulating capital. They first tried to enlarge and sustain the operations of the War Finance Corporation; such a move would not only have given them the kind of direct aid they wanted, but would also have reassured smaller investors in the general security market that the government supported the undertakings. While that effort failed, the bankers (along with some of the weaker corporations) did not give up trying to get what the *Journal of Commerce* called "federal credit" as a means of accumulating "the capital necessary" for major overseas operations. But it was not until after the start of the Great Depression that such funds became available.

The financiers were more successful in preventing government control of their operations. Hoover wanted to set limits on the bankers, restricting them to loans that were in line with the tactics of the Open Door Policy, and which actually promoted viable economic development in the poor, under-developed nations. He tried hard to obtain such authority during the first years of the Harding Administration, even though he was aware that it might set a dangerous precedent for government intervention. The bankers blocked him by appealing to the fears (and to the narrower philosophy) of Harding and others in the administration. Their argument was stated with considerable power by John Foster Dulles, who in those years was a leading lawyer for the financial community. "Control of foreign loans," he explained with obvious concern, "involves a vast power over our national economy." It "would obviously be unfortunate if [an] established precedent warranted the use of control over foreign loans as a medium for carrying into effect any economic or financial policies which might happen at the moment to be those of the heads of our executive departments." It proved difficult for Dulles, as for others in the financial community, to attain the more inclusive, long-range view of Hoover. In the 1920s, at any rate, the interests of the bankers obscured their vision. "No foreign policy could be intelligently conceived and carried out," Dulles judged, "by a Department of State which was ignorant of or indifferent to the past and current acquisitions by American interests in foreign lands."

These conflicts incident to the maturation of America's corporate economic system manifested themselves in Asia in a complex fashion. At one level they appeared as a battle between the banker Thomas Lamont, who was aligned with Japan, and several corporations which proposed to do business in China. But Lamont was supported by those corporations which had developed significant trade connections with Japan. Other corporations pushed trade with China, however, and those firms lined up with the companies interested in direct investment in that country.

Such economic crosscurrents caused Hughes and Hoover considerable trouble throughout the 1920s. Official strategy was to push American penetration in China while holding a checkrein on Japan. But Hoover and Hughes also wanted all the foreign markets they could get, including those in Japan. Hence they acquiesced in Lamont's tie with Japan, and in exports to Japan, hoping meanwhile to encourage and extend America's position in China. Ultimately, of course, American leaders thought to resolve the dilemma by influencing Japan through its economic ties to the United States. But this posed serious difficulties of its own, and the United States finally went to war to preserve the open door in Asia.

In other areas of the world, meanwhile, such as in Latin America, eastern Europe, and the Middle East and Africa, the policies of the United States were formulated to facilitate the "internationalization of business" through the expansion of the American corporation. Aware of the voracious appetite of American industry, and of its commensurate waste, Hoover, Hughes, and corporation leaders united in a concerted program to discover, develop, and control various key raw materials throughout the world. This drive was integrated with the traditional campaign for markets, and both were heightened by the determination to protect direct, on-the-spot operations from foreign competition and revolutionary opposition.

Latin America posed in classic form two basic difficulties connected with such corporate expansion. It was necessary to control and mitigate the region's opposition to the predominance of the United States and, at the same time, extend and rationalize the system of American authority. The effort to expand American exports, develop and control raw materials, and initiate corporate enterprises—while at the same time developing a regional political system based on local rulers loyal to the basic interests of the United States—made Latin America the laboratory of American foreign policy for all underdeveloped areas.

That comparison offers considerable insight if the foreign policy experiment of the 1920s is thought of as an effort to change the methods and style of American intervention developed by Roosevelt and Wilson while at the same time sustaining and even extending the long-range influence of the United States.* In many respects, moreover, the effort of the 1920s represented the same kind of convergence between reform ideas and hard-headed economics that characterized American policy toward Morocco at the time of the Algeciras Conference in 1905–1906. The developments of the 1920s in

---

* The laboratory metaphor itself is borrowed from Fred Harvey Harrington. Two earlier books bearing on Latin American policy are: D. M. Dozer, *Are We Good Neighbors?* (Gainesville: University of Florida Press, 1959); and B. Wood, *The Making of the Good Neighbor Policy* (New York: Columbia University Press, 1961). An excellent recent study is D. Green, *The Containment of Latin America* (Chicago: Quadrangle Books, 1971).

the Latin American policy of the United States were simply
an adaptation of American policy to altered circumstances
that was continued in the Good Neighbor Policy of the New
Deal and culminated in the Alliance For Progress proposed
by President John F. Kennedy.

In the 1920s, as well as in the 1960s, this modification of
policy was brought about by two main considerations. First,
new ideas about the nature of American predominance in the
Western Hemisphere led different groups in the United States
to propose and initiate policy changes. Second, and inter-
acting with the first, the failure of traditional and existing
policies to achieve the desired results prompted alterations.
Specifically, American policy-makers became convinced by
the end of the 1920s that the 21 military interventions undertaken between 1898 and 1924 had not served either to stabilize
the region or to institutionalize American power and influence.

The beginning of the shift in approach might usefully be
dated from the recognition of the Mexican Government of
Alvaro Obregon by the Harding Administration on August
31, 1923. While it is true that Mexico agreed as a condition of
recognition to respect subsoil rights acquired by Americans
prior to 1917, the move did terminate the direct and even
violent intervention carried on by President Wilson. Almost
immediately, however, incoming President Coolidge indicated
that his outlook was closer to the turn-of-the-century expansionism of Roosevelt than to the approach that Hoover and
Stimson were to reveal after 1928. Since he is usually thought
of as a pinched-in personality, such a comparison of Coolidge
with Roosevelt may appear rather strange. But Coolidge actually entertained an expansive conception of American foreign
policy. He described the process of American businessmen
going abroad and "opening up underdeveloped countries"
as—and note the similarity with the language of Roosevelt—
"the natural play of the forces of civilization." The United
States, he asserted, was "a patron of tranquility abroad."
People who questioned that judgment were "treading the way
that leads back to the jungle." Holding that American "investments and trade relations" made it "almost impossible to
conceive of any conflict anywhere on earth which would not
affect us injuriously," Coolidge concluded that "the one great

duty that stands out requires us to use our enormous powers to trim the balance of the world."

In keeping with that sense of responsibility, Coolidge sent Marines into Honduras in 1924 because, in the phrase of the State Department, "a condition of anarchy seems likely to develop." In the same year, the administration also formally advised Plutarco Calles, the newly elected Mexican President, that recognition was contingent upon continuing protection and respect for American lives and property. That blunt warning served only to strengthen the groups in Mexico that wanted to push ahead with measures limiting foreign economic penetration and influence. Three such laws were passed by the Mexican legislature to take effect on January 1, 1927. One limited foreign concessions to 50 years; another specified that foreign corporations (such as American oil firms) must forego any appeal for protection to their own governments; and the third, a more general land law to break up large holdings, impinged directly upon American agricultural and mining operators.

Even before the laws went into effect, the tension and fear arising from the conflict between Washington and Mexico City had prompted Coolidge in 1926 to send Marines into Nicaragua. The President and others in the State Department were afraid that the Mexican Revolution would spread— directly as well as in spirit—throughout Central America; they were determined to prevent the challenge to the United States from growing any stronger. The intervention in Nicaragua was undertaken to put conservatives friendly to the United States in power. It is simply described as a military and diplomatic maneuver undertaken to achieve a political objective that, it was expected, would in turn prevent long-range economic difficulties and losses.

The actual results were quite different. For one thing, the Marines stayed six years. The intervention in Nicaragua also created fears of a war with Mexico. The reaction against that possibility (as well as against the move into Nicaragua) accelerated and strengthened a movement among diverse groups that opposed military intervention and sought instead to restore and strengthen American influence through more peaceful and sophisticated means. One of those elements, a coalition of pacifist and reform organizations, mobilized considerable public opinion against Coolidge and his policy. They were probably aided, at least to some extent, by the way that England and other countries referred to the President's actions as "frankly imperialistic."

Such general expressions of disapproval were reinforced by criticism from two other sources whose influence was considerable though their size was smaller. Reform politicians of both parties attacked Coolidge vigorously. Senator Borah's opposition was especially militant and had added significance because of his influential position on the Senate Foreign Relations Committee. "The great problem in international affairs at present," he observed bluntly in February 1927, "[grows] out of the relationship between strong and weak nations. . . . It is not war between the great powers but spoliation of the weak nations which seems most vital and imminent in international affairs at this time." Borah was supported in the Congress, moreover, by men like Senators George W. Norris, Hiram Johnson, and Joseph Robinson, and Democratic Representative Fiorello H. La Guardia. They provided the leadership that produced on January 25, 1927, a unanimous vote (79-0) in support of Robinson's resolution calling on Coolidge to settle the dispute with Mexico through arbitration.

Since most Senators were more conservative on matters of foreign policy than Borah or Norris, it is helpful in explaining that vote to realize that many large corporations and other business interests also opposed the nature and implications of Coolidge's policy. Perhaps the most convincing evidence of the central importance of such corporation opinion takes the form of a State Department memorandum prepared during the period when Hoover and Stimson were trying to evolve a less militant approach to relations with Latin America.*

"The participation of American corporations in the development of Latin America involves an incalculable corrective to existing trade figures and implies a distinct and direct American influence in Latin American policies. Irrespective of

---

* This document, dated January 12, 1930, can be found in the National Archives (Record Group 59; Decimal File 710.11/1518).

the policy at Washington and the personality of the statesmen, the operations of such enterprises as the United Fruit Company or the several American oil companies create independent political interests in the territories subject to their economic operation which supplement and often determine official policy both at Washington and in the various Latin American capitals."

In the Mexican-Nicaraguan affair, such firms as Standard Oil and the Boston Bank opposed continued militance on the grounds that it would "injure American interests" far more than it helped them. Another indication of this opinion in the business community was provided indirectly in the editorials of the *New York Times*. At the outset of the crisis they were brazenly nationalistic, even imperialistic. By the end of January 1927, however, the editors were advising a change in policy because a continuation of the existing one "might easily tip the balance in favor of European exporters." Such economic considerations apparently contributed to their advocacy of a "prudent and conciliatory spirit." And finally, evidence of business influence appeared very clearly when Coolidge picked his trouble-shooters to resolve the crisis. He sent Henry L. Stimson, a lawyer for corporate interests, to Nicaragua in April 1927. And four months later he dispatched Dwight W. Morrow of the House of Morgan as a special emissary to Mexico.

The best general explanation of this attitude on the part of large corporation spokesmen (and their associates in law and politics) was probably offered by Leo S. Rowe, Director General of the Pan American Union. "We have advanced," he pointed out, "from the period of adventure to the period of permanent investment." As a man who probably understood the meaning of that change for foreign policy as well as anyone in his generation, Hoover moved very quickly after his election as President in 1928 to sustain the momentum away from the older tradition of open, forceful, military intervention. Even before he took office he made a long good-will trip throughout Latin America. "We have a desire," he assured his various hosts, "to maintain not only the cordial relations of governments with each other but the relations of good neighbors."

Hoover's desire to improve relations with Latin America in a manner that would also strengthen the economic expansion of the United States was wholly sincere. It was based upon a perceptive and sophisticated estimate of the phenomenon that was in later years called "the revolution of rising expectations." He recognized that World War I had broken open the long-festering wounds of economic inequity between the advanced and the poor countries, and between classes within the underprivileged societies. "The great inequalities and injustices of centuries," he explained in 1921, "[have been] flogged beyond endurance by the conflict and freed from restraint by the destruction of war." He also saw the corollary of that new determination and self-consciousness on the part of the suffering millions: that the United States, emerging from the war as the richest and most powerful country in the world, could easily become the focus of that bitterness, frustration, and antagonism. "A large part of the world," he warned the country at large (as well as businessmen), "has come to believe that they were in the presence of the birth of a new imperial power intent upon dominating the destinies and freedoms of other people."

Hoover's problem was to meet that danger while at the same time sustaining the overseas economic expansion that he and other American leaders considered essential to prosperity and representative government at home. He attempted to resolve that dilemma by modifying the methods of expansion so that they were more in line with his ideals. "The basis of an advancing civilization," he observed in 1923, "must be a high and growing standard of living for all the people, not for a single class." From that it followed, as he emphasized in 1928, that an "essential part of the sound expansion of our foreign trade [is] that we . . . interest ourselves in the development of backward or crippled countries by means of loans from our surplus capital." "In stimulating our exports, we should be mainly interested in development work abroad such as roads and utilities which increase the standards of living of people and thus increase the demand for goods from every nation, for we gain in prosperity by a prosperous world, not by displacing others."

A decade later, after the harsh recession of 1937–38 revealed that the depression had by no means been overcome, New Deal policy-makers finally began to use government powers and public monies in line with the analysis that Hoover offered in 1928–29. Quite rightly, they won credit for the developmental loans they granted to some Latin American countries. But to conclude that they were also the men who first thought of, or acted on, the approach is both historically inaccurate and personally unfair to Hoover.

In many ways, moreover, Hoover faced a much more difficult task. He had, in the short space of four years, to close out and reverse a tradition of military intervention and to initiate a new program. "It ought not to be the policy of the United States to intervene by force to secure or maintain contracts between our citizens and foreign states or their citizens. Confidence in that attitude is the only basis upon which the economic cooperation of our citizens can be welcomed abroad." Hoover infused that rhetoric with substance in many ways, but one of his earliest acts involved releasing for publication in 1928 the anti-interventionist *Memorandum on the Monroe Doctrine*. Prepared in the State Department by J. Reuben Clark, and held up by the Coolidge Administration, the document openly and officially disavowed the approach of Theodore Roosevelt.

In moving toward his objective, Hoover was confronted by more than the obvious handicaps of tradition and an inherited intervention in Nicaragua. Secretary of State Stimson, for example, had a good bit of the crusading upper-class reformer in his temperament that had to be restrained if not overcome. But Stimson had the relatively rare kind of courage that enabled him to modify or change his opinions on some vital issues when they were battered beyond a certain point by reality. Nicaragua's factional politics, and its resistance to the Marines, gave some of his assumptions that kind of a beating. He concluded by 1931 that it was time to withdraw. Any effort to keep Nicaragua pacified, and to establish American-style political life, would involve the United States in "difficulties and commitments which this Government does not propose to undertake." They would impose "a very serious burden." In a similar way, Stimson wholly agreed with Hoover that the United States should not intervene in the Cuban

Revolution which erupted in 1929–30. And in a way that offered a striking contrast with the later interference by New Deal policy-makers, they did not intervene *or* intermeddle.

As the *London Times* remarked on April 21, 1931, the approach to relations with Latin America revealed by Hoover and Stimson amounted to a "reversal of the methods" of the past. Stimson offered his own neat summary of the difference in connection with the Cuban uprising. "The situation in Cuba ought to so develop that less and less pressure would be necessary on the part of the United States to keep matters straight." Whether or not Hoover and Stimson are given formal credit for founding what later became known as the Good Neighbor Policy is probably not a vital issue. Given the consequences to Cuba and the United States of Roosevelt's support of Batista as he made his initial bid for power in 1933–34, perhaps even they would not press the claim too vigorously. The important things are that they broke with past methods, that their analysis and reasoning also served to guide later policy-makers, and that their objective was to sustain the overseas economic expansion and political influence of the United States under the strategy of the Open Door Policy.

Elsewhere throughout the world during the years after World War I, American policy developed within that framework. In every instance, the key move was the assertion of the policy of the open door. And in each case, the objectives were markets for American industrial exports, raw materials for American factories, and the right to enter directly into the economic life of a country by establishing factories and other enterprises. That economic expansion made it possible to exercise a growing influence on local political and economic decisions, served to provide a base for further penetration, and ultimately took on military significance. But its initial character and importance was only extended—it was neither changed nor abandoned.

The basic approach toward eastern Europe was characterized by Hoover's insistence that the American economic penetration of Russia should be handled directly rather than through Germany. Germany was needed to block Russia, and to strengthen the community of industrial powers, but it remained a competitor. Within that framework, American activity in eastern Europe included industrial and communications development and the search for raw materials such as phosphate and oil. Having penetrated the economies of the area, as in Poland, Bulgaria, Romania, Yugoslavia, and Albania, the businessmen turned to Washington for help against restrictive legislation enacted by these nations and against competition from Germany, Britain, and France. The first official move usually was a note to the country in question, reminding it of the principle and practice of the Open Door Policy. If that hint proved insufficient, American leaders resorted to economic pressure: directly, by withholding approval of projected loans or similar projects; or indirectly, by threatening, subtly or blatantly, to break diplomatic relations. Reinforcing their own vigorous political and economic activities on the scene, such diplomatic support enabled American businessmen to establish and develop significant interests in eastern Europe throughout the 1920s.*

Better known, and certainly more dramatic, was the postwar pattern of open-door expansion in the Middle East. Oil was the major objective of American policy, but American leaders did not overlook the long-range importance of a "new and as yet unorganized market of prodigious size." For these reasons, as well as in behalf of its own logistic and other interests, the Navy supported such expansion. Its program, along with President Wilson's assumption that Russia would be kept "bottled up" in the Black Sea, was based on the proposition that the strongest navy would control the straits of the Dardanelles. With this general support, Secretaries Hughes and Hoover in Harding's Cabinet first acted to force Britain and France to accept and honor the policy of the open door in their colonies and in the areas assigned to them under the League of Nations system of mandates. After several false starts, American interests finally began their penetration of the area by infiltrating European companies rather than by independent operations. Economic power opens its own doors.

Several factors account for the initial preference for indirect action. For one thing, it was cheaper and easier; it gave American companies a share of current production while

---

* This involvement should not be forgotten when considering American differences with Russia at the end of World War II.

enabling them to conduct private and secret explorations designed to outflank their European "partners." Also, American companies were occupied for the moment in the Western Hemisphere, fighting Mexico and exploring and claiming title to newly discovered reserves throughout the rest of the region. And finally, Hughes and Hoover continued and extended the practice of favoring, however subtly and covertly, one American corporation as the "chosen instrument" of the Open Door Policy in any given area.

In the case of the Middle East, the partiality benefited the complex of Standard Oil companies. Outfits such as Barnsdall, which wanted to work with the Russians in the Baku region, or Sinclair, which tried to do the same thing in the Far East, were blocked by the Department of State. Barnsdall discovered that it was permissible to do some trading with the Bolsheviks but not to help them develop important natural resources. And Secretary Hughes bluntly told Sinclair that he would not support the company in its battles with the Japanese, who claimed the sole right to exploit oil reserves in the Russian half of the island of Sakhalin.

There is some evidence which suggests that the official bias in favor of Standard Oil helps explain Sinclair's efforts to secure access to American domestic reserves held by the government itself—a campaign which ended in the Teapot Dome scandal of 1924. One thing is certain: favored by the government, Standard Oil could afford the luxury of delaying active production in the Middle East until it had penetrated and canvassed such areas as Saudi Arabia. That result might be described as a successful example of corporate capitalism in action. The nature and consequences of those activities became diplomatic issues for the Roosevelt Administration and its successors.

Though neither as dramatic nor as extensive as the undertakings in Latin America, eastern Europe, and the Middle East, American penetration of Africa and Southeast Asia also increased during the 1920s. After considerable maneuvering by Liberian leaders (as well as by Hoover and Hughes), designed to prepare the natives for foreign economic intervention, the Firestone Tire and Rubber Company began its development of rubber plantations in that nation. It was more difficult to penetrate European colonies in Africa and southeastern Asia in such direct fashion, but the patterns of investment, purchasing, and marketing which originated in the 1920s ultimately made those raw-material producing areas vitally important to the existing methods and processes of the American corporate economy.

There were other ways of providing for the continuing development of the American economy, but they were never seriously considered, let alone adopted. Thus the ties with the colonies of western European powers and other underdeveloped regions gradually came to be viewed as the *only* source of raw materials, services, and markets, whether or not current operations were based on such connections. And the threatened loss of supplies earmarked for future development was considered as dangerous as the possible loss of current ones, both by the corporations and the American Government. Perhaps more so, for the method and the rate of current exploitation were based in part on the assumption that the future was under control—that the frontier was unlimited.

When such assumptions, as well as current operations, were threatened by Germany and Japan (and by revolutionary agitation), American leaders routinely defined the issue as one involving the principle of the open door and the strategic position of the nation itself. Men who began by thinking about the United States and the world in economic terms, and explaining its operation by the principles of capitalism and a frontier thesis of historical development, came finally to define the United States in military terms as an embattled outpost in a hostile world. When a majority of the leaders of America's corporate society reached that conclusion, the nation went to war—at first covertly, then overtly.

Far from being unimportant, therefore, the Open Door Policy became increasingly more significant and crucial in the years after it was first enunciated by Secretary of State John Hay. The pattern of American expansion under the principles and procedures of the Open Door Notes came to maturity during the 1920s. And it was the threat posed to that program by the combined impact of the Great Depression and the competing expansion of Germany and Japan, both of which gained strength by falsely identifying themselves with one or more of the broad revolutions against classical liberalism, which ultimately accounted for American entry into World War II.

CHAPTER FIVE

The only thing we have to fear is fear itself.

FRANKLIN DELANO ROOSEVELT, 1933

When everyone began to realize finally that the country was really filled up, that there were no more good homesteads and no frontier to fill up in times of depression, there was great uneasiness.

HENRY AGARD WALLACE, 1934

Foreign markets must be regained if America's producers are to rebuild a full and enduring domestic prosperity for our people. There is no other way if we would avoid painful economic dislocations, social readjustments, and unemployment.

FRANKLIN DELANO ROOSEVELT, 1935

The rest of the world—Ah! there is the rub.

FRANKLIN DELANO ROOSEVELT, 1936

The reason for all this battleship and war frenzy is coming out. We Democrats have to admit we are floundering. The Democratic administration is getting down to the condition that Mr. Hoover found himself [in]. We have pulled all the rabbits out of the hat and there are no more rabbits.

REPRESENTATIVE MAUREY MAVERICK, 1938

THE WAR FOR
THE AMERICAN FRONTIER

There can be no military disarmament without economic appeasement.

SECRETARY OF STATE CORDELL HULL, 1938

Unless substantial economic offsets are provided to prevent this nation from being wholly dependent upon the war expenditures we will sooner or later come to the dilemma which requires either war or depression.

JOHN L. LEWIS, C.I.O., 1940

What interests us primarily is the longer-range question of whether the American capitalist system could continue to function if most of Europe and Asia should abolish free enterprise.

FROM THE FIFTH FORTUNE ROUND TABLE DISCUSSION
ON THE U.S. AND WAR, 1940

Yes, war did come, despite the trade agreements. But it is a fact that war did not break out between the United States and any country with which we had been able to negotiate a trade agreement. It is also a fact that, with very few exceptions, the countries with which we signed trade agreements joined to-

*gether in resisting the Axis. The political line-up followed the
economic line-up.*

CORDELL HULL, 1948

A visitor from afar might have concluded in 1929 that the
foundations and the superstructure of the *Pax Americana,* so
candidly avowed by Secretary of State Hughes in 1924, were
firmly established. And so they were, a truth demonstrated by
America's ability to meet two major challenges during the
next 15 years and emerge as the first nuclear superpower in
world history.

President Hoover had barely established a routine of administrative procedure before the basic assumptions underlying
the open-door conception of America and its role in the world
were undercut in a fundamental way by the Great Depression. The entire policy was predicated on the proposition that
the overweening economic power generated by the American
economic system would enable it to overcome competitors
and wrong-headed revolutionaries and bestow prosperity and
democracy upon the entire world. Yet within two years the
American economic system was not providing for its own
citizens.

A second event dramatized and extended the domestic crisis
of the corporate order. For by the end of Hoover's term in
office, it was apparent that the broad revolutionary challenges
to America's program for the world, which first appeared to
plague President Wilson, were being taken up, in part or in
toto, by other major powers. However they distorted or mis-
used the upsurge of dissatisfaction with the status quo, the
leaders of Germany, Japan, and Italy were working with the
most powerful weapon available—the determination, born
equally of desperation and hope, of large numbers of people
to improve, radically and immediately, the substance and tone
of their daily lives. And though a great hardship and suffering, these revolutions seemed to have survived and converged
in a Russia beginning to assert its right and ability to lead the
world out of economic and spiritual depression into a better
future.

The key decision made by American leaders, and accepted by the rest of the nation, involved a bipartisan agreement to preserve the existing system of corporate capitalism governed according to the existing practices of constitutional democracy. Far from being a revolution, the New Deal was a consensus and a movement to prevent a revolution. Thus it is most aptly defined and described as a movement to provide for the emergency relief, the short-run rehabilitation, and the long-term rationalization of the existing corporate society. Its objective was to define and institutionalize the roles, functions, and responsibilities of three important segments of any industrial society—capital, labor, and the government—and to do so according to the principles of capitalism. In fundamental ways, therefore, the New Deal continued and developed the central approach and outlook formulated by advocates of a corporate society such as Theodore Roosevelt, Herbert Croly, Herbert Hoover, Bernard Baruch, Gerald Swope, and Samuel Gompers.

While the initial necessity to grapple with the domestic crisis temporarily de-emphasized the foreign policy that was an integral part of that outlook, the New Deal did not make any fundamental change in the traditional policies of economic and ideological empire. Even in the depths of the depression, and increasingly so in subsequent years, the overseas expansion of the American corporate system was considered a basic means of recovery and further development. Franklin Roosevelt quickly reasserted, moreover, the kind of aristocratic *noblesse oblige* that his cousin Theodore had infused into American diplomacy. He also displayed a good bit of the crusading fervor for the extension of American ideas and ideals that had characterized the outlook and actions of Woodrow Wilson.

Roosevelt's sense of *noblesse oblige* and mission gave his foreign policy a more assertive and expansive tone than was produced by Hoover's emphasis on efficient economic expansion. This difference did not become readily apparent until the mid-1930s, but its early manifestations can be observed in the events of 1929 to 1933. President Hoover's response to Japanese military expansion in Manchuria was conditioned by his long-term objective of establishing a community of interest with Japan in Asia, and by his fear of war as the pump-primer for revolution. He neither liked nor approved of

Japan's actions, but he concluded that Japanese expansion was much the lesser evil when judged against Chinese revolutionary nationalism or the Soviet Union. War by itself was dangerous enough, but undertaken in the context of depression it would produce general disaster.

Roosevelt and Stimson shared some aspects of Hoover's outlook in general. Both men favored working with Japan throughout the 1920s and agreed with Hoover's emphasis on the importance of peace—both generally and in the circumstances of the depression. But they differed with Hoover over the best means of insuring peace. The divergence was the product of two factors: Roosevelt and Stimson came to question Japan's willingness and ability to accept America's conception of the world without coercion of some sort; and they entertained an active sense of America's mission in China. Those considerations led them to disagree with Hoover over what should and could be done to sustain peace, even though they were willing to accept his policy under the existing circumstances. Nevertheless, they inclined toward economic pressure and a show of force to push Japan back toward an acceptance of American leadership in the world community. In 1932 and 1933 this divergence of opinion among American leaders was not severe and dramatic, and it was not acted upon either by Stimson or by Roosevelt, but it did reveal a difference of opinion that became extremely significant within five years.

That willingness to employ economic coercion against Japan at the end of the 1930s seems to be the main explanation for what is a rather general impression that Roosevelt recognized the Soviet Union in 1933 for the purpose of exerting similar pressure on Tokyo. It is true that some Americans like Senator Borah suggested the maneuver; and the Russians did their best to foster that interpretation at the time to improve their own position in dealing with Japan. But it was not the reason Roosevelt acted.

The recognition of Russia was largely the result of a persistent campaign by large and small business interests who felt that it would lead to a vast increase in their export of goods, capital, and services. Their efforts began in 1926, when the first signs of economic trouble appeared in many industries.

For that matter, Hoover began financing such exports through the Reconstruction Finance Corporation before he left office (though neither the President nor Secretary Stimson responded favorably to Borah's proposals). Roosevelt did not recognize the Soviets simply, or only, as an economic move (the first Export-Import Bank, however, was organized explicitly to handle the anticipated export boom). His upper-class urbanity, for example, led him to consider the game of make-believe about the nonexistence of such a major country as something more than slightly ridiculous on the part of the world's most powerful country. And he did want to establish some kind of communication and discussion about peace between the United States and all major nations. But he never considered the kind of an entente sought by the Russians, as was indicated by his persistent refusal to respond to their overtures for a nonaggression pact with China and the Soviet Union.

Short-term as well as traditional long-run economic considerations also played an important role in Roosevelt's dramatic moves to improve and regularize relations with Latin America. The Good Neighbor Policy was infused with the tone and substance of *noblesse oblige* and announced in the rhetoric of America's mission to defend and extend democracy, but its context was defined by the immediate and specific needs of American businessmen and by the long-range objective of a broad integration of the economy of the United States with that of Latin America. It was Roosevelt's Latin American policy, not his recognition of Russia in 1933, which offered the strongest hint that he entertained from an early date the idea of a major intervention in world politics at some later time. From the outset, the leadership of the United States was asserted, defended, and extended in terms of meeting the European challenge to America's open-door empire in the Western Hemisphere. And the continued development of that interpretation and argument culminated in the treaty organization of the American system. Even so, the European challenge of the early 1930s was economic, not military.

Roosevelt's conception of America's general role in the world, and of its economic expansion, became clearer and more forceful in 1934, when it seemed that the early policies of the New Deal were generating recovery from the depression. This illusion of success enabled the Roosevelt Administration to give more attention to world affairs than it had during its first year in office. The most striking feature of this development was the degree to which Roosevelt and his advisors reasserted the traditional foreign policy of the United States. As with Theodore Roosevelt and John Hay, they assumed the necessity, desirability, and ability of the American economic system to expand throughout the world. And with Woodrow Wilson, they asserted America's leadership in the establishment and maintenance of an orderly peace. At home and abroad, peace and order were the main objectives of the New Deal.

In general, therefore, the United States at first gave ground before the assertiveness of Germany, Japan, and Italy. Neither private corporate nor official political leaders approved all the actions of those powers, but the bipartisan consensus among American leaders during these years was based on acquiescence in Axis actions and appeasement of Axis demands. The underlying attitude was that world problems would be taken care of by American recovery. Various critics did agitate for unilateral action in Europe or Asia, for an entente with the Soviet Union, or for more vigorous alignment with Great Britain and France, but they effected no significant modification, let alone a fundamental change in American policy.

Quite in keeping with traditional policies, American leaders undertook a vigorous campaign during these same years to renew and extend America's economic expansion. The corporations, for example, steadily extended their overseas operations after 1934. During the 1920s, moreover, Roosevelt and Hull had talked of solving domestic economic problems in terms of "exportable surpluses"; and once in power they stressed the importance of foreign trade and investment for domestic revival and for controlling conditions abroad which caused wars and revolutions. Based on the proposition that "the political line-up followed the economic line-up," this program for the expansion of the American economic system was presented as the answer to specific and general problems. Inherent in the approach was a definition of trade that went far beyond the idea of an exchange of commodities and services. The denotation of the definition emphasized trade as the expansion and control of markets for America's corporate *system*, while the connotations stressed the control and development of raw-material supplies.

Secretary Hull's reciprocal trade program was designed to meet both needs. The strategy was simple: in return for lowering American tariffs on selected items exported by a foreign country, that nation would decrease its tariffs on certain American exports. And by insisting upon the unrestricted most-favored-nation clause, the United States sought to extend its own potential or actual market even further. In practice, America traded tariff reductions on items which it needed (such as selected raw materials) or on goods which did not seriously challenge producers at home, in return for foreign reductions on American surpluses.

The reciprocity program offers basic insights into New Deal foreign policy and also serves to document its continuity with the decade of the 1890s. First proposed as a key element in foreign policy during the late 1880s, and then tentatively written into law in a limited way in the McKinley Tariff Act of 1890, the concept of reciprocity treaties was taken up by the National Association of Manufacturers in 1895 as an integral part of its drive for foreign markets. From the beginning, moreover, the principle of the unconditional most-favored-nation clause (by which America gained any benefits extended to other nations) was closely associated with the idea of reciprocity.

Neither Secretary of State Hull nor any other New Deal policy-maker ever improved very much upon McKinley's clear and candid explanation of the policy. "It is to afford new markets for our surplus agricultural and manufactured products," he had remarked in 1896, "without loss to the American laborer of a single day's work that he might otherwise procure." The statement of purpose written into the first and basic New Deal trade act of 1934 was no more than a rather clumsy reiteration of the outlook and logic evolved by intellectuals, businessmen, and politicians during the Crisis of the 1890s. The law announced that it was "for the purpose of expanding foreign markets for the products of the United States (as a means of assisting in the present emergency in restoring the American standard of living, in overcoming domestic unemployment and the present economic depression, in increasing the purchasing power of the American public, and in establishing and maintaining a better relationship among various branches of American agriculture, industry, mining, and commerce)."

Secretary Hull had long advocated greatly expanded penetration of Latin American markets, with a complementary influence over that region's sources of raw materials. His move upward from Tennessee politics to the House of Representatives was in considerable measure a result of the reputation and backing he had won by pushing that issue. Actually, of course, his emphasis on exports to Latin America was merely one facet of his almost religious faith in the nineteenth-century doctrine of free trade as a solution to the political and social, as well as economic, ills of the United States and the world. That commitment led him, not unnaturally, to make unfavorable moral judgments of any and all countries which opposed his plan, which tried other techniques of handling foreign trade (such as balancing accounts with each country separately), or which had economic systems that limited the activities of American businessmen (such as Russia and Mexico).

Hull's outlook further provided him with a circular argument involving cause, effect, and prescription that seemed to him, at any rate, unanswerable either by example or logic. Long before the Great Depression actually began, for instance, he predicted and explained such a crisis in terms of his theory. Speaking on January 3, 1929, he first documented the great gap between America's productive capacity and its actual output. Then he noted that there were great surpluses in spite of the idle facilities. "These glaring facts and conditions," he concluded, "soon will compel America to recognize that these ever increasing surpluses are her key economic problems, and that our neglect to develop foreign markets for surpluses is the one outstanding cause of unemployment." Because they were confusing and seemingly indecisive, President Roosevelt's early actions in the foreign trade area apparently upset Hull considerably. In one of his most famous campaign speeches delivered before the Commonwealth Club in San Francisco, for example, Roosevelt referred explicitly and with considerable emphasis to the end of the frontier and implied

that this called for a more self-contained and planned economy. It developed later, however, that he had neither written
nor studied and evaluated the speech before he delivered it.
Even so, a careful reading of the document reveals that the
argument pointed not so much toward national planning as
toward finding a new frontier in such areas as foreign trade.

And despite his concern and preoccupation with immediate
domestic relief measures, Roosevelt quickly indicated that he
was thinking along those lines. Hull understood this. The true
source of the Secretary's anxiety (and resentment) resided in
the signs that Roosevelt was attracted to the idea of expanding
foreign trade through bilateral balancing and bartering with a
steadily increasing number of countries. *The issue was never
whether or not to continue America's overseas economic expansion, but rather the question of how it should be furthered.*
The showdown came over such a bilateral deal negotiated with
Germany by George N. Peek, who was challenging Hull for
control of foreign trade matters. Hull won. The victory not
only opened the way for the reciprocal trade program, but
offered one of the earliest indications that Hull was not in fact
the kind of secondary figure in New Deal diplomacy that many
commentators and historians later assumed. Roosevelt swung
over to Hull's policy with an enthusiasm based upon his own
commitment to the basic objective. "The full measure of
America's high productive capacity is only gained," he warned
in 1935, "when our businessmen and our farmers can sell
their surpluses abroad." The President went on to reveal (and
dramatize) his acceptance of the same either-or attitude that
had characterized American thinking on the subject ever since
the 1890s. Prosperity and democracy were contingent upon
the program. "Foreign markets must be regained if America's
producers are to rebuild a full and enduring domestic prosperity for our people. There is no other way if we would avoid
painful economic dislocation, social readjustments, and unemployment."

Administration leaders connected with the trade program
left no doubt as to its underlying philosophy. Diplomat
George S. Messersmith held, for example, that any other approach "would call for a complete rearrangement of the entire
economic setup of the United States." But the most significant

spokesman was Assistant Secretary of State Francis B. Sayre, a law professor and the son-in-law of Woodrow Wilson, who became chairman of the President's Executive Committee on Commercial Policy. Sayre's departmental and public documents offer an illuminating example of how American policymakers had consciously accepted, and were acting upon, the same analysis developed in the 1890s. "By that time [the 1890s]," Sayre explained, "our national surpluses which could not be sold profitably in this country had come to assume formidable proportions, and it was becoming clear that the loss or curtailment of foreign markets would mean severe economic dislocation." He even quoted McKinley to cinch the point: "The expansion of our trade and commerce is the pressing problem." Sayre laid great and persistent stress on the idea that trade offered the only way to avoid changing the existing political economy. "Unless we can export and sell abroad our surplus production, we must face a violent dislocation of our whole domestic economy."

It is not surprising, therefore, that trade was defined in a most particular and narrow manner. On the one hand, it meant finding and expanding markets—*and making them "secure for the products of the United States."* [Italics mine.] On the other hand, it involved careful studies to pinpoint the countries supplying raw materials to American industry, followed by negotiations to tie those economies to the United States through reciprocal trade treaties.

This New Deal conception of trade as an integral part of the overseas expansion of the economy had three consequences of major importance. All of them operated and influenced events over the long-run as well as during the decade of the 1930s, and all of them contributed significantly to the maturation of the broader tragedy of American diplomacy.

The first was the role of the New Deal in reinvigorating, extending, and sustaining, in the mind of the general public as well as the policy-makers, the traditional view of overseas economic expansion. Lord Keynes and other economists who stressed the role of public spending and other measures to counteract underconsumption and underinvestment did influence New Deal thinking and policies. But they did so within the old system of thought. Their ideas did not displace the existing outlook. Thus the pattern of either-or thinking about representative government and economic welfare was reasserted and even intensified. Different solutions were dismissed because they would undercut the existing order of business and politics.

Secondly, the emphasis on trade expansion, and upon the Open Door Policy, served to define the nature and the causes of danger and conflict in international affairs. As Sayre explained, the trade expansion program was "an instrumentality for throwing the weight of American power and influence against the current disastrous movement toward economic nationalism." It was "only" as the American program was adopted that the United States could "recover her foreign markets." For the New Deal administration as for its predecessors, therefore, American recovery and prosperity were made dependent upon the acceptance of American policies by the rest of the world. By externalizing good, so also was evil externalized: domestic problems and difficulties became issues of foreign policy. In the immediate context of the mid-1930s, and as Roosevelt, Hull, Sayre, and others explicitly noted as early as 1935, that meant that Germany, Italy, and Japan were defined as dangers to the well-being of the United States. This happened before those countries launched military attacks into or against areas that the United States considered important to its economic system. It occurred instead as those nations began to compete vigorously with American entrepreneurs in Latin America and Asia. In the broader sense, the American outlook defined as a danger any nation (or group) that challenged or limited such expansion. The successful drive by the United States in 1962 to define any "Marxist-Leninist" government as an alien and dangerous outlaw in the Western Hemisphere was a projection of the same basic idea.

The third major consequence of New Deal trade philosophy was the way it sustained, and even deepened, the pattern of free trade imperialism or informal empire that had evolved out of British economic policy in the nineteenth century. America's relationship with the chief suppliers of raw materials became economically and politically ever more imbalanced in its own favor. And, at the same time, the policy reinforced the existing *internal* political economy of those poorer, weaker nations. For the changes introduced by American penetration served primarily to create islands of modernism that intensified the skewed and inequitable character of those societies.

In response, many people in these nations began to wonder if the United States was not merely a more subtle—and hence more dangerous—imperial power. Americans were shocked or angered by this reaction, arguing that their policies increased the national wealth and prestige of the raw-material areas. On the surface, this seemed to be true in most cases, but the American operators took much of the wealth back to the United States. Their actions, and those of American political leaders, also strengthened groups and classes in the underdeveloped regions that prevented the wealth that remained from being distributed equitably—or even wisely from a conservative point of view—or used in a way to initiate and sustain the balanced development of a poor country. For the most part, moreover, the pro-American groups were not very democratic in political and social matters. This further weakened American leadership.

Not only did this aspect of New Deal foreign policy serve to stockpile explosives for future social upheavals, but it can almost be said to have lit the fuses. The tragedy is that none of it was done with evil intent. Good intentions granted, however, that was nevertheless the basic dynamic inherent in the program. For having defined overseas economic activity as essential to the welfare of the United States, American policymakers were exceedingly prone to view social revolution in those countries as a threat to the vital national interests of their own nation. The irony is that while the New Deal did gradually become less militant in defending *individual* American business interests against the actions of underdeveloped countries, it continued at the same time to consolidate the traditional definition of such economic activities as essential to domestic prosperity and political welfare of the United States.

However more openly humanitarian (and more adept with the polished phrase), New Deal leaders did not in action go very far beyond the foreign policy of Hoover until the economic needs of American overseas business enterprise, and the competition from Axis rivals, forced it to do so. Since this may seem too severe a judgment, particularly for the generations which either led or came to maturity under the New Deal, it may be useful to make two points very explicit. The first concerns the sincerity and the liberal sentiments of New Deal policy-makers. No question, direct or indirect, is raised about either characteristic. The second involves something that is generally overlooked; namely, the basic denotation about conduct that is inherent in the famous phrase, "The Good Neighbor Policy." Here the issue is very important even though it is implicit. By American definition, and practice, good neighbors do not rock the boat.

But rocking the boat is precisely what Latin Americans were doing, at least by the standards current in the United States, throughout the 1930s. It was only after many years of intervention and intermeddling that New Deal leaders began to act as well as talk like good neighbors in a more mature and sophisticated manner. The early attitude was revealed by Hull's remark after he had signed a hemispheric pledge in 1933 holding that "no state has the right to intervene in the internal or external affairs of another." Speaking privately, the Secretary commented that the proposition was "more or less wild and unreasonable."

Hull, Roosevelt, and Ambassador Sumner Welles proceeded to act in keeping with the Secretary's judgment in connection with the Cuban Revolution that was under way when they came into office. Pressure exerted through and by Welles first contributed to the final collapse of the old regime headed by Gerardo Machado y Morales. But it was in dealing with the new government headed by Grau San Martín that New Deal interference became persistent and determined. Though it ran Cuba from September 1933, through January 1934, the Grau Government was never recognized by the United States. Secretary Hull and Ambassador Welles made it clear that the ability of Grau to maintain order was *not* the issue. "No government," Welles remarked to Hull during a phone conversation in mid-September, "will be able to maintain absolute order here for some time to come." Both men accepted that as natural under the circumstances. Welles was extremely upset, however, by any and all indications that "a social revolution" was in progress. "Our own commercial and export interests in Cuba," Welles warned in October, "cannot be revived under this government." Viewing the Grau Government as composed of "the most irresponsible elements," the Ambassador was determined to replace it by an instrument of "all the better classes of the country."

Three Cuban groups opposed Grau: the officer corps, the communists, and the business community and its associated politicians. Grau crushed two attempted coups by the officers, a demonstration of power and general support that impressed the British representative but served only to intensify American antagonism. And though certainly spearheaded by Welles, the opposition to Grau was supported by Hull and Roosevelt. Indeed! By the end of 1933, for example, the United States had some 30 Navy ships on station around Cuba. Even more important, at least in some respects, was the way that nonrecognition disrupted the Cuban economy. For that weakened the Grau Government as effectively, if more subtly, as detachments of American Marines doing guard duty throughout the country.

By all accounts, it would seem that President Roosevelt enjoyed his games of verbal hide-and-seek with American reporters who asked him whether or not his policy amounted to intervention. He once told them adamantly that the United States was not intervening at almost the precise hour that Welles was busily engaged in trying to organize a coalition against Grau. Even Welles once admitted to Hull that he was rather embarrassed by "the measure of control" he was exercising in Cuba. Finally, after many false starts, the support and encouragement that Welles and the United States gave to Batista led to the overthrow of the Grau Government.

By the end of the decade, Roosevelt had modified his method of handling Latin American affairs. The change nevertheless came very slowly. Bolivia found that out in March 1937, when it annulled the oil concession held by Standard Oil and confiscated the company's property. The United States supported the firm in two ways. It brought pressure on other Latin American countries to prevent Bolivia from obtaining help in developing or selling its oil, and it refused to give Bolivia any economic aid (loans or technical assistance). The latter position was stated bluntly in a memorandum of December 26, 1939. "In order to secure the necessary support and cooperation of American private interests [for such aid]," the State Department explained, "it is believed to be essential before American financial assistance is given that a settlement will have been reached." That document revealed not only the kind of economic intervention that was used against Bolivia, but also the relationship between official policy and the views of large corporate spokesmen. This connection between big business leadership and the government is often misconceived as a simple, direct kind of push-or-pull relationship in which outsiders lean on insiders—or vice versa. Many businessmen as well as many reformers are prone to make that kind of an interpretation. But it is misleading, particularly by the time of the mid-1930s, even though there were (and still are) many examples of such interaction.

But thinking of the New Deal so narrowly (or wholly) as a reform movement tends to blind both its critics and its defenders to the way that it steadily drew more and more of its leadership from the community of large, established corporation executives, their counsels, and their economic advisors. This does not necessarily mean that the New Deal became less reformist. It does mean, however, that the reforms were of a certain kind; namely, they rationalized the system as it existed, and did not lead to significant modifications of its character.

This aspect of New Deal leadership offers an important insight into the developments in American policy specifically toward Latin America, but also more generally, between 1937 and 1941.* It helps explain, for example, the gradual willingness (after mid-1939) to grant a loan to Bolivia on the basis of a gentleman's agreement that Standard Oil would then be given prompt satisfaction on its claims. This slow and halting

---

* My general knowledge and understanding of New Deal diplomacy has been vastly increased as a result of many long discussions with Professor Lloyd Gardner. We have exchanged research notes and ideas on an extensive and wholly reciprocal basis. He has contributed greatly to my comprehension of the development of American policy in Latin America during the years 1937-1941.

process of change was brought about by four principal factors. On the basis of the available evidence, they can be ranked in the following order of importance.

There was first a general reassertion during and after the sharp and serious recession of 1937–38 of both central themes of American diplomacy as it evolved during and after the Crisis of the 1890s: that vigorous overseas economic expansion was essential to the functioning of the system; and that, as stated so explicitly by Secretary of State Root in 1906, policy had to be formulated so "that the door, being open, shall lead to something." This feeling, and the new urgency behind it, was manifested by government spokesmen and also by leaders of the corporate system who did not hold public office. Official policy-makers like Lawrence Duggan, Eric Johnston, and Nelson Rockefeller, for example, advanced this view with great vigor. But corporation leaders outside the government shared the same outlook. A group of them meeting in 1939 under the auspices of *Fortune* magazine agreed that it was important to "provide adequate economic opportunities to the so-called 'have-not' countries."

Secondly, American private and official leaders were by 1939 very disturbed by German and Japanese economic competition in Latin America (as well as in Asia). It may be, indeed, that this factor was most important of all. On the other hand, there were many important Americans who felt as late as 1940 that it would be possible to work out some kind of economic compromise with the Axis powers. Two things, however, are certain: Axis competition worried a significant number of men in policy-making positions after 1938, and that concern served to convince some of them that it was necessary to modify some of the existing practices of America's overseas economic expansion in order to protect the expansion itself. Sumner Welles offers a good example of the way that kind of interaction altered earlier attitudes and actions.

The third consideration was the determination on the part of some of the larger Latin American countries, such as Mexico, to stand firm in their efforts to reform, control, and restrict American business activities in their countries. This resistance unquestionably speeded up the modification of American policy.

Fourth, the humanitarian idealism of American policy-makers affected their decisions. Never absent in the making of American policy, it enjoyed a renaissance in the late 1930s. This is no doubt partly explained as a reaction against Axis domestic and foreign policies whose nature was growing more obvious and more disturbing after 1936. But it was also the result of a few strong and even assertive reformers having positions of some authority, probably the best example being Josephus Daniels as Ambassador to Mexico. He not only softened some of Hull's outbursts to the Mexicans, but also enjoyed a direct correspondence with Roosevelt. More significant, however, the existence of a growing crisis by nature involved Roosevelt more directly in all relations with Latin America. And that brought his sense and spirit of *noblesse oblige* more actively into the policy-making process.

The developing and on-going interaction of these four factors can be seen and followed in the renewed crisis with Mexico over American oil properties. The election in 1934 of President Lázaro Cárdenas led to a resurgence of revolutionary enthusiasm and a program of vigorous reform legislation. After concentrating on domestic property issues for two years, Cárdenas pushed through in November 1936, a law providing the government with authority to move against foreign companies that controlled oil resources. The American response was prompt and negative. Hull minced no words. "It would be extremely unfortunate," he commented in August 1937, "if any action should be taken by the Mexican authorities which would jeopardize the [American oil] industry in any manner."

Hull was concerned about the Mexican situation for several broad and fundamental reasons. The threat in Mexico was only the specific issue. For one thing, he was worried about the impact of Mexico's action in countries like Venezuela, where Standard Oil had developed huge operations, or in Bolivia, which would be encouraged in its own expropriation battle. It might also slow down or disrupt entirely the efforts that were under way to win a favorable settlement of outstanding economic issues with Brazil. Thus the United States made it clear, even before any expropriation had actually taken place, that loans to Mexico would be held up indefinitely.

Other considerations made it difficult, however, to settle upon a policy of unmitigated opposition to Mexico. Ambassador Daniels in Mexico City and Secretary of the Treasury Henry Morgenthau were both beginning to fear Axis economic competition. Daniels argued that it was imperative to expand trade with Mexico, both for its own sake and to keep the door closed against Germany and Japan. Morgenthau was even more emphatic, probably because of his deep horror at Nazi persecution of Jews. "We're just going to wake up and find inside of a year," he fretted in December 1937, "that Italy, Germany, and Japan have taken over Mexico." In a similar way, State Department policy-makers like Adolph A. Berle, Jr., and corporation leaders like Juan Trippe of Pan American Airways, were upset by German airline activity in the region. "We initiated a campaign," Berle remarked tartly, "to clear these lines out."

Some policy-makers were emphasizing the need for developmental loans that would lead to expanded trade and investment throughout Latin America. This need had been intensified by the recession of 1937. Along with businessmen who experienced the difficulties in their daily operations, men like Duggan understood one of the fundamental problems of dealing with the Latin American economies. They were in many respects so backward and rudimentary that it was almost impossible to link them up with the economic system of the United States in any effective, efficient, and profitable manner. It did little good, for example, to have the Export-Import Bank grant a loan to an American manufacturer to finance a shipment if he could not even transport the goods inland to potential consumers. Similar difficulties faced Americans who wanted to expand and rationalize the collection and shipment of raw materials. Beginning in 1938 with a loan to Haiti for building roads and drainage projects (and followed by a similar arrangement that Welles negotiated with Brazil in March 1939), the New Deal began to finance the very kind of operations that Hoover had called for a decade earlier. There was, of course, one rather significant difference. Hoover wanted American entrepreneurs to make the loans. The New Deal used public funds supplied by taxpayers.

The complications and complexities of these efforts to cope

with the problems of economic expansion in Latin America were certainly sufficient to account for the intensity of the American reaction to Mexico's move against the oil companies. Granted Hull's assumptions, it does not require much imagination to understand his anger, worry, and concern. Those feelings were intensified, at the very time it became clear that Mexico was going to use the expropriation law, by Japan's renewed military operations in China in July 1937. Hull's commitment to the Open Door Policy in Asia was complete and unequivocal, and Japan's attack unquestionably influenced the New Deal's handling of the crisis with Mexico. Indeed, President Cárdenas expropriated American oil properties on March 18, 1938, at the very moment the Congress was considering President Roosevelt's request for a dramatic increase in the Navy. In response, Hull forgot the rhetoric of the Good Neighbor Policy and fired off an ultimatum. It was fortunately deflected by Ambassador Daniels and finally ricocheted into the Mexican Foreign Office as an unofficial document. Daniels was deeply concerned with better relations and "increased trade" with Mexico, and he realized that Hull's initial fear and anger might create a situation which could be resolved only through force. And Daniels had learned about the diminishing returns of military action while serving in the Navy Department when President Wilson had tried that method of dealing with Mexico.

Hull acquiesced in Daniels' maneuver (a fact often slurred over by those who praise the Ambassador); but he and other policy-makers in Washington retreated only far enough to pick up the weapon of economic coercion. They planned to force Mexico to accept arbitration of the issue. The ban on loans was continued. An effort was made to cut into Mexican dollar reserves by manipulating the price it received for its silver exports. And, finally, the government gave unofficial approval to the efforts by the oil companies to keep Mexico's newly nationalized industry from developing the country's resources and entering the world market with its petroleum.

There the crisis rested until July 1940, when the United States agreed, in view of "circumstances presently impending," to go along with the Mexican counterproposal to settle the conflict by appointing a joint commission to work out a compromise.* That diplomatic phrase about circumstances obviously referred to the accelerating pace of German and Japanese expansion, and to the increasing opposition manifested by the United States. Those were the most important considerations in determining the *timing* of the American decision to sit down with the Mexicans at the negotiating table. Even so, the community of American policy-makers was still split as late as the fall of 1941 over whether to hold out in the joint commission talks until Mexico's need for American investment capital modified its offer on compensation to the oil companies.

Considered alone, the combined economic and strategic challenge from the Axis could, and might well, have prompted the United States to maintain its intransigence (and even to increase its economic pressures). That was, after all, the course followed in dealing with Argentina. Such a might-have-been proposition is useful primarily to help clarify the reason that it did not occur. And that seems clearly to have been because Roosevelt was reached and persuaded by those policy-makers who insisted upon the need for a sophisticated reform in the methods of America's overseas economic expansion. The Duggan-Rockefeller-Johnston group had worked out a broad tactical conception which, as Professor Lloyd Gardner has described it, amounted to modifying the *laissez faire* system of Adam Smith so that separate national economies rather than individuals were defined as the entrepreneurs.

Now it is true, at least in one sense, that this was not so much an adaptation of Adam Smith as simply a decision to honor in practice the precepts of the theory as originally stated. Smith did lay great emphasis on the international division of labor, and that one point could be (and was) interpreted to mean that raw-material producing countries remained raw-material producing countries even though they became more efficient. But Smith also stressed freedom of enterprise where the resources existed, and many nations which in 1939 were still raw material producers enjoyed human and material resources that were capable of building and sustaining far more diversified economies. *To a certain extent, and one still to be controlled and structured by the economy and*

* Mexico's offer to embargo the shipment of certain strategic minerals to the Axis powers contributed to the change in American policy.

the policies of the United States, this latter interpretation of Smith is the one advanced by the sophisticated American reformers. The idea was to create somewhat more diversified political economies under the direction of the United States. The economic objectives were more markets and more efficiently produced raw materials. The political objective was middle-class government stabilized in a pro-American posture.

Roosevelt himself put it as neatly—and as revealingly—as anyone ever did in his casual remark of 1940. "[There is] a new approach that I am talking about to these South American things. Give them a share." It was to be a more generous share. It was to be a more intelligently defined share. And it was to be a share that might ultimately produce more psychological and social welfare along with a larger gross national income in the South American countries. But it was still a share to be granted by the United States.

Since Mexico is often pointed to as the glowing example of the success of this New Deal version of the Open Door strategy, it seems useful to digress briefly and examine the claim. Mexico unquestionably benefited from its ever more intimate economic integration with the United States after 1940. The economy became more diversified, the national income increased significantly, and the daily lives of some Mexicans became easier and more affluent. Let this be granted as the achievement.

The caveats and questions which remain are nevertheless very crucial. First: it should be recalled that the policies of the open door and the good neighbor were supposed to create prosperity and welfare in the underdeveloped countries as well as in the United States, and to do so short of war. They should be judged by their own claims. And by that standard they have not succeeded. The difference between the Mexico of 1935 and the Mexico of 1972 is not the result of the Open Door Policy and the Good Neighbor Policy functioning in a period of peace. *The improvement that has been made since 1935 is very largely the product of World War II and the Cold War.*

Second: the claim as stated neglects entirely the psychological, social, and even economic results of American expansion into Mexico. Here again the evidence is strongly negative.

Mexicans discovered by 1961 that they were steadily losing effective control of some areas of their economy. Indeed, it was a conservative government that began in that year to consider and act upon measures designed to regain some measure of that authority. As for the oil industry itself, American companies won their secondary objective: because of being excluded from the private international government of oil and because of Mexico's shortage of investment capital over which it exercised full control, the nationalized industry has never contributed its potential share of the nation's development.

Third, and in a more general sense (that is often neglected), it is hardly too much to say that the Mexican political economy maintains a precarious stability only because it sloughs off into the United States, in the form of legal and illegal migratory and transient labor, a sizable portion of its own population. That group of *braceros* is increasing by a million people a year. Americans think of those men, women, and children as employed workers. But they actually form a huge unemployment problem in Mexico. Neither the existence of that mass of ill-used human beings, nor the way they are dealt with, can be adduced as proof of a sound and healthy system.

Finally, millions of Mexicans still live in poverty. They are not just middle-class people in debt beyond their means. They are not simply poor. They live in poverty. Hence it is both practically and morally necessary, before praising American policy as the benefactor of the Mexican Revolution, to consider the sober and yet deeply moving estimate presented by anthropologist Oscar Lewis in his classic study of *The Children of Sánchez*. His judgment on the migratory workers, for example, is this: "Were the United States suddenly to close its borders to the *braceros,* a major crisis would probably occur in Mexico." But his most telling comments come in the context of his stark review of American penetration. American investment totalled almost $1,000,000,000 as of 1960. And the major television programs are sponsored and controlled by American firms. But the chronic inflation since 1940, when American influence began to rise so dramatically and continually, has raised the cost of living for workers in Mexico City some 400 per cent. And the "uneven distribution of the growing national wealth has made the disparity between the incomes of the rich and the poor more striking than ever before." "At least the lower third of the rural and urban population" know only what Lewis calls "the culture of poverty." He characterizes it as a "constant struggle for survival, unemployment and underemployment, low wages . . . child labor, the absence of savings, a chronic shortage of cash . . . crowded quarters, a lack of privacy, . . . a high incidence of alcoholism, [and] frequent resort to violence." As for the improvement and development that has occurred, Lewis offers a judgment that is far closer to the truth than any explanation which stresses the role of American influence. "It is the poor who emerge as the true heroes of contemporary Mexico, for they are paying the cost of the industrial progress of the nation." Unfortunately, the New Deal adaptation of Adam Smith did not prove sufficient unto the task of transforming the promises of the Open Door Policy into reality.

American policy-makers also discovered, again in a way contrary to its axioms and expectations, that the strategy of the open door did lead to war. None of them wanted war. They did not plot to involve the United States in armed conflict with the Axis. Indeed, and as symbolized by Roosevelt's support of the Munich Agreement of 1938 between Nazi Germany and Great Britain, they tried very seriously and persistently to accomplish their objectives without war. But given their *Weltanschauung*, their explanation of how the prosperity and welfare of the United States was to be achieved and maintained, they had no recourse but war. And as it happened, the United States was engaged in a shooting conflict with Germany before Japan struck Hawaii. The question of how and when that combat would have formally been joined if the Japanese had not attacked Pearl Harbor is fascinating but nevertheless irrelevant to an understanding of how American leaders came to accept the necessity of violence. It is also possible, perhaps even probable, that they would have reached that decision even if they had not entertained a frontier-expansionist conception of history. But again, and however pertinent it may be for later consideration, that hypothetical question is not germane to an explanation of how the United States did actually become involved in World War II.

Perhaps the most helpful way to approach that problem is

by reviewing the attitudes toward foreign policy that existed after Roosevelt had been in office two full years. Encouraged by the economic revival that seemed in 1935 to herald a general recovery from the depression, the community of public and private decision-makers looked ahead to a continuing extension of overseas economic activities. Those men also reasserted their conviction that such expansion would prevent foreign revolutions (and future depressions in the United States itself) and that peace was essential to recovery at home and profitable operations abroad.

Beyond those areas of agreement, however, the policy-makers split into differing—and often bitterly antagonistic—groups. Two main features of their dialogue and argument must be kept in mind if the evolution of policy is to be understood.

First: these divisions over policy not only cut across political lines, but also across what was by then an increasingly artificial boundary between private economic (including labor) leadership and formal office holders. The decision-making community at all times included men of great power and influence outside the government as well as those inside the nation's official establishment. Thus the support for a given policy always came from men in both groups. The natural corollary was that both the private leadership and the government bureaucracy disagreed among themselves as well as with members of the other bloc. One striking result of this hammering out of a consensus on policy between 1935 and 1941 was that a consolidated corporate group emerged under the banner of bipartisanship for security and prosperity. That coalition was an elite which came to enjoy a very extensive measure of control over foreign policy. Often, for example, the internal debates were not even known to—let alone participated in by— their critics or the general public. And the elite's broad authority over both private and official information and news media further closed down the discussion of alternatives.

It is vital to understand this pattern of power if the role and the authority of the military itself is not to be exaggerated. Beginning in 1938 and 1939, the evolving corporate elite of private and official leaders called in the military to execute a policy that they—*the civilians*—were formulating and adopting. *It was the civilians who defined the world in military terms, not the military who usurped civilian powers.* Once the military had been called in, they quite naturally gained more influence because the situation had been defined in a way that put a premium on their particular knowledge and experience. But a change in the definition of reality would decrease the power of the military. Even granting a generous measure of new authority, the military did not even in the 1960s establish themselves in an independent and superior position.

Second: the argument within the policy-making community developed around four issues. At the outset, by 1935, the debate concerned whether or not it was possible to work out some compromise with the Axis powers. That discussion shaded into an argument about whether the effort to remain neutral in another war would lead to an economic depression through the loss of overseas markets. Then, in 1937, the majority, who still held that it was feasible to arrange some kind of accommodation without war, began to divide over whether or not to coerce the Axis into an acceptable settlement by using economic sanctions and the threat of military force (if not its actual use in combat short of a formal declaration of war). Finally, and beginning in 1939 after the Nazi victory over Poland, there opened a final argument over whether or not it would be necessary for the United States to become a total and formal belligerent. Though that angry debate was settled by the Japanese, it seems apparent that the policy-makers and the public were reaching, however reluctantly, the conclusion that war was necessary.

The detailed reconstruction of that evolution into trial by arms has yet to be made by any historian or group of historians.* But it is possible to characterize the changing attitudes of various groups and personalities within the corporate leadership of the country, and to outline the main phases of the debate. One of these was the argument over neutrality

---

* The two volumes by W. L. Langer and S. E. Gleason, *The Challenge to Isolation,* and *The Undeclared War* (New York: Harper and Bros., 1952, 1953), have a general but undeserved reputation as being the last word. Another approach, fairly represented in a collective volume edited by H. E. Barnes, *Perpetual War for Perpetual Peace* (Caxton, Idaho: Caxton Printers, Ltd., 1953), is challenging but by no means definitive. The best single volume is P. W. Schroeder, *The Axis Alliance and Japanese-American Relations* (Ithaca: Cornell University Press, 1958).

policy that began early in the 1930s with a discussion of blocking the sale of munitions to belligerents in another war. American leaders (and the public at large) generally agreed on the wisdom of that restriction, but they rapidly drew back from any commitment to full neutrality when it became apparent that such a policy would undercut existing and prospective overseas economic expansion.

Along with the strikingly frightened reaction of American leaders to the threat posed to exports and foreign investments by the outbreak of World War I, this marked fear in the 1930s about the economic consequences of real neutrality offers impressive proof of the degree to which Americans *thought* their domestic welfare depended upon overseas economic activity.† Theoretical and statistical arguments concerning the actual extent of that dependence are of course relevant, particularly in connection with any consideration of alternate foreign policies, but this idea about its great importance is the crucial factor in understanding and interpreting American foreign policy in the 1930s—and in subsequent decades. Americans thought and believed that such expansion was essential, and their actions followed from that supposition.

This became apparent early in the discussion which developed around the ideas of Charles Warren, an international lawyer who had served President Wilson as an Assistant Attorney General prior to 1917. Warren argued that the only way to avoid involvement in a future war was to abandon all claims to neutral rights and rest content with whatever trade the belligerents would permit. In the face of prompt opposition, he shortly modified his original proposal by suggesting that trade with belligerents be limited to the average amount carried on during a five year period prior to the outbreak of hostilities.

Secretary Hull and other key advisors in the State Department, and such quasi-official figures in the corporation community as Allen Dulles, continued to criticize even Warren's revised plan as a surrender of traditional rights and as a body

† Some of the most revealing evidence concerning this response to the World War I situation is to be found in the *Hearings before the Special Senate Committee Investigating the Munitions Industry* (39 parts: Washington: Government Printing Office, 1934–1936).

blow to American commerce. As might have been expected, many businessmen joined the attack on Warren. No doubt influenced by Senator Gerald P. Nye's investigation of the traffic in munitions at the time of World War I, and even in the period of peace thereafter, the pro-trade group accepted the need for an arms embargo. But everyone involved in the debate, if not all those who followed it in the popular press, knew that the commerce in arms was not the central issue.

The crucial point involved trade in other manufactured goods, and in raw or semi-processed materials. Not only were those the products sought by belligerents, but they were the items that Americans wanted to sell abroad. Senator Nye understood and defined the dilemma as early as 1935. "My own belief," he concluded, "is that a complete embargo on trade is the only absolute insurance against the United States being drawn into another prolonged major war between great powers. I am convinced that drastic legislation to accomplish this could not be passed even in time of peace." *

Nye had strong reasons for reaching such a conclusion. Secretary Hull and Herbert Feis of the State Department argued quite openly that restrictions of that kind on American overseas economic activity would be extremely harmful if not disastrous to the nation's economy. In a typical bit of calculated understatement, for example, the Secretary observed that a general embargo would be "undesirable." The bipartisan nature of this resistance to real economic neutrality was indicated by the agreement of Henry Cabot Lodge, Jr. And Roosevelt was warned in 1935 by the President of the New York Chamber of Commerce that "exporters and merchants on our eastern seaboard are now more interested in the free-

* This analysis and interpretation was originally prepared from materials in the National Archives, manuscript collections of such figures as President Roosevelt and Senator Borah, the *Congressional Record*, and the various investigations into neutrality undertaken by the Congress during the late 1920s and the 1930s. Just as this manuscript was going to press in 1962, however, I had the good fortune to receive an advance copy of R. A. Divine, *The Illusion of Neutrality* (Chicago: University of Chicago Press, 1962), which deals with the fight over neutrality within a similar framework. I have borrowed this quotation from Nye, and a later one from Pittman, from Professor Divine, who found them during his research in the manuscript files of the congressional committees.

dom of the seas for American ships than at any time since the World War." The same view was advanced by General Motors, the giant cotton firm of Anderson, Clayton, and even by the Business Advisory Council of the Department of Commerce.

One of the bluntest analyses of these economic considerations was offered by Edwin Borchard, an outstanding professor of international law at Yale who was deeply concerned to strengthen American neutrality. Commenting in 1936 on proposed legislation that followed some of Warren's early ideas, Borchard warned that "we are likely to begin to lose our markets the minute this bill is passed." "Nobody," he feared, "has apparently thought through the full effects of this legislation." Those consequences would be "revolutionary" because they involved the issue of "self-sufficiency." Neutrality of that kind was dangerous because it would "incite disorders and distress at home."

Senator Key Pittman's judgment of the situation in 1936 made it clear that Borchard underestimated the extent to which government and business leaders had very carefully "thought through the full effects of this legislation." "The necessity for foreign commerce is so great and political pressure at this particular time is so strong," Pittman explained, that it was unrealistic to expect real neutrality legislation. The compromise was Cash-and-Carry Neutrality, a concept and an idea apparently conceived by Bernard Baruch. The long-term result of that approach was clear even at the time of its adoption by the Congress—it created an economic alliance between the United States and Great Britain.

Even before that implicit connection led to formal political and military discussions and agreements, however, American leaders were defining the Axis powers as dangerous economic rivals in Latin America. That conflict played an early and significant role in the thinking of decision-makers about the possibilities and probabilities of war with Germany and Italy, and even with Japan. Much of the shift toward a policy of vigorous opposition short of formal belligerence took place in connection with Axis activities in Latin America. In the intellectual and emotional sense, that is to say, an important number of American leaders began to go to war against the Axis in the Western Hemisphere.

This attitude was intensified in those who already held it, and adopted by others, as a result of two events during 1937–1938. One was the Spanish Civil War, and the other was the Japanese attack in China. Although the Spanish conflict generated more emotional involvement and more vociferous agitation, particularly in the populous Eastern part of the country, the Japanese action made a more significant impact within the policy-making community. This was in part due to the triumph in Spain of General Francisco Franco, who was openly supported by Germany and Italy. His victory liquidated the issue. If the Republican Government had held out for a longer period, as did the Chinese, it is conceivable that the Spanish Civil War would have brought the United States into a general European coalition against Germany before Japan attacked Pearl Harbor. Possible but not probable. Spain served to arouse and involve two rival groups in the United States, but they were quite unevenly matched in power and influence. The reformers who opposed fascism and thought it was time to slow or halt its ideological, political, and military momentum mounted a dynamic public campaign in behalf of their policy. But it is highly doubtful that a majority of those reformers favored direct American intervention. The opposition, and especially the hierarchy of the Catholic Church and a broad segment of private and public Protestant leaders, enjoyed much more influence. As a result, the Roosevelt Administration followed a policy of strict and formal neutrality which weakened the Republican Government. American policy in its deeper nature is rather well characterized by a bit of chronology: Franco captured Madrid on March 28, 1939, and the United States recognized his government on April 1, 1939.

Japan's attack in China on July 7, 1937, which followed upon its withdrawal from the London Naval Conference in 1936, had a far greater effect on American policy-makers. Several considerations explain this difference. The most important of these was the emphasis on Asia as the Eldorado of America's overseas economic expansion ever since the time of the Sino-Japanese War in 1894, which had led to the strategy of the Open Door Policy. This had always been focused on China, even though tactical and other considerations had prompted economic and political dealings with Japan that sometimes seemed to create a different impression. It is at most a slight exaggeration to say that China was by 1937 firmly established in the minds of most American policy-makers, *and even below the level of conscious thought,* as the symbol of the new frontier of America's ideological and economic expansion. This was as true for those who advocated working through and with Japan as it was for others who presistently agitated for a stronger direct effort in China. The commitment to China was much greater than the identification with any European power except England—and possibly France. This cast of mind and emotion, this utopian image, was strengthened and infused with new substance between 1935 and 1937 by very practical economic developments. A significant number of private and official decision-makers became convinced during those years that the long-awaited blossoming of China as a market was finally under way. There was, as one of them phrased it, a "new spirit" of confidence that the open door was about to lead to vast and profitable economic activity.

This enthusiasm was the offspring of two developments. One involved the way that China had finally begun to modernize its own system; that meant it was buying more and more industrial goods and services from the United States. The other concerned American trade with China. After a slump during the 1920s, it began to increase very rapidly. In 1932, for the first time in over a decade, American-Chinese trade totalled more than Chinese-Japanese trade. That exciting trend continued, moreover, through the next two years. This led, in 1935, to a little remembered but very significant liaison between the National Foreign Trade Council and various people and groups (including a bloc in the State Department) within the Roosevelt Administration. Men inside the government who favored implementing the Open Door Policy by dealing directly with China and taking a firmer stand against Japan became more active in policy discussions. And the N.F.T.C. organized a quasi-official American Economic Mission to the Far East. Headed by W. Cameron Forbes, it visited Japan and China for the purpose of gathering data upon which to base future policy.

Upon his return, Forbes announced that there was little enthusiasm for the mission in Japan. "In China, on the other hand," he reported, "American participation and American investment along all lines was sought." He then spelled out the implications by reminding American businessmen that in 1935 they had outscored Japan in trade with China to the amount of some $22,000,000. Finally, he made it clear that it was time to use firm pressure to keep the door open. "This policy of the open door does not seem to have been observed in the conduct of affairs in Manchuria." Should that Japanese conduct be extended to more of China, he warned, "there will inevitably be built up a greater and greater resistance." Japan's attack was particularly disturbing to Forbes and men who shared his outlook because it came at a time when American economic activity in China "was considered especially bright." "Probably never in its history," Forbes remarked in his judgment on the assault, "has China offered greater promise for its future trade, industry, and general economic progress than . . . just prior to the outbreak of the present hostilities." Nor were the implications limited to China, or to Forbes and his followers. In 1937, for example, Asia furnished 51.5 per cent of all raw and crude materials imported into the United States. British Malaya and the Dutch East Indies supplied 86 per cent of its crude rubber and 87 per cent of its tin. Asia provided, in addition, 85 per cent of its tungsten, a third of its mica, 99 per cent of its jute, and 98 per cent of its shellac.

This confrontation between America's specific and general economic interests and expectations and Japan's move south into China, directly affected the posture and the policy of the United States. Through September and October 1937, the issue was debated vigorously within the State Department in preparation for the Brussels Conference on the Far East. The argument took the traditional form: some wanted to make a strong stand with China, a smaller group suggested working with the Russians, and others reiterated that it was necessary to follow the tactic of trying to control Japan.

At this juncture, the Soviet Union renewed its bid for an entente with the United States. Its spokesmen warned American officials at Brussels that, while the offer was wholly sincere, it might well represent the last stand of those in the Kremlin who advocated collaboration with the Western Powers against the Axis. Russia felt it "had taken some terrible beatings" while striving to work out such an alliance, and it might very soon change its policy and emphasize unilateral moves to insure its own security. (The general assumption that the Soviets can never be trusted in such situations is not borne out by the Brussels experience. The failure of the conference did verify the warnings given to American policy-makers. The decline in influence of Maxim Litvinov, and of the pro-Western views he advocated, can be dated from that time. American policy-makers nevertheless continued to make this kind of error in dealing with the Soviet Union.)

Roosevelt seems to have considered, however briefly, a more positive response to this overture. But his final instructions followed the pro-Japanese line. He defended his choice by arguing that, short of war, Japan could be stopped only by arranging a truce in China. Even so, the American policy at Brussels was based on extracting extensive concessions from China. It may be that the President had even then concluded that war was all but inevitable, and was only buying time with a down payment provided by the Chinese. It seems more probable, however, that Roosevelt and Hull felt that unilateral American economic and military pressure would force the Japanese to retreat. They were no doubt encouraged in this traditional assumption behind the strategy of the Open Door Policy by the speed with which Japan accepted American demands for an apology, reparations, and promises for the future in connection with the sinking of the Navy river gunboat *Panay* in December 1937.

There is no doubt, in any event, that the United States proceeded very quickly after the Brussels Conference to reassert and act upon both its frontier-expansionist outlook and its traditional strategy of the Open Door Policy. Hull clarified that with one blunt remark on February 19, 1938, shortly after the administration had asked for a huge increase in naval construction. "There can be no military disarmament," he explained, "without economic appeasement. . . . Only healthy international trade will make possible a full and stable domestic economy." And by "healthy international trade," Hull obviously and exclusively meant trade defined in American terms.

Assistant Secretary Sayre reviewed the events of 1937 and 1938 a bit more laconically: "The economic world became a battlefield in which the issues were sometimes political as well as economic." And military as well as political, he might have added. But the most classic explanation of the crisis was offered by William S. Culbertson, who had begun his service as an economic advisor and policy-maker on trade matters under President Wilson, had continued to exercise such influence in the 1920s, and was still active in the New Deal period. "Our economic frontiers," he remarked, "are no longer coextensive with our territorial frontiers." No one ever offered a more succinct description and interpretation of the single most important aspect of twentieth-century American diplomacy—either in general, or pertaining explicitly to the nation's involvement in World Wars I and II.

Administration leaders in Congress made the same point in less striking style during the consideration in the late winter of 1938 of Roosevelt's bill for the expansion of the Navy. In a long debate that was far more revealing of the nature of American foreign policy than were the arguments over the Neutrality Acts of 1935, 1936, and 1937, New Deal Senators David I. Walsh and Tom Connally stressed two factors. They began by pointing to German and Japanese activity in Latin America and cautioned that it was necessary to be "very careful" about such competition. Their conclusion was a warning that the danger might rapidly become greater.

Then they compared the American economic system to the British Empire. "We, too, have trade routes," Walsh explained. "It is estimated by our experts that unless we are able to keep open certain trade routes the United States could not maintain itself more than two years without being defeated by a powerful enemy." Any delay in building a big Navy would court final surrender. "We cannot build battleships in time of war unless we keep the trade routes open to bring in manganese. We cannot make munitions in time of war unless we keep the trade routes open to bring in certain essential raw materials." Backed by such leadership and logic, the bill passed the House of Representatives 294 to 100, and the Senate 56 to 28.

Armed with this steel in his diplomatic glove, Secretary Hull called for a moral embargo on shipments to Japan in June 1938. Six months later the United States loaned China $25,-

000,000. And in July 1939, it denounced its commercial treaty with Japan. One group of policy-makers was clearly moving to stop the Japanese by economic pressure and the threat of force. One spokesman who was also an active member of the Council on Foreign Relations put it bluntly. "Seen in its Far Eastern setting," William Diebold, Jr., explained, "our concept of commercial policy expands. . . . It becomes our most potent instrument of foreign policy, a long-range weapon with which to settle the fate of nations."

That intensity and tempo of opposition was not apparent, however, in dealings with Germany in 1938 and 1939. And it slacked off for more than a year in affairs with Japan. The reason for this lies in the ambivalence and the split among the policy-makers. Fears of war and hopes of compromise with the Axis were still very strong. John L. Lewis and other leaders in the C.I.O., for example, manifested that combination of attitudes very clearly. Aware and concerned by 1939 that the United States was "gradually being driven out of trade relationships with the various markets of the world," Lewis did not turn to war or preparations for war as a solution. He first accepted the reality that "the open door is no more" in Asia. Then he advocated an increased effort in Latin America to take up the slack. Government loans should be granted to provide the peons with buying power. Lewis shared the feeling of the steel workers that foreign policy should not "be formulated or made dependent upon the protection of the vested or property interests in foreign countries of the large corporations in this country." Of course, labor leaders feared such preparations for war as the draft, because the government—and its industrial contractors—could then control the conditions and the market for labor. Lewis saw the squeeze and disliked it. "Unless substantial economic offsets are provided to prevent this nation from being wholly dependent upon the war expenditures," he cried out in anguish in 1940, "we will sooner or later come to the dilemma which requires either war or depression."

Corporation leaders and their associates were caught in the same corner, as were other policy-makers in the government. The great majority of American leaders emerged from World War I fearing war as the midwife of international revolution and domestic unrest. A good many of them remained uncon-

vinced even by 1939 that it was the greater part of wisdom to
make war in order to make peace. Worried about "world-
wide ruin," and frightened of the political and social consequences of "another generation of misery," such leaders
opposed war as a "great destroyer and unsettler of their affairs." Bernard Baruch, for example, thought that "the institutions of government, as we have known them, [would] fall
down . . . and that the whole moral attitude of the world
would change." Many corporation leaders and a significant
though probably smaller number of national politicians extended that line of reasoning on through the 1930s. They
argued that serious preparation for war would subvert the
kind of political economy they equated with freedom and democracy. "As certain as night follows day," asserted the editors
of *Iron Age* in 1939, "while we were fighting to crush dic-
tatorships abroad, we would be extending one at home."

"It is fairly certain," agreed a corporation executive who was
prominent in the financial and policy affairs of the America
First Committee, "that capitalism cannot survive American
participation in this war." Others broadened the analysis, seeing American intervention as leading "to the end of capitalism
all over the world" with a resulting "spread of communism,
socialism, or fascism in Europe and even in the United States."
Winthrop W. Aldrich spoke from a similar estimate in his remarks to the National Foreign Trade Council shortly after the
Munich Agreement of 1938 had been signed. "We ought to
take full advantage of the opportunity for the continuance
of peace which has resulted from the events of the last few
weeks," he advised in very strong terms. "It is of paramount
importance that the efforts of the diplomats and of the heads
of governments should speedily be reinforced by measures of
economic appeasement." The depth and power of the crosscurrents within the community of policy-makers is clearly
revealed by Aldrich's remarks. He was head of the Chase
National Bank, which not only was a very powerful element
in the Federal Reserve System, but also handled most of the
Soviet Union's transactions in the United States. He was advising conciliation with the Axis while Secretary of State Hull
was militantly fighting the pressures for such economic appeasement.

Tormented by their estimates of the consequences of intervention, leaders of the Aldrich bent argued, when pressed to the wall, that America could and should avoid war by building and integrating an impregnable empire in the Western Hemisphere or that it could and should assert America's ultimate supremacy by waiting for the belligerents to exhaust themselves. Senator Harry S Truman was one of the politicians who inclined toward the latter proposal. "The role of this great Republic," he explained in October 1939, "is to save civilization; we must keep out of war." Later, after the Nazis attacked Russia, he went so far as to suggest aiding both of them in such a way as to promote their mutual exhaustion.

The way those attitudes began to change was nicely revealed in the course of a discussion among leading businessmen held late in 1939 under the auspices of *Fortune* magazine. The participants formally and vigorously rejected entry into the war. But almost everything else they said indicated either that they expected American involvement or that they were still trying with considerable success to avoid facing the fact that the things they did want could not be obtained short of war. No war, they agreed, and then voted "unanimously" to oppose giving way to Japan's New Order in Asia. No war, they reiterated, and then flatly refused even to discuss the possibility of a more self-contained economy. Overseas economic expansion was mandatory. No war, they repeated, and then agreed that the Philippines had to be defended in order to protect "the rich resources" of Southeast Asia. No war, they concluded, and proceeded to reject "abandonment of the U.S. world position through surrendering neutral rights, adopting economic self-containment, or acquiescing in Japanese demands in the Orient."

The contradictions became almost ridiculous when they went on to discuss "the important tasks confronting the next peace." "What interests us primarily," the businessmen explained in perfect candor, "is the longer-range question of whether the American capitalist system could continue to function if most of Europe and Asia should abolish free enterprise." Their conclusion was not too surprising: the next peace settlement would have "to organize the economic resources of the world so as to make possible a return to the system of free enterprise in every country."

It required very little more Axis expansion to push men who were that ambivalent over to the side of intervention. They were further exhorted and encouraged by industrial leaders like James A. Farrell of the steel industry, who had been agitating for more expansion, and more militant opposition to the Axis, for at least two years. "Our internal economy," Farrell explained in 1938, "is geared to export trade on an increasingly higher level. . . . We must be prepared," therefore, "to increase our outlets abroad for manufactured products or make adjustments of far-reaching consequences." Hence to Farrell it was "imperative that business interests and government agencies act together to assure American business a proportionate and equitable share in the [world's] trade. . . . The door of equal opportunity to all trading areas should be kept open." Farrell strongly implied that war was certain. "It suffices to say that no compromise seems possible between [economic] doctrines so wide apart in principle."

The Business Advisory Council of the Roosevelt Administration gave Farrell the assurances he wanted. "An enlargement of our opportunities for trade and investment in foreign countries is *now essential* to maximum national prosperity." In addition, many of those who had in 1938 and 1939 feared the totalitarian consequences of going to war had by 1940 turned the argument upside down. They began to assert that staying out of the war would bring the end of free enterprise and democracy. Lewis W. Douglas, who had served as Budget Director in the early days of the New Deal, typified such thinking. "To retreat to the cyclone cellar here means, ultimately, to establish a totalitarian state at home."

Such a convergence of thinking among corporate policymakers encouraged the administration to act more openly. It continued to lie about, and in other ways conceal, some of its key policy decisions. But Roosevelt and Hull felt strong enough by September 1940, to embargo aviation gasoline and end iron shipments to Japan. Germany's rapid conquest of France brought even more support for their policies. Hitler might be said to have provided the deciding vote that passed the first peacetime draft in the same month of September. Thereafter events and decisions moved in an ever-accelerating spiral downward into war. Within a year, on September 4,

1941, the United States was engaged in undeclared naval warfare with Germany. Japan attacked three months later.

The final explanation of the tragedy at Pearl Harbor has yet to be made. It most certainly lies in some combination of American arrogance and negligence and of Japanese brilliance. But there is no doubt about the final convergence of thought between the Roosevelt Administration and the leaders of America's corporate economic system. For by mid-1943, when the issue of postwar foreign policy came to the fore and was thrashed out in Congressional hearings and departmental discussions, it was apparent that the Roosevelt Administration was dominated by men whose personal experience and intellectual outlook were conditioned by their careers as leaders or agents or students of the large corporation. Dean Acheson, Averell Harriman, Donald M. Nelson, Edward Stettinius, Adolf A. Berle, Jr., John Foster Dulles, Eric Johnson, Paul Hoffman, William C. Foster, and James Forrestal are but the most obvious names from the top layer of American leadership in foreign affairs.

These men symbolized a consensus that had been foreshadowed in the winter of 1939–1940, when American economic leaders began to support Roosevelt's policy toward the Axis. By January 1940, key leaders of America's large corporations were defining crucial problems in terms of economic stagnation at home and postwar peace terms. Having had the central issue spelled out for them in that fashion, the editors of *Fortune* devoted their attention to the questions of "The Dispossessed" at home and a redefinition of "The U.S. Frontier."

From the candid admission that the American system was in serious trouble ("For nearly one-fourth of the population there is no economic system—and from the rest there is no answer"), the editors of *Fortune* drew three major conclusions. First, they acknowledged that "the U.S. economy has never proved that it can operate without the periodic injection of new and real wealth. The whole frontier saga, indeed, centered around this economic imperative." Second, and in consequence of this fact, the editors defined two new frontiers. A new emphasis on enlarged consumer sales at home would have to be paralleled by a tremendous expansion of "foreign trade and foreign investment." Secretary of State Hull's trade agreements program was "a step in the right direction," but to "open up real frontiers, under a general policy of raising the standard of living of other countries, we shall have to go much further."

In outlining its conception of such a program, *Fortune* argued that "the analogy between the domestic frontier in 1787, when the Constitution was formed, and the present international frontier is perhaps not an idle one. The early expansion of the U.S. was based upon firm political principles; and it may be that further expansion must be based upon equally firm—and equally revolutionary—international principles." *Fortune's* third point concerned the importance of having more and more corporation leaders enter the Roosevelt Administration and subsequent governments.

As they devoted more of their attention and energy to the challenge of extending the new American frontier, many economic leaders became enthusiastic converts to the mission to reform the world. The convergence of a sense of economic necessity and a moral calling transformed the traditional concept of open door expansion into a vision of an American Century. In this fashion, the United States entered and fought World War II. Americans were convinced that they were defending an anticolonial democracy charged with a duty to regenerate the world. They also had come firmly to believe that their own prosperity and democracy depended upon the continued expansion of their economic system under the strategy of the open door.

CHAPTER SIX

The President [Roosevelt] . . . said that he himself would not be in favor of the creation of a new Assembly of the League of Nations, at least until after a period of time had transpired and during which an international police force composed of the United States and Great Britain had had an opportunity of functioning.

REMARKS TO WINSTON CHURCHILL, AUGUST 1941,
AS REPORTED BY SUMNER WELLES

For unless there is security here at home there cannot be lasting peace in the world.

FRANKLIN DELANO ROOSEVELT, JANUARY 1944

It is important that I retain complete freedom of action after this conference [in Moscow] is over.

FRANKLIN DELANO ROOSEVELT, OCTOBER 1944

We cannot go through another ten years like the ten years at the end of the twenties and the beginning of the thirties, without having the most far-reaching consequences upon our economic and social systems. . . . We have got to see that what the country produces is used and sold under financial arrangements which make its production possible. . . . My contention

THE NIGHTMARE OF DEPRESSION
AND THE VISION OF OMNIPOTENCE

*is that we cannot have full employment and prosperity in the
United States without the foreign markets.*

DEAN ACHESON, NOVEMBER 1944

*. . . if the Russians did not wish to join us they could go to
hell.*

HARRY S TRUMAN, REMARK OF APRIL 23, 1945,
AS REPORTED BY CHARLES E. BOHLEN

*In Rumania and Bulgaria—and rather less decisively in Hungary—the Russian Government has sponsored and supported
Governments which are democratic in the Russian rather than
in the English-speaking connotation of the term and whose
friendship for Russia is one of their main qualifications. This
policy would fit in well enough with a "zones of influence"
conception of the [peace] settlement; and it would be idle to
deny that other great nations, both in the remoter and in
the recent past, have pursued the same policy in regions of the
world which they deemed vital to their security. During the
past few weeks, however, the English-speaking Powers have
adopted an attitude towards Balkan affairs which seemed to
imply the contrary view that any of the three Powers may
claim a right of intervention even in regions especially af-*

203

*fecting the security of one of the others; and the clash of these
opposing views, each of which can be formidably sustained by
argument, underlay all the difficulties of the Foreign Ministers
in their discussion of Balkan affairs.*

LONDON TIMES EDITORIAL, OCTOBER 3, 1945

*. . . the United States has it in its power to increase enor-
mously the strains under which Soviet policy must operate, to
force upon the Kremlin a far greater degree of moderation and
circumspection than it has had to observe in recent years, and
in this way to promote tendencies which must eventually find
their outlet in either the break-up or the gradual mellowing of
Soviet power.*

GEORGE FROST KENNAN, FEBRUARY 1946—JULY 1947

*The situation in the world today is not primarily the result
of the natural difficulties which follow a great war. It is chiefly
due to the fact that one nation has not only refused to co-
operate in the establishment of a just and honorable peace,
but—even worse—has actually sought to prevent it.*

HARRY S TRUMAN, MARCH 1948

I. ROOSEVELT AND STALIN CONFRONT
   THE DILEMMAS OF VICTORY

Politicians become statesmen, not by honoring pious shib-
boleths, nor even by moving men to action with inspiring
rhetoric, but by recognizing and then resolving the central
dilemmas of their age.

When measured against this demanding standard, Franklin
Delano Roosevelt's performance after 1940 poses a difficult
problem in judgment for the historian. On the one hand, he
seems clearly enough to have sensed the contradiction between
his intellectual, emotional, and policy commitment to America's
traditional strategy of the open door, and the new circumstances arising out of World War II which called for the acceptance of limits upon American expectations and actions,

and for the working out of a concert of power with other major nations. Though it was not in any sense unique, Roosevelt's recognition of that new reality does entitle him to a place of honor within the community of American policymakers. It also explains and justifies the praise of his partisans.

On the other hand, Roosevelt did not resolve the dilemma posed by that contradiction between tradition and reality. He occasionally spoke candidly of the problem. He offered a few very general ideas about the kind of things that could be done to adapt American thinking and policy to the new conditions. And he suggested a few concrete proposals for dealing with specific aspects of the developing crisis. But he never worked out, initiated, or carried through a fresh approach which combined necessary domestic changes with a fundamental re-evaluation of American foreign policy. He did not resolve the dilemma. At the time of his death, he was turning back toward the inadequate domestic programs of the New Deal era, and was in foreign affairs reasserting the traditional strategy of the Open Door Policy.

Explorations into the forest of conditional history are sometimes fruitful, for they occasionally suggest new insights into what did occur. This is perhaps the case with the debate over what would have happened if Roosevelt had lived. The most sympathetic interpretation explains Roosevelt's ambivalence as a result of his declining health. That was a relevant consideration, but there is little evidence that Roosevelt seriously entertained even the idea of initiating a re-evaluation of America's conception of itself and the world. For the further such an inquiry is pushed, the more it becomes apparent that Roosevelt had not abandoned the policy of the open door; and that, even if he personally had been on the verge of trying to do so, few of his advisors and subordinates had either the intention or the power to effect such a change.

The leaders who succeeded Roosevelt understood neither the dilemma nor the need to alter their outlook. A handful of them thought briefly of stabilizing relations with the Soviet Union on the basis of economic and political agreements, but even that tiny minority saw the future in terms of continued expansion guided by the strategy of the Open Door Policy.

The great majority rapidly embarked upon a program to force the Soviet Union to accept America's traditional conception of itself and the world. This decision represented the final stage in the transformation of the policy of the open door from a utopian idea into an ideology, from an intellectual outlook for changing the world into one concerned with preserving it in the traditional mold.

American leaders had internalized, and had come to *believe*, the theory, the necessity, and the morality of open-door expansion. Hence they seldom thought it necessary to explain or defend the approach. Instead, they *assumed* the premises and concerned themselves with exercising their freedom and power to deal with the necessities and the opportunities that were defined by such an outlook. As far as American leaders were concerned, the philosophy and practice of open-door expansion had become, in both its missionary and economic aspects, *the* view of the world. Those who did not recognize and accept that fact were considered not only wrong, but incapable of thinking correctly.

The problem of the Soviet leaders was defined by the confrontation between the expansive prophecy of Marx about world revolution (which was supported by the traditional Great Russian and Slavic ideas of world leadership) and a realistic, Marxian analysis of world conditions (which was reinforced by sober calculations of nationalistic self-interest). Russian leaders clearly recognized their dilemma, and realized that rehabilitation and military security were the points upon which its resolution had to hinge. But American policy offered the Russians no real choice on those key issues. Particularly after the atom bomb was created and used, the attitude of the United States left the Soviets with but one real option: either acquiesce in American proposals or be confronted with American power and hostility. It was the decision of the United States to employ its new and awesome power in keeping with the traditional Open Door Policy which crystallized the cold war.

To say that is not to say that the United States started or caused the cold war. Nor is it an effort to avoid what many people apparently consider the most important—if also the most controversial and embarrassing—issue of recent and contemporary history. For, contrary to that general belief, the problem of which side started the cold war offers neither a very intelligent nor a very rewarding way of approaching the central questions about American foreign relations since 1941.

The real issue is rather the far more subtle one of which side committed its power to policies which hardened the natural and inherent tensions and propensities into bitter antagonisms and inflexible positions. Two general attitudes can be adopted in facing that issue. One is to assume, or take for granted, on the basis of emotion and official information, that the answer is obvious: Russia is to blame. That represents the easy, nationalistic solution to all questions about international affairs. That attitude also defines history as a stockpile of facts to be requisitioned on the basis of what is needed to prove a conclusion decided upon in advance.

The other approach is to consider history as a way of learning, of mustering the intellectual and moral courage to acknowledge the facts as they exist without tampering with them. If they are unpleasant or disturbing, then new facts—in the form of our ideas and actions—must be created that modify the unsatisfying scene. This is the more difficult and the more demanding method. Recognizing this, John Foster Dulles offered in 1946 a classic bit of encouragement to push on with the effort: "There is no nation which has attitudes so pure that they cannot be bettered by self-examination." *

In undertaking such self-examination, the first and essential requirement is to acknowledge two primary facts which can never be blinked. *The first is that the United States had from 1944 to at least 1962 a vast preponderance of actual as well as potential power vis-à-vis the Soviet Union.* Nothing can ever change the absolute and relative power relationship between the two countries during that chronological period. This relative weakness of the Russians did not turn them into western parliamentary democrats, and it did not transform their every action into a moral and equitable transaction. But it does con-

---

* Dulles apparently mislaid his own advice in subsequent years.
* An early and cogent estimate of this relative balance of military power between America and Russia is P. M. S. Blackett, "Steps Toward Disarmament," *Scientific American* (April, 1962).

front all students of the cold war, be they academicians or politicians or housewives, with very clear and firm limits on how they can make sense out of the cold war if they are at the same time to observe the essential standards of intellectual honesty. For power and responsibility go together in a direct and intimate relationship. Unless it tries all the alternatives that offer reasonable probabilities of success, a nation with the great relative supremacy enjoyed by the United States between 1944 and 1962 cannot with any real warrant or meaning claim that it has been *forced* to follow a certain approach or policy. Yet that is the American claim even though it did not explore several such alternatives.

Instead, and this is the second fact that cannot be dodged, the United States used or deployed its preponderance of power wholly within the assumptions and the tradition of the strategy of the Open Door Policy. The United States never formulated and offered the Soviet Union a settlement based on other, less grandiose, terms. For that matter, it never made a serious and sustained effort even to employ in dealing with the Russians the same kind of tactics that had been used for a generation before World War II in relations with the Japanese.

It is true that the offer to include the Soviet Union in the Marshall Plan can be interpreted as a similar move. For, if the Soviets had accepted the conditions set forth for receiving such assistance, the United States would have been in a position to exercise extensive influence over internal Soviet affairs, as well as over its foreign policy. To cite but one known example, American leaders would have demanded that the Russians allocate large quantities of raw materials to western Europe. That in itself would have delayed and complicated Soviet recovery, let alone its further development.* Even so, American policy-makers greeted the Russian refusal to participate on such terms with an audible sigh of relief. They never made the kind of serious effort to negotiate a satisfactory compromise with the Russians as they had done with the Japanese. If it be objected that the effort would have failed anyway because it had not worked with the Japanese, then those who

---

* See, for one of many pieces of evidence concerning this attitude: J. M. Jones, *The Fifteen Weeks* (New York: Viking Press, 1955), 253.

advance that argument must go on to confront one of three conclusions that are inherent in their logic. It must be admitted either that the strategy itself cannot succeed without war, or that it can succeed without war only if the other country accepts and works within limits set by the United States. Otherwise, the policy must be changed—formally or informally.

Instead of being changed, however, the traditional strategy was merely reasserted and put into operation at the end of the war under the famous and accurate phrase about "negotiation from strength." But negotiation from strength meant in practice that there would be no meaningful negotiations. The concept defined negotiation as the acceptance of American proposals, and American leaders acted upon that definition. The broad and fundamental failure of the policy demonstrated the basic misconception of man and the world inherent in the policy of the open door. For it established beyond cavil that the policy of the open door, like all imperial policies, created and spurred onward a dynamic opposition to which it forfeited the initiative. Not even a monopoly of nuclear weapons enabled America to prove itself an exception to that involuting momentum of empire.

Even before they formally entered World War II, American leaders assumed that the United States would emerge from the conflict in a position to extend, stabilize, and reform the empire of the open door. Roosevelt's assumption that Anglo-American forces would police the world for a "transition period" after the defeat of the Axis was given overt expression in August 1941. That was almost four months before Pearl Harbor but after the decision had been made to help the Russians defeat Hitler in Europe. His casually optimistic outlook foresaw the ultimate creation of an international organization committed to the policy of the open door, a circumstance that would enable the United States to proceed with the work of developing the world.

Supported by a thoroughly bipartisan assortment of liberals and conservatives, this reassertion of the traditional open door strategy guided the community of American policy-makers throughout the war and on into the cold war era. Ultimately it became, in the best tradition of the open door, and in the words of G. L. Arnold, a sympathetic British observer, a view of the world resting "upon the expectation of a prolonged era of peace, Anglo-American hegemony (with the aid of China) in the United Nations and in the world generally, free trade outside the Soviet orbit and gradual liberalization within, a weakened and profoundly pacific Russia far behind the Western powers in the utilization of atomic energy." The assumption of virtuous omnipotence, implicit in the Open Door Notes and formulated explicitly on the eve of American entry into World War I, reached full maturity in that image of an American Century. As with Theodore Roosevelt's concern to save civilization and Wilson's crusade to make the world safe for democracy, however, the urge to give the future a New Deal was powered by a persuasive sense of the necessity to expand economically in order to sustain democracy and prosperity in the United States.

In keeping with this outlook, the United States declined in the winter of 1941–42 even to consider the Soviet Union's bid to settle the postwar boundaries of eastern Europe on the basis of the situation as it existed just prior to Hitler's attack.* Russia raised the question in conversations with the British during November and December 1941, at which time Soviet spokesmen made clear and pointed references to being left out of the Atlantic Conference discussions of August 1941, between Churchill and Roosevelt.

Stalin suggested five major areas for agreement: (1) the boundaries of the Soviet Union should be guaranteed largely as they existed just prior to Hitler's assault in June 1941 (including the Curzon Line in Poland); (2) Austria should be restored as an independent nation; (3) Germany's industrial and military base should be weakened by splitting off the Ruhr manufacturing complex, by incorporating East Prussia into Poland, and perhaps by breaking off one other large province; (4) Yugoslavia and Albania should be re-established as inde-

---

* The best printed sources for this crucial episode are: W. S. Churchill, *The Grand Alliance* (Boston: Houghton Mifflin Co., 1950); *The Memoirs of Cordell Hull* (New York: Macmillan Co., Vol. II, 1948); S. Welles, *Seven Decisions That Shaped History* (New York: Harper and Bros., 1951); and especially *Foreign Relations, 1942: Vol. III, Russia* (Washington, Gvt. Printing Office, 1961).

pendent countries, and Czechoslovakia and Greece should have their prewar boundaries reaffirmed; and (5) Russia should receive reparations in kind from Germany.

These proposals pose a fascinating "iffy" question: what if Russia had been committed to those conditions, and they had been honored by both sides? Certainly the postwar era would have developed in a significantly different manner. Another consideration is more relevant to what did happen, because the Soviets continued in large measure to emphasize their proposals of 1941 during the war and on into the subsequent period.

At the time, however, the American response was wholly negative. Hull considered it "unfortunate" even to discuss such "commitments," and simply refused to agree to them. He first put strong pressure on the British to delay and then spurn the Soviet offer. There is no mystery about his adamance. American leaders did not want to negotiate any settlements until they were in the strongest possible position, and they thought that would be at the end of the war. And they were guided by the Open Door Policy, and they had neither the desire nor the intention to negotiate away any equality of opportunity in eastern Europe.

Stalin nevertheless continued to press his proposals during discussions with Anthony Eden in Moscow in December 1941, and on into 1942. Hull never gave way. He secured Roosevelt's support in April 1942, for the view that such commitments were "both dangerous and unwise." A month later the Secretary and his advisors in the State Department prepared a protest "so strong that we were in some fear lest the President disapprove it." The concern was unfounded. Roosevelt, so Hull reported, "quickly returned it with his O.K." The Soviets were blocked. The postwar configuration of eastern Europe was left moot—to be settled by other means.

This episode was extremely significant in American-Soviet relations, and English and American leaders realized that at the time. In many ways, the crisis can be understood most clearly in terms of the paradoxical attitude of the United States toward the Baltic States. Before World War I, Estonia, Latvia, and Lithuania had been provinces of Russia. Then, at the time of the Bolshevik Revolution, Germany had forcibly annexed them. During the subsequent years of intervention, the Allies encouraged and finally established the three countries as part of the *cordon sanitaire* designed to contain the Soviet Union.

Acquiescing in, but not accepting, that loss of its traditional "window on the West," the Soviets signed peace treaties with the new states in 1920. But the United States did not recognize the independence of those nations for several years, insisting that they were legitimate parts of the Russian state. Ultimately, however, America gave way and established diplomatic relations with the three countries. Having re-established its traditional authority over the Baltic states in 1939, the Soviet Union fully expected and intended to retain that control after the defeat of Hitler. In the discussions that took place during the winter of 1941–1942, however, the United States refused to return to its original position. Stalin's blunt reaction to being blocked on this issue by Hull and Roosevelt (and thereby the British) casts an exceedingly bright light on subsequent tension between East and West.

"It is very important to us," Stalin explained at the outset of the negotiations, "to know whether we shall have to fight at the peace conference in order to get our western frontiers." *

The record of the discussions reveals that the Russians became convinced that such a battle would be necessary.

"Surely this is axiomatic," Stalin shot back when Eden continued, as the advance guard for Hull and Roosevelt, to balk at an agreement. "We are fighting our hardest and losing hundreds of thousands of men in the common cause with Great Britain as our ally, and I should have thought that such a question as the position of the Baltic states ought to be axiomatic. . . . [I] am surprised and amazed at Mr. Churchill's Government taking up this position. It is practically the same as that of the Chamberlain Government. . . . This attitude of the British Government toward our frontiers is indeed a surprise to me so I think it will be better to postpone the proposed agreements."

"It now looks," he added in a remark that implicitly tied Roosevelt and the United States to the British position, "as if

* This and subsequent quotations from Stalin come from the stenographic report of the discussions printed in *Foreign Relations, 1942: Russia.*

the Atlantic Charter was directed against the U.S.S.R." Stalin was of course aware of America's responsibility for preventing an agreement. Any doubts are removed by Eden's blunt summary of the whole affair. The American attitude, he warned on March 12, 1942, "will surely appear to Stalin so uncollaborative a state of mind as to confirm his suspicions that he can expect no real consideration for Russia's interests from ourselves or the United States."

Roosevelt took an almost identical position three years later, in the fall of 1944, when the issue was reopened by the Russian counteroffensive against Hitler. The British repeated their warning about the dangers inherent in Roosevelt's efforts to avoid a commitment: the Russians were on the scene, and the only possible way of sustaining Western interests was through serious negotiations based on a series of *quid pro quos*. Instead, Roosevelt and Hull again stood by the strategy of the open door. They insisted that any agreement between Stalin and Churchill would have to be limited to a period of three months duration. It seems very probable that Stalin concluded that he would "have to fight at the peace conference in order to get our western frontiers."

In the meantime, the refusal to negotiate a basic settlement with the Soviet Union in the winter of 1941–1942 was almost immediately followed by another serious difference between the two countries. For, later in the spring of 1942, the Russians were given ambivalent and confusing assurances about when a second front would be opened in Europe. By August, when it had become apparent that Allied troops would not land on the continent that year, relations with Moscow had encountered very rough sledding. Even so, several developments reduced the tension and produced an interlude of improved relations between America and Russia. Foremost was the Russian victory at Stalingrad. That triumph convinced everybody, including the Russians, that Hitler would be defeated. As a result, and even before they launched their major counteroffensive, the Soviets embarked upon a fundamental debate over what to do after the war. Their discussions ranged across political, philosophical, and economic lines, but its essential nature was defined by Russia's tremendous physical and human losses in the war.

After Stalingrad, the Russians knew they would survive, but as a terribly weakened nation. Hence they were aware that the way they handled the recovery problem would influence all other decisions. Perhaps the most revealing insight into Russia's basic outlook at that time was offered (unconsciously, in all probability) by Molotov on February 18, 1956—after the Soviets had developed their nuclear weapons, and after the Chinese Communists had triumphed in Asia. "We now have an international situation," he remarked, "of which we could only have dreamed ten or fifteen years ago." Implicit in Molotov's comment was the fact that the Russians had viewed their position in the 1940s as one of weakness, not offensive strength.

Though there were various shades of opinion as to how the central issue of reconstruction should be dealt with, the Russians divided into three broad groups. One of them, occasionally called "our softies" by their Russian opponents, held that it was necessary and desirable to undertake reconstruction at a relatively moderate tempo, obtaining assistance from the United States. The softies stressed the need and desirability of relaxing the pervasive and extensive controls that had been exercised over Soviet life ever since the first Five Year Plan and the wisdom of revising, decentralizing, and rationalizing the industrial system that had been built. They also emphasized the danger of deteriorating relations with the United States. Perhaps most significant of all, they advanced the thesis that Western capitalism could probably avoid another serious depression, and hence the appeal and the safety of the Soviet Union depended upon its ability to improve the quality of life in Russia and thereby induce other peoples to accept communism by the force and persuasiveness of example.

Others within Russia argued that the softies were wrong in theory or in fact. Some of these men, who may be called the conservatives, agreed with the softies that it was desirable to ease up at home and were half convinced by the more favorable analysis of foreign capitalism, but they doubted that the Western nations, and in particular the United States, would help the Soviet Union solve its reconstruction problems. Hence they concluded that Russia would have to establish a basic security perimeter in Europe, the Middle East, and Asia and once again pull itself up by its own bootstraps.

Opposed to the softies and the conservatives was a group which may be called the doctrinaire revolutionaries. The die-hards scoffed at the analysis and proposals advanced by the moderates and asserted that the only practical and realistic program was to secure a base for militant revolutionary activity throughout the world. Such doctrinaires stressed the need to force the pace of reconstruction while doing all that was possible to export revolutions.*

Stalin's temperament and experience inclined him toward resolving the dilemma posed by the problem of reconstruction and the tradition of revolution in a conservative manner. But that approach depended on two things for success: (1) limiting and controlling revolutionary action by foreign communists, which otherwise would antagonize the United States, and (2) reaching an economic and political understanding with America, an agreement that would enable Russia to handle the problem of recovery and at the same time relax certain controls and pressures inside the country. To use the language of Wall Street, Stalin was a bull on communism. He was confident that if given a peaceful opportunity to develop its program in Russia, communism would gradually appeal to more and more countries of the world. He felt this was particularly likely in the underdeveloped areas and in poorer industrialized nations. If this could be managed by getting aid from America and by restraining foreign Communists from seizing power through revolutions, then the movement toward socialism and communism would move slowly enough to avoid frightening the United States into retaliation against the Soviet Union itself.

Two important aspects of this ferment and clash of views within the hierarchy of Soviet leadership have to kept in mind throughout any discussion of American-Soviet relations after

* Perhaps the best introduction to the nature and feel of debate within the Soviet Union is A. Erlich, *The Soviet Industrialization Debate, 1924–1928* (Cambridge: Harvard University Press, 1960); then, in addition to the materials cited below, see on the World War II phase of such dis-agreements the following items: Z. K. Brzezinski, *The Soviet Bloc. Unity and Conflict* (Cambridge: Harvard University Press, 1960, and paper-back, 1961); V. Dedijer, *Tito* (New York: Simon & Schuster, 1953); I. Deutscher, *Stalin* (New York: Oxford University Press, 1949); M. Gordey, *Visa to Moscow* (New York: Alfred A. Knopf, 1952); E. Snow, *Stalin Must Have Peace* (New York: Random House, 1947); and A. Werth, *The Year of Stalingrad* (New York: Alfred A. Knopf, 1947).

1941. They are particularly important to an understanding of the interaction between the two countries during the period between April 1945 and the summer of 1948.

The first is that this conflict over policy within the Soviet Union cannot be discounted or dismissed on the grounds that it did not produce Western-style representative government in Russia. Both the American public in general and its individual leaders tend very strongly to interpret the absence of Anglo-Saxon institutions in another country to mean that there is also an absence of significant or meaningful disagreement and debate about important issues. This is simply wrong. The ways in which differences of interest and opinion are organized and exert influence are many and varied. Even in the United States, for that matter, many crucial issues came increasingly after 1929 to be debated and decided by an elite almost wholly outside the institutions of local, state and national elections. Furthermore, as events since 1952 have demonstrated, such debate in Russia did continue and did begin to take on institutional form and substance. It also affected policy.

This development leads directly to the second main point. American policy exerted an early, continuing, and significant influence on the course of debate in the Soviet Union. Indeed, it had done so since the very first weeks of the Bolshevik Revolution in 1917. American policy therefore influenced Soviet policy and action. These considerations can not be re-emphasized every time they appear in the subsequent pages of this essay, but it is extremely important to understand them and use them as intellectual tools in thinking about later events.

In order to bypass all the misunderstanding that it is possible to avoid, let these points be stated as simply and as directly as possible. As Stalin made clear in the winter of 1941–1942, the Soviet Union fully intended to re-establish what it considered to be its minimum natural and desirable frontiers in eastern Europe. He further concluded that the United States and England would resist that effort. His opposition raised in the minds of Soviet leaders the very natural question as to whether or not they did not need an even firmer security perimeter.

Hence the problem for American leaders was one of developing an attitude and a broad set of proposals involving such security and economic aid for the Soviet Union that would enable them to negotiate some kind of modus vivendi with the Russians. The failure of American leaders to do that is the central theme of American diplomacy after the abortive negotiations of 1941–1942. If studied and written as a critique of Soviet policy, the emphasis involved in treating these matters would be different. In that case, the story might very well focus on the way that the breakdown of the talks of 1941–1942 strengthened those Soviet leaders who laid primary stress on extending communism as the Red Army moved westward. That might very possibly be the real tragedy of Soviet diplomacy. But since this essay is about American diplomacy, and—even more—since it was the United States that refused to offer any clear and unequivocal basis for such fundamental negotiations, the essay has to concentrate on America's actions and the ideas behind them.

Returning, then, to the events of the winter of 1942–1943, there were several developments which encouraged Stalin in his propensity to resolve his dilemma in a conservative (i.e., nationalist) fashion. One was the Western landing in North Africa, which did apparently modify his suspicion and anger over the failure to make an assault on the European continent. More important, however, was an American approach concerning postwar economic relations with Russia which seemed to suggest that the Soviet Union could obtain help in dealing with its reconstruction problems. Stalin responded quickly and decisively. But he was ultimately forced to conclude that the American overture did not represent a changed outlook on the part of the majority of America's corporate leaders.

In its origins the plan was a continuation of the old idea that America's economic system had to have a constantly expanding foreign market if it was to survive and prosper. At bottom, therefore, it was the fear of another depression (or the resumption of the old one) that prompted a few American leaders such as Donald M. Nelson and Eric Johnston to think of large-scale exports to Russia. Johnston, for example, was convinced after careful investigation in 1944 that the primary concern of Soviet leaders was "to rebuild Russia." They also worried about the depletion of certain raw materials and thought that Russia could continue to supply such items as manganese after the war. This small minority of American leaders began to realize that, whatever his many faults, Stalin was not another Hitler and that the Soviet Union had not developed by the same dynamic as Nazi Germany.

During 1943, therefore, Nelson and a few other Americans pushed the idea of a large loan to Russia. Stalin told Nelson that he was very much in favor of the plan and even gave him a list of priority needs as a first step in working out a specific program. Their negotiations had much to do with the improvement in political relations between the two countries, exemplified by Stalin's voluntary promise to Secretary of State Hull in October 1943 that Russia would enter the war against Japan. A bit later, in November, the conversations at the Teheran Conference also reflected the improved atmosphere.

For his part, Roosevelt was by that time revealing a more realistic attitude about including the Soviet Union as a full partner in any plans for the postwar world. He did not talk any longer, for example, about the way that England and America would between themselves police the world at the end of the war. In a similar way, he apparently grasped the fact that Stalin was "most deeply interested" in Russian recovery problems, and indicated at least some recognition of the way that issue was tied in with Soviet foreign policy. The President also seemed to be gaining some awareness that more reforms were needed in the United States. He talked, at least to some extent, about the importance of an "economic bill of rights" to balance, supplement, and reinforce America's traditional political freedoms. In certain respects, he appeared to be echoing the argument of the speech he had read at the Commonwealth Club in San Francisco during the 1932 presidential campaign. "America's own rightful place in the world," he asserted, "depends in large part upon" its handling of domestic issues. "For unless there is security here at home," he explained, "there cannot be lasting peace in the world."

Such remarks can be interpreted to mean that Roosevelt was beginning to understand that America's traditional policy of open-door expansion had contributed significantly to its domestic and international difficulties. Even so, his concrete proposals for development at home were pale copies of old New Deal legislation. And while he said he was "sorry" that he did not have time to discuss Russia's postwar recovery problems with Stalin at Teheran, the fact is that he never took—or made —time to do so during the remaining sixteen months of his life. He did not even see to it that his subordinates committed and prepared themselves to discuss and negotiate the issue with the Soviets. Roosevelt's declining health may account in part for this, but in that event it is clear that such an approach to the Russians was very low on the President's list of priorities.

There is at least one account, moreover, which suggests that Roosevelt's position was very similar to those who wanted to use Russia's needs to win major political and economic concessions. The story is told by James Byrnes in his second volume of memoirs, *All In One Life*. He reports that Leo Crowley, who was to terminate Lend-Lease shipments to the Soviet Union as soon as Germany surrendered, told him of a conversation with Roosevelt that took place about April 1, 1945, shortly before the President died. "Crowley told me that . . . he told the President about a rumor that our government was considering a loan to the Soviets of $10 billion, and that he [Crowley] thought it wise to refrain from making any loan until more was known of their postwar attitude. He said the President agreed." This account should not be taken as full proof of Roosevelt's attitude. But it does, even when evaluated with caution, support the main point at issue. It is simply not possible to account for the continuance of the Open Door Policy by blaming Roosevelt's successors, for the President did not carry through on persistent Russian overtures for major economic assistance to help them rebuild their shattered economy.

Had Roosevelt done this, it would be more meaningful to charge his successors—or the Russians—with sabotaging his plan for the future; for it is quite true that the small group around Nelson favoring some rapprochement with the Russians was opposed by a much larger number of America's corporate leaders. It seems likely that Averell Harriman, one of the many wealthy industrial and banking leaders who supported Roosevelt, and who was one of the President's top advisors, was one of the more influential leaders of the anti-Russian group. Harriman's natural antagonism to the Soviets was reinforced by his vigorous belief in the necessity of open-door expansion, a belief that may have been heightened even more by an unhappy experience with the Russians in the 1920s, when his attempt to control a sizable segment of the world's manganese market by developing Russian supplies ended in mutual dissatisfaction. Harriman was but one of many corporate leaders, however, who had gone into the Roosevelt Administration with anti-Russian views. Others included James B. Forrestal and Bernard Baruch. All of these men were skeptical of Nelson's approach to dealing with the Soviets and were supported in their view by State Department experts such as George F. Kennan (who was in Russia much of the time with Harriman).

These men shared Harriman's extremely reserved reaction, early in 1944, to the news that the Russians "were anxious to come to a prompt understanding" about postwar economic relations. His view became even clearer when, a bit later that year, Stalin made a formal request for a loan of six billion dollars. Harriman advised cutting the initial amount under discussion to one-tenth of that sum and proposed that the project should be defined as a credit, rather than as a loan, so that if it ever actually went through, the United States could exercise extensive controls over Russia's use of the money. Thus, while he agreed with the Nelson group that "the question of long-term credits represents the key point in any negotiations with the Soviet Government," he also shared the State Department's view that the lever provided by Russian weakness and devastation could and should be used to insure a predominant role for America in all decisions about the postwar world.

Harriman and most American leaders knew precisely what kind of choice they made. One of the most unequivocal pieces of evidence on this point comes from Admiral William H. Standley, who served as American Ambassador to Russia during the first part of the war. Speaking publicly on November 14, 1944, he offered a candid review of the situation. Some kind of rivalry with the Russians was unavoidable simply because they would be the only other victorious power on the continent of Europe. But that tension could be kept within bounds, Standley argued, if the United States accepted its primary responsibility in the situation.

"We must assume two important premises," he pointed out. "First, that Russia's security is vital to her and that she cannot turn to industrialization and development of her raw material resources unless she has that security. . . . After victory, security is their next consideration. . . . [And unless we help establish it] they will have to proceed on their own to provide it."

Harriman based his policy on an identical analysis. He candidly acknowledged "that the sooner the Soviet Union can develop a decent life for its people the more tolerant they will become." That interpretation obviously implied a basic policy of helping the Russians recover from the devastation of the war. But quite unlike Standley, Harriman proposed instead to exploit Russian weakness and force them to accept American policies. The Russians "should be given to understand that our willingness to co-operate wholeheartedly with them in their vast reconstruction problems will depend upon their behavior in international matters." "I am opposed to granting her that credit," he stated flatly in May 1945. "I would apportion that credit out piecemeal, demanding in return concessions on the political field."

From the very beginning of the discussions with Stalin in 1943, Roosevelt was aware of the Soviet overtures for economic aid and of the importance Stalin attached to such negotiations. Yet the President never took the lead himself in handling the issue. Nor did he direct the State Department or a special committee to push the matter. In the end, therefore, there was no concerted American effort to match the Russian approach of handling related political and economic questions on an integrated basis.*

Roosevelt's attitude, which so clearly reflected the traditional outlook of the Open Door Policy, was revealed even more vividly in the spring of 1944, when the Soviet Army began to advance into eastern Europe. Confronted by Churchill with the need to come to some clear arrangement with the Russians, Roosevelt at first agreed to the idea of a clear and precise division of authority. Then, in an abrupt turnabout,

---

* On these matters consult the very illuminating, but all too often neglected volume by E. F. Penrose, *Economic Planning for the Peace* (Princeton: Princeton University Press, 1953).

he asserted that he must have "complete freedom of action," whatever the agreement arranged by Churchill and Stalin. After considerable effort, Churchill and Stalin worked out an understanding—"a good guide," said Churchill, "for the conduct of our affairs"—whereby Russia would exercise predominant authority in southeastern Europe, Great Britain would do so in Greece, and the Allies would share responsibility in Yugoslavia. Roosevelt reluctantly accepted this division of power on the basis of a three-month trial.

During subsequent months, the British intervened to crush a revolution in Greece and prepare the way for the installation of a government they wanted and could control. Though he urged the British to take a more liberal line, Roosevelt went along with Churchill on the need to control affairs in Greece and acquiesced in the Prime Minister's action. *Both in fact and in the eyes of the Russians, that committed Roosevelt on the eve of the Yalta Conference to the agreement worked out between Churchill and Stalin.* For his part, Stalin refrained from attacking or blocking the British move in Greece. Churchill reported that Stalin "adhered very strictly to this understanding." Stalin also moved to forestall trouble with the Western Allies arising from foreign communist agitation and revolution. He advised, and apparently even warned, Tito and Mao Tse-tung to abstain from revolutionary action in their nations and instead to accept subordinate positions in coalition governments led by pro-Western parties.

Against this background, and in the context of Germany's imminent defeat, Roosevelt met Churchill and Stalin at Yalta in February 1945. In addition to their knowledge of the Churchill-Stalin agreement, and of Stalin's self-containment during the Greek episode, American leaders were aware that the Chinese communists, after a long debate, had concluded in September 1944, that they preferred to work with the United States rather than with Russia in the future development of China. Thus it is absolutely clear that Roosevelt and his advisors knew that the Soviet Union was prepared to negotiate seriously about the character of postwar relations with the United States and that America had an equally fruitful opportunity in Asia. But during the conference American leaders were not concerned to push such negotiations. They were not prepared to abandon, or even seriously to modify, the traditional strategy of American expansion.

Disturbed by America's ambivalence and Churchill's increasingly open opposition, which increased the difficulty Stalin had in controlling the doctrinaire revolutionaries within his own camp, Stalin went to Yalta with two approaches to the postwar world. One was based on receiving a large loan from the United States. His overtures in this direction were answered with vague and unrewarding replies. Stalin's alternative was to obtain, by agreement or by self-exertion, economic reparations from Germany and a strong strategic position in eastern Europe, the Black Sea area, and the Far East. America went to Yalta, on the other hand, guided by little except a sense of mission to reform the world, a growing fear of postwar economic crisis, and an increasing confidence that Russian weakness would enable America to exercise its freedom and solve its problems by further open-door expansion.

Commentators have criticized President Roosevelt very severely on the grounds that he was naive in believing he could persuade Stalin to co-operate with the West after the war. Such attacks are weak and misdirected in several important respects. In the first place, it is almost absurd to think—or charge—that a man with Roosevelt's mastery of political infighting was naive. He may have overestimated his power or his skill, but he was not naive. Significantly, too, Roosevelt had *not* abandoned, at the time of his death, the intention of reasserting American power and influence in eastern Europe. It was suggested to him that the United States should file a vigorous protest over the Soviet action early in 1945 of reconstituting the Rumanian Government along pro-Soviet lines. Roosevelt did *not* reply that the basic issue should be forgotten. His position was quite different. *He said merely that the Rumanian episode, because it involved supplies for the Red Army that was still fighting Germany, did not offer the best kind of ground upon which to take a stand.*

Roosevelt's idea of reaching an accommodation with Stalin was not based on some utopian dream of perfect and everlasting agreement on any and all issues. However, Roosevelt simply did not understand the nature and workings of a modern, complex industrial economy. The result in domestic affairs was that his political acumen and skill were never focused on the central and vital issues of getting the political economy into some kind of fundamentally dynamic balance. The same weakness plagued him in dealing with the Russians. He never got his priorities straight. Short of war, economic aid was the one effective tool he had in negotiations with the Soviets. But he never used it.

Roosevelt's successors understood and used that lever, but they treated it as a weapon to force the Soviets to accept American policies. The conflict over affairs in eastern Europe which developed out of that attitude is usually stressed in discussing the origins of the cold war. Yet it may be that the issues of German reparations and American expansion in the Middle East were equally important as determining factors. Failing to obtain a loan from America, Stalin had to decide among three possible courses of action.*

He could give way and accept the American interpretation of all disputed points, abandoning foreign communists to their fate and attempting to control the extremists in his own nation. He could respond with an orthodox revolutionary program throughout the world. Or, relying on large economic reparations from Germany, he could continue the effort to resolve his dilemma in a conservative manner even though he did not have any formal understanding with the United States. This approach would also do much to keep Germany from becoming a threat to Russia in the immediate future. It left him, however, with the need to effect some basic settlement concerning eastern Europe, the Far East, and the Black Sea region.

Stalin was able to reach such an understanding with the United States in but one of those areas. This was in Asia, where he traded American predominance in China (and Japan) for strategic and economic rights in Manchuria. Concerning eastern Europe, however, Stalin accepted an ambivalent proposal on the Polish issue which represented America's unwillingness to acknowledge his agreement with Churchill as much as it did Russia's security needs. He was no more successful in the Middle East, where American oil companies had moved back into Iran in 1943. Supported by the State Department and

* Here see M. F. Herz, *Beginnings of the Cold War* (Bloomington: Indiana University Press, 1966).

special emissaries, the companies were well along in their efforts to obtain extensive concessions. Roosevelt was "thrilled" by the chance to work along with the oil companies and make Iran an example of what America could do for underdeveloped areas of the world, an attitude which helps explain why the United States was not willing to allow the Russians to obtain oil rights in northern Iran. Stalin gave way on the issue at Yalta and also refrained from pushing his desire to gain more security for Russia in the Black Sea area.

Despite his failure to get any positive response from the United States on the question of a postwar loan, or a clear understanding on other vital issues, Stalin still hoped to effect a conservative resolution of his dilemma. Throughout the first half of 1945, for example, *Izvestia* stressed the vitality of the American economy (in striking contrast to the fears being expressed in Congressional hearings), emphasized the importance of resolving outstanding issues by negotiation, and reiterated the fruitfulness of economic co-operation. The British press attaché in Russia reported that Soviet comment remained restrained and hopeful until America initiated a campaign of vigorous criticism and protest aimed at Soviet predominance in eastern Europe.

But the most significant indicators of the predisposition to work out some modus vivendi with the United States, and then to concentrate on internal recovery and development, came in the debates within the Soviet hierarchy, and in the relatively restrained policies followed in eastern Europe after the Nazis were defeated. One of the earliest indications of Russian emphasis on domestic affairs appeared in 1943 in the form of a discussion (in the journal *Under the Banner of Marxism*) over the proper way to teach economics. This took special note, among other things, of Stalin's praise of the United States. The crucial feature was the heavy stress laid upon the extent of the recovery crisis, and upon the need to concentrate on domestic affairs. Many American observers immediately understood and pointed out the nonrevolutionary implications of the argument, but official policy-makers in the United States took little if any cognizance of the matter.*

---

* The reader who does not have access to, or cannot read, Soviet sources (upon which this discussion is based), can follow the debate in these

An even more revealing debate occurred after the publication in 1946 of a major study of capitalism by the Soviet economist Eugene Varga. The date of 1946 is significant in two respects. It means, in the first place, that the discussion had been going on at least since 1944, a consideration which underscores the ambivalent, undecided, and cautious nature of Soviet thinking at the end of the war. It also indicates that the Russians had not made a firm decision on their basic approach as late as 1946; even though, as will be seen, the United States had been exerting strong pressure on the Soviet Union ever since the London Foreign Ministers' Conference in September 1945.

Varga's central point was that capitalism in general, and in the United States in particular, was capable of stabilizing itself in the postwar era. He went on to argue that the role of the government could be positive and creative under capitalism, and in that fashion suggested that the classic Marxian prophecy about the inevitable collapse of capitalism might need to be revised and modified. Varga's argument pointed very directly toward the need to stabilize relations with the United States, and to concentrate on domestic Soviet development.*

---

items: L. A. Leontiev (et. al.), "Teaching of Economics in the Soviet Union," [*Under the Banner of Marxism*, Nos. 7–8 (1943)], translated and printed in *The American Economic Review* (September, 1944); P. Baran, "New Trends in Russian Economic Thinking?", *American Economic Review* (December, 1944); R. Dunayevskaya, "A New Revision of Marxian Economics," *American Economic Review* (November, 1944); and A. Zauberman, "Economic Thought in the Soviet Union," *The Review of Economic Studies*, Nos. 39–41 (1948–50).

* The Varga Controversy, as it came to be called, has received considerable attention from American students of the Soviet Union. Varga's book was published as *Changes in the Economy of Capitalism Resulting from the Second World War*. An English translation of the stenographic report of a vigorous debate on the book, in which Varga participated, and which took place on May 7, 14, and 21 of 1947, appeared as *Soviet Views on the Post-War World Economy* (Washington: Public Affairs Press, 1948). The reader who wants real insight into the extent to which Soviet leaders do disagree among themselves, and into the vigorous nature of their discussions, should consult the translation. Of the many comments on the debate, the reader may find it useful to begin with these: F. C. Barghoorn, "The Varga Discussion and Its Significance," *American Slavic and East European Review* (March 1948); H. Marcuse, *Soviet Marxism. A Critical Analysis* (New York: Columbia University

These examples point up a very important kind of continuity in Soviet affairs that is often missed or forgotten. The revisionist debate that erupted within and between communist countries in the mid-1950s was actually no more than a continuation of the discussion that began in 1943–44 within the Soviet Union, and which was pursued very vigorously as late as 1947 and 1948. The two illustrations mentioned here should not be taken as isolated, atypical events. Early in 1945, for example, a very long and strongly argued revisionist article appeared in the magazine *Foundations of Marxism*. Similar debates took place around short stories and novels. And the philosopher Aleksandrov, who had good things to say about Western capitalist thinkers, was in high favor as late as the first months of 1947.† The popular idea that Soviet leaders emerged from the war ready to do aggressive battle against the United States is simply not borne out by the evidence. Varga himself was not attacked in public in any serious way, for example, until after Winston Churchill's militant Iron Curtain speech in 1946, and the enunciation of the Truman Doctrine in March 1947.

Soviet officials who later chose to live in the West often offered the same kind of evidence bearing on Russian policy at the end of the war. One of the American experts who interviewed many such men offered this general judgment about Soviet policy in Germany. "The paramount consideration was not the extension of the revolution to Germany and the establishment of a Soviet Government there, but the rehabilitation of the Soviet Union's war-ravaged industry and transportation . . . regardless of the effect this policy might have on . . . establishing a Soviet Germany." For that matter,

---

Press, 1958); and B. Moore, *Soviet Politics—The Dilemma of Power* (Cambridge: Harvard University Press, 1950). Quite surprisingly, D. F. Fleming does not examine these internal debates in his massive and impressive study, *The Cold War and Its Origins, 1917–1960* (New York: Doubleday and Co., 2 Vols., 1961). He does provide, however, a vast amount of supporting evidence in his discussion of Soviet policy at the end of the war. Further material is in I. Deutscher, *Russia: What Next?* (New York: Oxford University Press, 1953); and B. Moore, *Terror and Progress: USSR* (Cambridge: Harvard University Press, 1954).

† See, as representative: V. Alexandrova, "The Russian People and the 'Lost Peace'—In Literature," *Modern Review* (1949); and P. E. Corbett, "The Aleksandrov Story," *World Politics* (1949).

the Red Army's railroad lines across Poland into Germany were ripped up in 1945. And in eastern Europe, the Soviet approach was modeled on the popular front governments of the 1930s rather than upon the existing Soviet system.*

The point of these examples (and there are many more) is not to suggest, let alone try to prove, that Stalin and other Soviet leaders behaved either as Western democrats or as men uninterested in exercising influence in eastern Europe. The point is to indicate and to stress the importance of three quite different things: first, the very significant extent to which Soviet decisions from 1944 through 1947 were based on domestic Russian conditions; second, the degree to which the Soviets were assuming that capitalism would stabilize itself around the great and undamaged power of the United States; and third, the way in which those two factors pointed in the mind of many Russians—including Stalin—to the need to reach some kind of agreement with America. They never defined such an understanding on the basis of abandoning Russian influence in eastern Europe or acquiescing in each and every American proposal just as it first emanated from Washington. But neither did they emerge from World War II with a determination to take over eastern Europe and then embark upon a cold war with the United States.

Beginning in 1946, Stalin grew ever more skeptical about the possibility of negotiating any basic understanding with American leaders. But he never became a fatalist about war with the United States. And the so-called softies in the party were not finally downgraded, and then subjected to vigorous and extensive attacks (including imprisonment) until the late summer and early fall of 1947. It was not until even later that the Soviet Union moved ruthlessly to extend and consolidate its control over eastern Europe.

---

* The quotation is from R. Slusser (ed.), *Soviet Economic Policy in Postwar Germany. A Collection of Papers by Former Soviet Officials* (New York: Research Program on the USSR, 1953). Also see: R. A. Rosa, "The Soviet Theory of 'People's Democracy'," *World Politics* (1949); H. G. Skilling, "People's Democracy, The Proletarian Dictatorship and the Czechoslovak Path to Socialism," *American Slavic and East European Review* (1951); and Brzezinski, *The Soviet Bloc*.

II. THE OPEN DOOR POLICY AND THE ONSET OF THE COLD WAR

Stalin's effort to solve Russia's problem of security and recovery short of widespread conflict with the United States was not matched by American leaders who acceded to power upon the death of Roosevelt. The President bequeathed them little, if anything, beyond the traditional outlook of open-door expansion. They proceeded rapidly and with a minimum of debate to translate that conception of America and the world into a series of actions and policies which closed the door to any result but the cold war.

The various themes which went into America's conception of the freedom and the necessity of open-door expansion, from the doctrine of the elect to the frontier thesis, had been synthesized into an ideology before Roosevelt's death. Once it was frozen into ideology, it became very difficult—and perhaps artificial, even then—to assign priorities to its various facets. Even a single man, let alone a group, emphasized different themes at various times. Yet the open-door outlook was based on an economic definition of the world, and this explanation of reality was persistently stressed by America's corporate leadership as it developed its policy toward the Soviet Union and other nations. It was not the possession of the atomic bomb which prompted American leaders to get tough with Russia but rather their open-door outlook which interpreted the bomb as the final guarantee that they could go further faster down that path to world predominance.

Long before anyone knew that the bomb would work, most American leaders were operating on the basis of three assumptions or ideas which defined the world in terms of a cold war. The first specified Russia as being evil but weak. This attitude, predominant among American leaders from the first days of the Bolshevik Revolution in 1917, was reinforced and deepened by the nonaggression pact signed by Russia with Nazi Germany in 1939. There is little evidence to support the oft-asserted claim that Americans changed their basic attitude toward the Soviet Union during the war. Most of them welcomed Russian help against Germany, and some of them mitigated their antagonisms and suspicions, but several careful studies make it clear that large and crucial segments of the American public remained "dubious about the prospects of building the peace together with Russia." .

Even before the end of the war in Europe, many Americans were again comparing Stalin with Hitler and stressing the importance of avoiding any repetition of the appeasement of Nazi Germany. Others, like John Foster Dulles, who had sought persistently and until a very late date to reach a broad compromise with Hitler and Japan, changed their approach when it came to dealing with Russia. They made no such efforts to reach an understanding with Stalin. And by the time of the San Francisco Conference on the United Nations, such leaders as Averell Harriman were publicly expressing their view that there was an "irreconcilable difference" between Russia and the Western powers.

At the same time, however, very few—if any—American leaders thought that Russia would launch a war. Policy-makers were quite aware of the "pitiful" conditions in western Russia, of the nation's staggering losses and its general exhaustion, of its "simply enormous" need for outside help "to repair the devastation of war," and of Stalin's stress on firm economic and political agreements with the United States to provide the basis for that reconstruction. In their own discussions, American decision-makers drew an astute and crucial distinction between Soviet actions to establish a security perimeter in eastern Europe and an all-out aggressive move against the entire capitalist world. They were right in their estimate that Russia was concerned with the first objective. They were also correct in concluding that the Soviet Union—unlike Nazi Germany—"is not essentially constructed as a dynamic expansionist state." *

Far from emphasizing the imminence of a Russian attack, American leaders stressed the importance of denying any and all Soviet requests or overtures of a revised strategic agreement

---

* See, as a typical report of such discussions within the American policy-making community, the story in the *New York Times*, September 27, 1945 (p. 4), from which the quotation is taken.

in the Middle East, and at the same time concentrated on re-asserting American influence in eastern Europe while pushing the Russians back to their traditional borders. The first such American action came in the spring and summer of 1945 in the form of protests over Soviet influence that developed as the Red Army moved westward in pursuit of the Nazis. These protests were not prompted by the fear that Russia was about to overwhelm Europe or the world in general, but rather by the traditional outlook of the open door and the specific desire to keep the Soviets from establishing any long-range influence in eastern Europe.

Another basic attitude held by American leaders defined the United States as the symbol and the agent of positive good as opposed to Soviet evil and assumed that the combination of American strength and Russian weakness made it possible to determine the future of the world in accordance with that judgment. One important congressional leader, for example, remarked in 1943 that lend-lease provided the United States with a "wonderful opportunity" to bring the United States to "a greater degree of determining authority" in the world. He was quite aware that his view was "shared by some of the members of the President's Cabinet" and that important State Department officials were "fully in accord" with the same outlook. Another key congressman was thinking in terms of the "United States seeking world power as a trustee for civilization." * Following the even earlier lead of publisher Henry R. Luce, who had announced in 1941 that it was high noon of the American Century, various business spokesmen began stressing the need to become "missionaries of capitalism and democracy." Shortly thereafter, a leading oil-industry leader asserted that America "must set the pace and assume the responsibility of the majority stockholder in this corporation known as the world." Such remarks were not unique; they merely represented the increasing verbalization of one aspect of America's traditional policy.

The third essential aspect of the open-door outlook, which

---

* See, as typical of such remarks, the comments of Karl E. Mundt, A. A. Berle, Jr., John M. Vorys, and Charles A. Eaton, in *Extension of Lend-Lease Act. Hearings Before the Committee on Foreign Affairs. House of Representatives* 78th Cong., 1st Ses. (1943).

also made its appearance before the end of the war, was the fear that America's economic system would suffer a serious depression if it did not continue to expand overseas. Stressing the fact that there remained roughly nine million unemployed in 1940, one leading New Deal senator warned in 1943 that the danger of another depression could not be overemphasized. A government economic expert promptly supported this view with his own report that "it unfortunately is a fact that for the majority of the people in the United States the thing we have liked to refer to as the American standard of living is only possible in situations where two people in the family are working."

The reason for this concern, and the extent to which government participation in the financing of such expansion was crucial, is nicely revealed by two sets of statistics. The first figures concern direct exports. In 1928, when the United States enjoyed a net export surplus with every region of the world except some areas in the tropics, the nation sold 17.1 per cent of the world's exports. Ten years later, during the depression, that share had dropped, despite government loans and subsidies to exporters, to 14.9 per cent. The proportion in 1953, 21.3 per cent, seems at first glance to indicate a dramatic recovery and further gain. But 5.6 per cent of that total was paid for by government loans and grants financed by the American taxpayer. Hence the net share of world exports was only 15.6 per cent. Not until 1956, when it reached 17.9 per cent, did the net figure surpass the American export position of 1928.

The second kind of data concerns the extent to which various American corporations depend upon overseas operations. Total foreign sales, including those of directly owned overseas branches and subsidiaries as well as exports from parent American companies, amounted in 1956 to $58 billion. When classified according to the percentage of total sales accounted for by all foreign operations, the pattern is indicated by the following examples: 75 per cent—Standard Oil of New Jersey; more than 70 per cent—H. J. Heinz and Colgate-Palmolive; over 40 per cent—American Radiator, International Harvester, F. W. Woolworth, Gillette Razor, and National Cash Register; better than 30 per cent—Parke Davis Drugs, Sterling Drugs, and Otis Elevators; and between 15 and 30 per cent—Johnson and Johnson, Corn Products Refining, Firestone, Goodyear, International Business Machines, Coca Cola, and Eastman Kodak.*

The drive to achieve those postwar results began in earnest while the war was still being fought. For his part, Secretary Hull never eased off on the pace he had established in 1933. "The primary object," he reiterated in 1940, "is both to reopen the old and seek new outlets for our surplus production." One of his principal concerns was to break into the British trading system, a campaign in which he was vigorously encouraged and supported by American exporters. Hull's weapons included lend-lease, and Britain's growing need for a major recovery loan. The United States made its aid conditional upon the acceptance by England of the open-door principle.†

One of the most vigorous proponents of this assault upon the British imperial market was William L. Clayton, a self-made man who became head of the world's largest cotton export business and then moved into the Roosevelt Administration as a policy-maker. His underlying attitude was very similar to Hull's: "The international economic policies of nations," Clayton remarked in 1943, "have more to do with creating conditions which lead to war than any other single factor." He was committed, as one might expect, to the Open Door Policy as the way to expand exports. Clayton was unusual, however, in that he was considerably more candid than most American leaders when speaking about the nature of that overseas economic expansion. He admitted, for example, that the United States often tried to close the door to competition once it had gone through and established its own position. "As a matter of fact, if we want to be honest with ourselves, we will find that many of the sins that we freely

---

* A convenient, though merely surface, survey is: C. E. Silberman and L. A. Mayer, "The Migration of U.S. Capital," *Fortune* (1958). On investments, see the authoritative *U.S. Business Investments in Foreign Countries* (Washington: Department of Commerce, 1960). More helpful are M. Wilkins, *The Emergence of Multinational Enterprise* (Cambridge: Harvard University Press, 1970); and C. P. Kindleberger (Ed.), *The International Corporation* (Cambridge: The M.I.T. Press, 1970).

† Here see R. N. Gardner, *Sterling-Dollar Diplomacy* (Oxford: Oxford University Press, 1956).

criticize other countries for practicing have their counterpart in the United States."

Clayton's comment is particularly relevant to America's insistence that former Axis colonies, and other trustee territories, should be handled in such a way that the United States would be assured of unrestricted economic access. As Assistant Secretary Sayre explained the policy, it was centered on establishing "sound economic foundations." "Here again," he noted, "another distinctively American ideal, expressed at various times as the Open Door Policy, is made a binding obligation in all trust territories." The remarks of Sayre and Clayton serve to clarify and dramatize one of the issues that plagued American-Soviet relations after 1943. The United States interpreted Russian resistance to the Open Door Policy in eastern Europe as an unfriendly act, even though Stalin acquiesced in the principle throughout the Pacific and elsewhere in the world.

Another policy-maker dramatized this ever-increasing concern with overseas economic expansion by comparing the American system with the old British empire. America, he explained, was "a great island" dependent upon a "greater volume of exports" than even the British had needed in the nineteenth and early twentieth centuries. But what was very probably the clearest and most direct statement and explanation of the American approach to the postwar world was provided in November 1944—five full months before the death of Roosevelt—by Assistant Secretary of State Dean Acheson. Testifying before a special Congressional committee on Post-war Economic Policy and Planning, Acheson analyzed the situation in a remarkable and almost unique outburst of blunt candor. His remarks cast such a dazzling light on American foreign policy ever since that date that they warrant extensive quotation.*

Along with almost every other American leader, Acheson was gravely concerned lest the economy slide back into the depression of the 1930s or collapse in the new debacle at the end of the war. That was the danger, and Acheson repeatedly

---

* All of the testimony during these hearings, however, is very pertinent. *Post-War Economic Policy and Planning. Hearings Before the Special Subcommittee on Post-War Economic Policy and Planning. House of Representatives*, 78th Cong., 2nd Sess. (1944).

emphasized it during his entire career in the Department of State.† If that happened, he began his testimony in 1944, "it seems clear that we are in for a very bad time, so far as the economic and social position of the country is concerned. We cannot go through another ten years like the ten years at the end of the twenties and the beginning of the thirties, without having the most far-reaching consequences upon our economic and social system."

"When we look at that problem," he continued, "we may say it is a problem of markets. You don't have a problem of production. The United States has unlimited creative energy. The important thing is markets. We have got to see that what the country produces is used and is sold under financial arrangements which make its production possible." The solution, Acheson explained to the Congressmen, was not in doubt. "You must look to foreign markets."

Acheson then interrupted the main line of his analysis in a curious way. He voluntarily threw in a comment that seems remarkably similar to the admission made by Brooks Adams in 1900, when he was proposing exactly the same kind of expansion. Indeed, the full flavor and import of the episode can only be captured in the give-and-take between Acheson and the chairman of the committee.*

> ACHESON.   We could argue for quite a while that under a different system in this country you could use the entire production of the country in the United States.
> WORLEY.   What do you mean by that?

† When compared with their subsequent political and historical rhetoric about the success of the New Deal itself, the candid and sworn testimony of New Deal leaders after 1943 offers a valuable corrective. More historians should examine it.

* This parallel between Acheson and Adams becomes even more fascinating in the light of two other similar episodes. Adams in 1900 used the words *contain* and *containing* to describe how the United States should deal with Russia. George F. Kennan used precisely the same terminology in 1946 and 1947 in writing his famous "X" article which enunciated the policy that took the word *containment* as its name. In the same year, 1947, the New Deal newspaper columnist Marquis Childs republished Adams's essay, *America's Economic Supremacy*, as a guide to the proper policy for the United States in the cold war. My efforts to find out whether these episodes involved more than coincidence have not been successful. In either case, the continuity of American foreign policy is established beyond question.

ACHESON.   I take it the Soviet Union could use its
entire production internally. If you wish to control the entire trade and income of the United States, which means
the life of the people, you could probably fix it so that
everything produced here would be consumed here, but that
would completely change our Constitution, our relations to
property, human liberty, our very conceptions of law. And
nobody contemplates that. Therefore, you find you must
look to other markets and those markets are abroad. . . .
The first thing that I want to bring out is that we need
these markets for the output of the United States. If I am
wrong about that, then all the argument falls by the way-
side, but my contention is that we cannot have full employment and prosperity in the United States without the foreign
markets. That is point one, and if anyone wants to challenge
me on that we will go over it again.

WORLEY.   I think we are agreed on that.
ACHESON.   How do we go about getting it? What
you have to do at the outset is to make credit available.
. . . I don't believe private capital can possibly do it.
WORLEY.   Why not?
ACHESON.   I don't think there is enough private
capital willing to engage in that activity, which is quite risky.
There will be a lot of losses. . . .

As for the significance of the Open Door Policy in this drive
for markets, Acheson made that very clear:

WORLEY.   You don't think there would be a peace
agreement without collateral agreements of an economic
nature?
ACHESON.   I don't see how it would work, Mr.
Chairman. If we tried to do that it would really mean that
we would be relying exclusively on the use of force. I don't
believe that would work.

As the policy developed, however, American leaders did
come to rely extensively on the threat of force implied by
their short-lived monopoly of the atom bomb, and on the
development of conventional forces that were deployed in a
long sequence of operations and interventions. That attitude,

and the tension it produced in relations with Russia, ultimately provoked strong protests from Secretary of War Stimson and Secretary of Commerce Henry A. Wallace. Prior to their changes, however, both men supported the orthodox line of policy. Deeply concerned about the problem of preventing a depression, Wallace persistently talked between 1943 and 1947 about overseas economic expansion as the new frontier. "Private enterprise in the United States can survive only if it expands and grows," he argued, and pointed out that he was only trying to help the businessmen do what they themselves advocated. "The old frontiers must be rebuilt," as he put it, and pointed to American economic expansion into the poor, underdeveloped countries as "this unlimited new frontier of opportunities." Wallace of course wanted to reform and improve conditions abroad as part of that extension of American enterprise, and was in many respects the epitome of the New Deal version of Woodrow Wilson's reforming expansionism.

But it is very revealing that Wallace himself spoke favorably of Hoover's similar desire to improve the lot of the overseas poor as an integral part of extending American business operations. "I have considerable sympathy," Wallace remarked as he took over the same cabinet post in 1945, "with Herbert Hoover's problem as Secretary of Commerce." The one obvious difference in their outlooks was Wallace's willingness to provide the private entrepreneurs with public capital. "It is vital," he asserted, "that Government co-operate with the export trade . . . to put on an aggressive sales campaign abroad."

Wallace's version of the expansionist outlook won him sharp criticism from Senator Robert A. Taft. Along with his repeated warnings that American policy might well provoke the Soviets into ever more militant retaliation, and perhaps even war, Taft's attack on Wallace serves to illustrate the misleading nature of the popular stereotype of the Senator. Taft immediately spotted the contradiction between the rhetoric of the New Deal and the reality of its policies. "Dollar diplomacy is derided," he commented very pointedly in 1945, "although it is exactly the policy of Government aid to our exporters which Mr. Wallace himself advocates to develop foreign trade, except that it did not [in its earlier forms] involve our lending abroad the money to pay for all our exports."

Despite the perception of his analysis, Taft stood virtually alone. Congressman Clarence Murdock of Arizona offered what was perhaps the most striking summary of the majority view: "The proper foreign outlet is our safety valve." Milo Perkins, a New Deal businessman who for a time headed the Board of Economic Warfare, offered a pungent statement of the familiar either-or thesis that had originated in the 1890s. "We must sell great quantities of machinery and transport equipment and machine tools abroad if we are to avoid large-scale factory shutdowns here at home." Labor and farm leaders joined corporation executives and government officials in supporting that analysis. "We cannot possibly maintain full production and full employment," the United Auto Workers announced in 1945, "unless we have a world pool of free and prosperous consumers." "Foreign trade," the union explained, "can be the margin between a drop into economic chaos and a steadily expanding economy." Edward O'Neal, President of the American Farm Bureau Federation, was equally vehement. Agricultural surpluses "will wreck our economy unless we can find sufficient outlets in foreign markets to help sustain the volume of production." In his view, the "finest" policy proposal involved Wilson's old idea of extending the Monroe Doctrine to the world at large. "Let us spread it all over," O'Neal suggested to the congressional committee on postwar planning; "let us run it into China, if necessary, and run it around into Russia."

As it moved quickly to take over government affairs after the death of Roosevelt, the Truman Administration made it clear that it would sustain all these aspects of the traditional approach to foreign policy.* "The United States cannot reach and maintain the high level of employment we have set as our goal," Secretary of State James F. Byrnes reiterated, "unless the outlets for our production are larger than they've ever been before in peacetime." Byrnes had neither time nor inter-

---

* There is now a sizable body of literature on this theme. Begin with L. C. Gardner, *Architects of Illusion* (Chicago: Quadrangle Books, 1970); then go to G. Alperovitz, *Atomic Diplomacy: Hiroshima and Potsdam* (New York: Simon and Schuster, 1965), and his collection of essays *Cold War Essays* (Garden City: Anchor Books, 1970), and the items in the bibliography.

est for the idea of working out some agreement with the Russians that involved the recovery loan they had requested. He even sidetracked the basic memorandum dealing with the issue. "I had it placed in the 'Forgotten File'," he later revealed, "as I felt sure that Fred Vinson, the new Secretary of the Treasury, would not press it."

President Harry S Truman was for his part an enthusiastic and militant advocate of America's supremacy in the world. He seemed, indeed, to react, think, and act as an almost classic personification of the entire Open Door Policy. From a very early date, moreover, he led the rapid revival of the analogy between Nazi Germany and the Soviet Union (and Hitler and Stalin) which became one of the fundamental clichés of America's analysis of the postwar world. Given that analogy, which was very rapidly and very generally accepted, American policy can without much exaggeration be described as an effort to establish the Open Door Policy once and for all by avoiding what were judged—on the basis of the analogy—to have been the errors of appeasement made during the 1930s.

There were two central fallacies involved in that estimate of the world. Soviet Russia and Nazi Germany were significantly different in crucial aspects of domestic and foreign policy; and, unlike the situation in the 1930s, the United States was neither weak nor disarmed. Indeed, it enjoyed a great absolute as well as relative advantage in both economic and military power. As the United States Government candidly admitted even as late as 1962, the United States had been the strongest power in the world ever since 1944. For that matter, it was the existence and the knowledge of that strength that encouraged Truman and other leaders after 1945 to think that they could force the Soviets to accept American proposals without recourse to war.

It is no doubt wrong and inaccurate to conclude that the effort to establish the false analogy between Soviet Russia and Nazi Germany was the product of conscious distortion by America's private and official leaders. Many of them adopted and used that argument in complete sincerity. They simply accepted it without serious thought or critical evaluation. However mistaken in fact and logic, such men were not hypocrites. But it also is true that there were a good many men who shared the attitude of Senator Arthur K. Vandenberg. He thought it was necessary "to scare hell out of the American people" in order to win their active approval and support for the kind of vigorous anti-Soviet policy he wanted. Those men did consciously employ exaggeration and oversimplification to accomplish their objectives. Senator Taft would seem to have offered a sound judgment on that conduct. He remarked during congressional consideration of the European Recovery Program that he was more than a bit tired of having the Russian menace invoked as a reason for doing any- and everything that might or might not be desirable or necessary on its own merits.

Truman not only thought about Russia in terms of Nazi Germany, but he made it clear very soon after he took the oath as President that he intended to reform the world on American terms. He casually told one early visitor "that the Russians would soon be put in their places; and that the United States would then take the lead in running the world in the way that the world ought to be run." Then, on April 23, 1945, he told the Cabinet "that he felt our agreements with the Soviet Union so far had been a one-way street and that he could not continue; it was now or never. He intended to go on with the plans for [the] San Francisco [Conference] and if the Russians did not wish to join us they could go to hell." Senator Vandenberg, soon to become (along with John Foster Dulles) the Republican leader of that bipartisan approach to the Soviet Union, caught the spirit—and reflected the absurd exaggeration—of the outlook of his diary entry of the following day: "FDR's appeasement of Russia is over."

As one insider remarked, "the strong view prevailed" from the very beginning, though it did not take on the form and tone of a great crusade against the Soviet Union and international communism until the end of 1946. Thus, for example, additional lend-lease allocations and shipments to Russia were canceled in May 1945. Truman later referred to it as "my greatest mistake," and claimed that, given a second chance, he would have handled it differently. Nevertheless, all lend-lease to the Soviets was closed off promptly once the Japanese surrendered. It is also clear that, on a comparative basis, Russia was treated far less considerately than England and France during the process of termination. In those respects, therefore, the action was repeated.*

But in the first instance, and as Truman later explained, the authority to act had been sought by Leo Crowley, the Foreign Economic Administrator, who proceeded to interpret it very broadly and to use it very vigorously. Truman's oblique comment that the whole affair was "clearly a case of policy-making on the part of Crowley and Grew" implies an explanation that can be substantiated by other evidence. Crowley's push for the power was supported by Admiral William D. Leahy, Assistant Secretary of State Joseph Grew, and Harriman. All those men wanted to use American economic power to coerce the Soviets on policy issues. This is established beyond any question in a Grew memorandum of his phone conversation with Crowley on May 12, 1945, as they were working to obtain a grant of authority from Truman. The document makes it absolutely clear that Crowley and Grew had Russia in the very forefront of their minds as they pressured the President. For his own part, Crowley refused to consider the Russian request for a loan as coming under the lend-lease law, even though he did negotiate such an arrangement involving $9 million with France. Crowley's general outlook was revealed when congressmen questioned him about loans in general. "If you did not like the government," he was asked, "you would not have to make them a loan at all?" "That is right," Crowley replied. "If you create good governments in foreign countries, automatically you will have better markets for ourselves."

Whatever further details may ultimately be added to the

* This reconstruction of the affair is based in the main upon the following sources: *Memoirs by Harry S Truman. Volume One. The Year of Decisions* (New York: Doubleday and Co., 1955); William D. Leahy, Manuscript Diaries, 1941–1945, State Historical Society of the State of Wisconsin, Madison; *Foreign Relations. The Conference at Malta and Yalta* (Washington: Government Printing Office, 1958); *Extension of the Lend Lease Act. Hearings Before the Committee on Foreign Affairs. House of Representatives.* 79th Cong., 1st Sess.; *Export-Import Bank of 1945. Hearings Before the Committee on Banking and Currency. House of Representatives.* 79th Cong., 1st Sess.; *Export-Import Bank. Hearings Before the Senate Committee on Banking and Currency.* 79th Cong., 1st Sess.; and materials from the Manuscript Papers of Henry L. Stimson and Joseph Grew, Harvard University Library.

story of the termination, there is no doubt that the action seriously antagonized the Russians. Stalin interpreted it as a move to put pressure on him to accept American policies, and bluntly called it "disturbing." Then, in a very revealing series of comments, Stalin told Harry Hopkins in May 1945 that such an approach would not produce Soviet acquiescence.*

Stalin first provided an insight into the differences within the Soviet hierarchy. The Russian leader said that "he would not attempt to use Soviet public opinion as a screen but would speak of the feeling that had been created in Soviet governmental circles as a result of recent moves on the part of the United States Government." "These circles felt a certain alarm," he explained, "in regard to the attitude of the United States Government. It was their impression that the American attitude towards the Soviet Union had perceptibly cooled once it became obvious that Germany was defeated, and that it was as though the Americans were saying that the Russians were no longer needed."

To be specific, Stalin continued, the way lend-lease had been canceled "had been unfortunate and even brutal . . . [and] had caused concern to the Soviet Government. If the refusal to continue lend-lease was designed as pressure on the Russians in order to soften them up, then it was a fundamental mistake."

In this episode involving lend-lease, as well as in additional examples reported by Truman, Byrnes, and other American leaders, Molotov emerges as the leader and spokesman of the militant wing of the Soviet hierarchy. It should be remembered in this connection that Molotov caught the full impact of Truman's vehement anti-Soviet attitude in a face-to-face meeting on April 23, 1945, that followed the crucial discussion of that policy among American leaders on the same day. There is considerable and convincing evidence, furthermore, that Molotov often took and persisted in a very tough line with the United States until Stalin intervened to modify and soften the Russian position. This interpretation of the disagreements

---

* The following quotations come from a stenographic record of the conversations reproduced in R. E. Sherwood, *Roosevelt and Hopkins. An Intimate History* (New York: Harper and Bros., 1948), 893–94.

among Soviet leaders is further and dramatically reinforced by events after Stalin's death, and particularly by the continued agitation by Molotov against Premier Nikita S. Khrushchev's efforts to establish the policy of co-existence and peaceful transition to socialism and communism.

In 1945, as in later situations of a similar nature, the position of Molotov and his supporters was unquestionably strengthened by the actions of the United States. Stalin was broadly justified in his fears expressed to Hopkins about the developing American attitude concerning the importance of Russia after the defeat of Germany. Truman and his advisors did not immediately and drastically downgrade Russian help. They continued to seek Soviet assistance against the Japanese until they learned that the atom bomb was a success. At that point, their attitude changed drastically: they clearly wanted to defeat Japan before the Russians entered the war. Even before that, however, at the end of April 1945, the change had begun to occur. Following the meeting of April 23, for example, the United States stopped pressing for air bases in Siberia, and ceased worrying about clearing the North Pacific shipping lanes to Russia's far eastern ports. In a similar way, American position papers prepared for the forthcoming meeting with Stalin at Potsdam revealed a determination to push for the open door in eastern Europe.

III. A NEW VISION OF OMNIPOTENCE AND A MISREADING OF HISTORY PROMPT THE UNITED STATES TO OVERPLAY ITS HAND

Following upon President Roosevelt's clear expression of a desire to retain "complete freedom of action," the United States Government under President Truman initiated and sustained a vigorous drive to undercut the Stalin-Churchill agreement of October 1944, concerning eastern Europe, and to replace it with the Open Door Policy. Churchill supported that determined effort to subvert the understanding which he himself had originally and voluntarily written out and pushed across the table to Stalin. Truman and Churchill undertook that course, moreover, in the full knowledge and open acknowledgment that Stalin had honored his part of the bargain in Greece.

This insistence upon applying the Open Door Policy to eastern Europe (and, of course, to Asia) was decided upon before anyone knew for sure that the atom bomb would work.* Along with the feeling among American policy-makers that Russia's war-caused weakness would enable them to secure major concessions from Moscow, that consideration must be kept constantly in mind when following the sequence of events after the defeat of Germany. The success of the bomb strengthened an existing attitude and a traditional strategy—it did not call forth a new approach.

Stimson's diary entry covering a conversation with Truman on June 6, 1945, indicates that American leaders were conscious of the relationship between the bomb and their general strategy at an early date. Truman "said that he had been thinking of that," Stimson noted, "and mentioned the same things that I was thinking of, namely the settlement of the Polish, Rumanian, Yugoslavian, and Manchurian problems." By the end of the month, in preparation for the Potsdam Conference, the American position concerning the countries of eastern Europe had become clear and firm. The United States planned "to insist on the reorganization of the present governments or the holding of free general elections." The broad objective was phrased in the classic terms of the Open Door Policy: "To permit American nationals to enter, move about freely and carry on commercial and government operations unmolested in the countries in question."

---

* This account of the Potsdam and London conferences, which took place between July and November 1945, is based upon a wide selection of primary and secondary materials. The reader without recourse to manuscript collections can find the main elements of the story, and most of the quotations used here, in these published volumes: J. F. Byrnes, *Speaking Frankly*, and *All In One Lifetime* (New York: Harper and Bros., 1947 and 1958); W. S. Churchill, *Triumph and Tragedy* (Boston: Houghton Mifflin, 1953); H. L. Stimson and M. Bundy, *On Active Service In Peace and War* (New York: Harper and Bros., 1948), *Memoirs of Harry S Truman*; and the most illuminating volumes, *Foreign Relations. The Conference of Berlin (The Potsdam Conference), 1945. Two Volumes* (Washington: Gvt. Printing Office, 1960), which also print revealing excerpts from Stimson's Diary.

The goal was "access, on equal terms, to such trade, raw materials and industry" as existed and developed. In the meantime, such access was sought "to modify existing arrangements." As part of that general effort, American officials planned to demand unrestricted movement for American newspapermen so that "the spotlight [can be] trained on these areas." And finally, the United States emphasized the specific objective of internationalizing the commercial waterways of the Danube River system with a Western majority on the board of control.

Similar stress was laid on guaranteeing the Open Door Policy in Asia. American leaders seem to have entertained a particularly vivid hope that the defeat of Japan would turn the clock back to 1903–1904; a maneuver that would enable the United States to step back on the mainland of Asia at the moment of its greatest success in Manchuria with the expectation that this time it would not be frustrated as before. The Russians posed the only danger to this idyllic picture. On the eve of the first general session at Potsdam, for example, Stimson seems to have set himself the role of special tutor to Truman and Byrnes on the importance of the Open Door Policy in the Far East. Even though the lessons had apparently been going on for some time, Stimson saw Truman again on July 14, 1945. "[I] went over [it] with him carefully," Stimson wrote in his diary, "again and again warning him to be absolutely sure that the Russians did not block off our trade."

Still concerned, Stimson wrote the President a special letter on July 16. Concentrating on "our clear and growing interests in the Orient," the Secretary all but hammered the words through the page in the course of his pounding on the crucial importance of the Open Door Policy. Ideally, of course, Russia should not have anything to say about handling Japan or the general problems of the Far East. At most, and only if it became absolutely necessary in the face of Soviet complaints, some kind of "token occupation" would be arranged.

Stimson next had a briefing session with Byrnes on July 17. The subject had not changed. Neither had the dedication of the tutor. "I impressed on him," Stimson recorded, "the importance of the Open Door Policy." A series of special reports made the same point. Harriman, for example, prepared one which placed—even in that context—a noticeable emphasis on "the development of commerce and trade of the United States." Perhaps his service as an artillery officer in World War I had inured him to such bombardments, for Truman seemed never to blink at the hammering on the same point. Obviously pleased, Stimson reported on July 18, 1945, that the President "was confident of sustaining the Open Door Policy."

Stalin arrived in Potsdam with a noticeably different set of priorities. He was still concerned about Russia's frontiers in Europe, about preventing Germany from trying it again in another 25 years, and about a major economic transfusion for the Soviet Union's battered economy. Apparently shrewd enough to realize that he had little chance to obtain a large loan from the United States, and in any event unable to plan on that basis in the summer of 1945, Stalin laid immediate and heavy emphasis on being treated as an equal and upon obtaining massive reparations from Germany and its former allies.

"This Council," Stalin remarked in explaining the Soviet view of the conference at its first general session, "will deal with reparations and will give an indication of the day when the Peace Conference should meet." The primary political issue, he continued, was that of dealing with Germany and its former allies. That was "high policy. The purpose of such a policy was to separate these countries from Germany as a great force." Referring often to the "many difficulties and sacrifices" brought upon Russia by those Axis partners, Stalin argued that the proper strategy was "to detach them once and for all from Germany." As for reparations, Russia would if necessary "compel" such deliveries.

The American response on reparations was crucial to the outcome of the Potsdam Conference, and also, very probably, to the whole course of subsequent events. "Reparations," Byrnes told Molotov on July 20, "do not seem to the United States to be an immediate problem." He then added that "the United States does not intend to make advances to any country in order that reparations may be paid by them." "We do not intend, as we did after the last war, to provide the money for the payment of reparations." The full significance of those remarks by Byrnes cannot be grasped without understanding both the background of each of them, and the interrelationship between them. It seems wise, therefore, to discuss them separately before putting them together.

First of all, and as revealed in Byrne's remark about loans, American policy-makers had misread the history of their experience with reparations after World War I. They concluded that American loans to Germany had simply ended up as reparations to England and France, who themselves had not repaid their debts to the United States. In the American view, therefore, the United States had been twice played the fool. The vigorous assertion by Byrnes reflected a determination not to fall into the same trap still another time.

That reaction was based on a seriously distorted interpretation of the World War I experience. It neglected, on the one hand, the creative role of American loans and the harmful effects of having actually collected money from England and France. On the other hand, and regardless of the estimate made of those and similar factors, the World War I situation blinded American leaders to the vastly different one that existed at the end of World War II. It was not so much that they had learned no lesson from history but rather that they had become almost obsessed with the wrong lesson.

The real point was that the capital for reconstruction at the end of World War II had to come from some place. Alternative sources were available. Either it could come from the United States under more relevant conditions and terms than had been arranged at the end of World War I, or it could come in the form of reparations taken by Russia—reparations which could be stopped only by recourse to another war. American policy-makers had used history to block their view of the present.

In order to avoid the second alternative, American leaders would obviously have had to negotiate a loan to Russia in conjunction with their discussion and settlement of other issues. But that approach was never even initiated, let alone put into sustained operation. The contradiction involved can be explained, however, by reference to the atom bomb. *Byrnes knew, when he told Molotov on July 20 that reparations were not "an immediate problem," that the atom bomb was a success.* The first news reached Potsdam on July 18. And as Stimson noted in his diary, Truman and other American leaders were "highly delighted" and "very greatly reinforced." It seems very likely, therefore, that the information on the bomb (even though the first dispatches were not complete accounts) served to convince the United States that it could hold the line on reparations and bargain from a position of formidable power.

But this reaction actually served, in a deeply ironic way, to close both the intellectual and the psychological jaws of the trap that American policy-makers had set for themselves. For in fact it left the United States with no moderate, flexible policy. It hardened both the feeling that the Russians would have to come to terms and the reading of history to the point that no loans should be granted if they would end up as reparations. That attitude left the United States with no choice but to acquiesce or use the bomb if the Russians refused to give way and accept American conditions for economic aid.

The extent to which this analysis explains American policy can be seen by the response to further news about the bomb test. Truman had already indicated, in a private conference with Churchill, that he was very favorably inclined toward the old Roosevelt idea of an Anglo-American entente. He was also aware of the understanding between Churchill and Roosevelt of September 18, 1944, concerning the bomb: "The suggestion that the world should be informed . . . with a view to an international agreement regarding its control and use," the two had agreed, "is not accepted."

Churchill seems to have insinuated in his masterful way that the secret might be kept from Stalin. This was by no means a novel idea. It had, after all, been kept from him up to that point. And Stimson records that he and others were very "doubtful" about sharing the news of the test bomb. However it evolved, and Truman appears to have refused to consider saying nothing to the Russians, the final compromise was to tell Stalin in a brief, casual way that the United States had developed a new weapon. Much has been made of the fact that Stalin already knew about the bomb through espionage. That is of course true, but he probably learned more of direct importance in observing how the news of the successful test firing affected the attitude and manner of Truman and Byrnes at the next session of the Potsdam Conference.

Stimson reports that Truman was "immensely pleased" and "tremendously pepped up by it." The President "said it gave him an entirely new feeling of confidence." This change is apparent even in reading the third-person stenographic account of the meeting with Stalin on July 21, 1945. One of the first questions to arise concerned the governments in eastern Europe, and this is the official account.

> PRESIDENT TRUMAN: The American Government was unable to recognize the governments of the other satellite countries [besides Italy]. When these countries were established on a proper basis, the United States would recognize them and not before. The President stated that the meeting would proceed and that this question ˜would be passed over.

After he returned to England, Churchill told the House of Commons that "we possessed powers which were irresistible." His comments to Stimson at the time, in Potsdam, are perhaps even more revealing. "He [Truman] stood up to the Russians in a most emphatic and decisive manner, telling them as to certain demands that they absolutely could not have and that the United States was entirely against them. . . . He told the Russians just where they got off and generally bossed the whole meeting."

Truman bossed the meeting but he did not change American policy on reparations. That oversight served to subvert the power of the bomb. An astute American observer warned on the next day, July 22, that the Russian position on reparations should not be discounted. It was backed by "intense popular feeling and fresh experience." But the old bloc against loans, when combined with the new vision of omnipotence, led the United States into a dead end. In order to avoid financing Russian reparations through loans to Germany, Italy, or other former Axis partners, and with the myopic confidence induced by the news of the bomb, Byrnes proposed to Molotov on July 23 that "each country tak[e] reparations from its own zone."

Now the fascinating thing is that the Russians fought that proposal for one whole week—from July 23 to July 31—before Stalin finally agreed to it. Even then, he remarked very sharply that it was "the opposite of liberal." *

---

* Italics added to the material quoted, as well as to my words.

Those two sentences have been set apart, and even further emphasized, for two reasons. First: the Byrnes offer to Molotov of July 23 clearly meant that the Russians would have a free hand in their zone of Germany and throughout eastern Europe. The freedom to control economics implied—demanded—political control. Assistant Secretary of State Clayton understood this point and commented on it with great perception in a memorandum of August 16, 1945, after the offer had been accepted by the Soviets. Although he was formally denying the point he was raising, the tone of his remarks needs no comment. "There appears to be," he noted ruefully, "an unfortunate tendency to interpret the reparations operating agreement as an indication of complete abandonment of four power treatment of Germany. This is not stated in the texts and should not be accepted as a necessary conclusion. . . ." But whether accepted or not, that was the meaning of the final arrangement.

To argue that the Russians did not understand the implications of the Byrnes offer of July 23 even though Clayton did is to argue that they were fools. To argue that they did understand it and still acted as they did is to argue that they played Byrnes and Truman and Stimson along for one entire week as a matter of private amusement. Those positions can be held and defended as viable explanations of Russian behavior. But the evidence indicates that the Russians very deeply wanted a firm commitment on reparations in the form of heavy industrial equipment from the restored production of the Ruhr Valley more than they wanted anything else. Such reparations would not only provide crucial help at home, but the agreement providing for them would be based on an Allied control of German industry that would in turn limit Germany's ability to start another war. Clayton himself, certainly as conservative and hard-headed an operator as the United States had produced, concluded in a memorandum of July 27, 1945, that this was the correct analysis. Molotov's behavior between July 23 and July 31 further supports that interpretation.

Molotov connected the issues of reparations and German war potential very simply: "The question of reparations was even more urgent because unless this was settled there could be no progress on economic matters" involving the future strength of German industry. Hence the Soviets wanted "clear replies to the questions." Byrnes gave them one by suddenly remarking that the United States now considered the Yalta figure of $10 billions for Russia to be "impractical." Molotov then shot back that the Soviets were "entitled to a clear answer" on what figure the United States did find acceptable. Failing to obtain one, Molotov then raised—very directly and without any frills—the central implication of the proposal that Byrnes had offered on July 23.

> MR. MOLOTOV: My understanding, Secretary Byrnes, is that you have in mind the proposal that each country should take reparations from its own zone. If we fail to reach an agreement the result will be the same. . . .
> THE SECRETARY [BYRNES]: Yes. . . .
> MR. MOLOTOV: said would not the Secretary's suggestion mean that each country would have a free hand in their own zone and would act entirely independently of the others?
> THE SECRETARY [BYRNES]: said that was true in substance. . . .

In spite of those candid and revealing remarks by Byrnes, the Soviet Union nevertheless continued its efforts to reach an agreement involving all of Germany. Molotov was still "anxious" about the issue on June 29 and 30. He wanted "a fixed sum or quantity agreed upon," including materials from the Ruhr, because the Soviets feared "they would be left with very little equipment as reparations in spite of the fact that the Germans had destroyed Soviet industries. They needed agricultural machinery and [goods] to rehabilitate their railroads." They also wanted to settle what Stalin had on the first day of the conference referred to as the issue of "high policy"—preventing Germany from attacking Russia in another 25 years.

Finally, in the face of continued American refusal to discuss the issues in that related way, Stalin accepted the Byrnes proposal of July 23, 1945. He then extended it in a way that clearly foreshadowed the division of Europe. The specific issue involved the assignment of German assets in other European countries, but the discussion immediately picked up overtones of a far broader nature.

PREMIER STALIN: . . . with regard to shares and foreign investments, perhaps the demarcation lines between the Soviet and Western zones of occupation should be taken as the dividing lines and everything west of that line would go to the Allies and everything east of that line to the Russians.

THE PRESIDENT [TRUMAN] inquired if he meant a line running from the Baltic to the Adriatic.

PREMIER STALIN replied in the affirmative. . . .

[BRITISH FOREIGN SECRETARY] BEVIN said he agreed and asked if Greece would belong to Britain. . . .

PREMIER STALIN suggested that the Allies take Yugoslavia and Austria would be divided into zones. . . .

MR. BYRNES said he thought it was important to have a meeting of minds. Mr. Bevin's question was whether the Russians' claim was limited to the zone occupied by the Russian Army. To that he understood Mr. Stalin to say 'yes.' If that were so he was prepared to agree.

PREMIER STALIN replied in the affirmative. . . .

THE PRESIDENT [TRUMAN] said that he agreed with the Soviet proposal.

The American decision to give the Russians a free hand on reparations throughout eastern Europe can in the end be explained only in one of three ways. The first would be to assert that the United States knowingly handed eastern Europe over to the Soviet Union. This is absurd on the face of it. It is also belied by Truman's actions during the conference, and by his blunt public remarks after the meeting was over. The eastern European countries, he announced on August 9, 1945, were "not to be spheres of influence of any one power." The Open Door Policy was thereby reaffirmed. A second explanation would be based on the idea that the United States made the reparations deal without understanding its political implications. But that interpretation is undercut by the analyses prepared by Clayton and other American officials who did see those possibilities.

The third explanation is supported by direct and indirect evidence. It is, simply, that the United States—confident in its vast economic and military superiority over Russia—made the reparations agreement to avoid any indirect financing of Soviet recovery. American leaders were certain that the bomb, and Russia's great recovery needs, provided them with the leverage to re-establish the Open Door, and pro-Western governments, in eastern Europe.

This vision of omnipotence was apparent in Truman's remarks of August 11, 1945. "We must constitute ourselves," he explained, "trustees of this new force to prevent its misuse." As for the possibility that the Soviets would construct their own bomb, Byrnes recalled that "no one seemed too alarmed at the prospect." But perhaps the best evidence of the American attitude came in connection with the use of the bomb against Japan. Byrnes later remarked that American leaders had eastern Europe as well as Asia in mind when they reached the decision to use the weapon as soon as possible.

That recollection is borne out by the evidence of the time. The decision to bomb Japan as quickly as possible was made during the Potsdam Conference, and at the very time of the toughest discussions about eastern Europe. In a very candid meeting on July 23, 1945, Truman, General George C. Marshall, Stimson and others generally agreed that the Russians were no longer needed in the war against Japan. They also talked very directly of using the bomb before the Russians could enter that conflict. Actually, however, that was not a new approach. Stimson had recommended as early as July 2, 1945, that the bomb should be dropped at a time when "the Russian attack, if actual, must not have progressed too far." And once it had proved out in the test, Truman was "intensely pleased" with the chance of using it before the Russians even entered the war.

This sense of urgency about using the bomb makes it possible to advance beyond the question of whether the United States dropped the bomb to end the war against Japan, or whether it did so in order to check the Russians. The evidence provided by the government archives and private American leaders converges on one explanation: The United States dropped the bomb to end the war against Japan *and thereby stop the Russians in Asia, and to give them sober pause in eastern Europe.*

Once it was known to work, the atomic offensive against Japan could have been delayed as much as a month or six weeks—if all that had been at stake was the saving of American lives which might be lost in the invasion of Kyushu that was projected for the fall. By that time, for example, the United States would have had a small arsenal of the weapons, so that it would have made little difference if the first drop during a demonstration had misfired, or otherwise failed. As for the saving of lives, they would still have been spared by using the weapon in September. But the bomb had to be used quickly, and if necessary repeatedly, if the war was to be ended before the Russians honored their promise to attack within three months after Germany was defeated.

Secretary of State Byrnes offered this very explanation of the dropping of the bomb—and with equal directness. Indeed, he did so twice. He was asked in 1960, on the fifteenth anniversary of the bomb, whether there was "any urgency to end the war in the Pacific before the Russians became too deeply involved?" "There certainly was on my part," Byrnes replied. "We wanted to get through with the Japanese phase of the war before the Russians came in." * Even earlier, in 1958, Byrnes revealed how the United States encouraged Chiang Kai-shek to drag out his negotiations with Stalin over their arrangements in Manchuria.* Referring to an American dispatch to Chiang of July 23, 1945, Byrnes explained the meaning and importance of a particular sentence. "The second sentence was to encourage the Chinese to continue negotiations after the adjournment of the Potsdam Conference. . . . If Stalin and Chiang were still negotiating, it might delay Soviet entrance and the Japanese might surrender. The President was in accord with that view."

American leaders were becoming so enthusiastic and confident over the power of the bomb that Secretary of War Stimson undertook a very courageous and searching review of the existing attitude. Even before Roosevelt died, Stimson was somewhat disturbed over the way various members of the government were reacting to the progress reports on the weapon. True enough, he felt that the bomb should be used against

* J. F. Byrnes, "We Were Anxious to Get the War Over," *U.S. News and World Report* (August 15, 1960). See also the remarks of Leo Szilard in the same issue for further evidence on the point.
* J. F. Byrnes, *All in One Lifetime*, 291–99; Truman's Memoirs, 315–19, 423–25; and *Foreign Relations. The Conference at Potsdam, Volume II*, 276.

Japan, and kept from the Russians until safeguards had been established; but he also fretted that the attitude of the majority of American leaders would lead neither to peace nor prosperity. During the next five months, Stimson grew progressively more convinced that American policy concerning the bomb was leading into another armament race, and perhaps even to a horrible war with Russia. On the eve of the Potsdam Conference, for example, he cautioned Truman that war would become inevitable if the United States took the position that all differences with the Soviet Union were irreconcilable. The Secretary's increasing concern was very probably caused by the interaction of four factors: the strong line taken by Truman and Byrnes at Potsdam; the awful destruction caused by the bombs at Hiroshima and Nagasaki; the clear evidence that Byrnes and the President had been encouraged by the bomb to maintain and even increase their pressure on Russia at the upcoming foreign ministers' conference scheduled for September in London; and his own searching thought and reflection on the problem, which was certainly provoked in part by his own great responsibility in recommending the use of the weapon.

The evidence suggests very strongly that Stimson devoted most of his intellectual and moral energy to the problem of the bomb from the end of the Potsdam Conference through the time when he received reports on the havoc caused in Japan. The result was a performance very similar, though of course more courageous and dramatic, to the one resulting from his experience in the late 1920s with armed intervention in Latin America. In that instance he concluded he had been wrong and set about to bring the Marines home from Nicaragua and to change the basic policy.

Stimson decided in the late summer of 1945 that the United States "was on the wrong path" in handling Russia in connection with the bomb. Having made that judgment, he undertook a brave, serious effort to persuade Truman and Byrnes to change their policy. He saw Byrnes on September 4, 1945, only to discover that the Secretary of State "was very much against any attempt to co-operate with Russia." Stimson noted that Byrnes was "full of his problems with the coming meeting of the foreign ministers and he looks to having the presence of the bomb in his pocket, so to speak, as a great weapon."

Byrnes left for London on September 5, unmoved by Stimson's arguments. Deeply concerned, and aware that his long government service was coming to an end, Stimson took his case directly to the President. His formal letter and memorandum to Truman dated September 11, 1945, made two crucial points. The first involved his conclusion, based on a careful evaluation and analysis of all the evidence he could obtain, that American efforts to force the pace, or determine the nature, of internal relaxation or liberalization in Russia by applying pressure "would be so resented that it would make the objective we have in view less probable." It followed from that estimate that the most vital issue of American foreign affairs concerned the way that the United States dealt with Russia in connection with the bomb. Stimson outlined the consequences of the then existing attitude and policy of Truman and Byrnes with a degree of accuracy that seems almost eerie in view of subsequent developments. "Unless the Soviets are voluntarily invited into the [nuclear] partnership upon a basis of co-operation and trust, we are going to maintain the Anglo-Saxon bloc over against the Soviet in the possession of this weapon. Such a condition will almost certainly stimulate feverish activity on the part of the Soviet toward the development of this bomb in what will in effect be a secret armament race of a rather desperate character. There is evidence to indicate that such activity may have already commenced."

He continued in a passage so important that he italicized it when making the document public in 1948. *"Those relations may be perhaps irretrievably embittered by the way in which we approach the solution of the bomb with Russia. For if we fail to approach them now and merely continue to negotiate with them, having this weapon rather ostentatiously on our hip, their suspicions and their distrust of our purposes and motives will increase."*

In conclusion, Stimson stressed the need for a direct approach *"to* Russia." '*I emphasize perhaps beyond all other considerations,"* he wrote, *"the importance of taking this action with Russia as . . . peculiarly the proposal of the United States. Action of any international group of nations, including many small nations who have not demonstrated their potential power or responsibility in this war would not, in my opinion, be taken seriously by the Soviets."*

Stimson's powerful argument may have caused Truman to pause, and perhaps momentarily to reconsider the militant anti-Soviet policy he had laid down on April 23, 1945. If so, the second thoughts were quickly set aside. Byrnes arrived in London determined to apply the strategy of the Open Door Policy in every area of the world. On the question of Axis colonies, for example, the American proposal was to place them under a trusteeship guaranteeing the open-door principle. And as far as Japan and the Asia settlement were concerned, the United States took its control so much for granted that Byrnes was truly "surprised" when the Russians asked for some share in making the decisions.

The clash in London was most fully revealed in connection with the two issues that had dogged American-Soviet relations ever since 1944. The first involved the continued efforts of the United States to abrogate the Churchill-Stalin bargain of October 1944, which had underwritten Soviet predominance in eastern Europe. The second was defined by the refusal of the United States to commit itself on the reparations issue, which for their part the Russians stressed above all else. On both questions, furthermore, Byrnes had in Labor Foreign Secretary Ernest Bevin an ally whose militance measured up to the standard set by Churchill.

As it happened in London, moreover, the United States used its power to attempt to displace an existing agreement. As Byrnes later explained to the Congress, the American objective was "the maintenance of the open door in the Balkans." Specifically, Byrnes was "disturbed" by, and sought to limit or stop completely, the Soviet moves to establish close economic partnerships with eastern European nations. In the positive sense, he sustained Truman's drive launched during the Potsdam meeting to internationalize the entire Danubian waterway system.

That move of Truman and Byrnes in 1945 was in many respects similar and comparable to Secretary of State Knox's attempt in 1909 to internationalize the Manchurian railway system. The analogy is illuminating. The American objective was the same in both cases: as the London *Times* described the postwar maneuver, to establish the conditions under which there would be "free entry into the Danube Valley and Eastern Europe for the goods and capital of the Western countries."

And just as it had been assumed in Manchuria, so it was also assumed in eastern Europe in 1945 that such free access for American economic power would in turn help to create and sustain political predominance. The American demand for free elections in eastern Europe was considered by American policy-makers as much a means to such economic and political ends as a philosophic or moral end in and of itself.*

But as Knox had failed in 1909, so did Byrnes fail in 1945. As they had done in 1909, the Russians in 1945 evaluated the American proposal for exactly what it was. And as in the earlier episode, so also in the later one—the Russians resisted. One exchange between Byrnes and Molotov summarized not only the impasse at London in 1945, but much of the diplomacy of the succeeding 15 years. The Secretary of State tried to persuade Molotov that the United States, despite its demands for the Open Door and its refusal to come to terms on reparations, was not trying to weaken or close out Soviet influence in eastern Europe. "I must tell you," Molotov replied, "I have my doubts as to this."

IV. THE DIPLOMACY OF THE VICIOUS CIRCLE

The New York *Times* correspondent Herbert L. Matthews wrote from London on September 25, 1945, what probably remains the best short analysis of what happened between the spring and the early fall of that fateful year. "France, Britain, and the United States, in seeking to absorb eastern Europe into a unified continental system, are aiming to weaken the Eastern bloc, and at the same time they are being forced with varying degrees of reluctance into the formation of that very Western block that Russia dreads.

"It is a vicious circle. . . ."

Soviet Russia's initial response to the American outlook and action was ambivalent. On the one hand, and by necessity, it launched a major program of reconstruction based on labor and capital extracted from a war-weary and weakened popu-

* On this point see: H. J. Morgenthau, "The End of an Illusion," *Commentary* (November 1961).

lace, supplemented where possible by reparations from Germany and eastern Europe. On the other hand, and as feared by former Secretary of State Hull as early as April 1945, it sought to "establish outposts, bases, and warm-water harbors in many areas and add buffer territory and otherwise prepare her own outward defenses just as fully as if the United Nations were not in existence." Yet in every case but one, that involving eastern Europe, Russia retreated from these efforts in the face of America's vigorous and militant opposition.

Thus Russia withdrew from Iran, leaving the Western powers in a predominant strategic and economic position. Thus it also retreated from its efforts to modify Western supremacy at the entrance (and exit) of the Black Sea. And thus it acquiesced, though under vigorous protest, when on May 3, 1946, the United States abruptly and unilaterally announced that it was terminating reparations to Russia from the Western zones of occupied Germany. These reparations, never large, had been arranged as part of interzone economic rehabilitation after the Potsdam Conference.

This decision, apparently taken on his own responsibility by General Lucius Clay, the Military Governor of the American zone, very probably had a crucial effect on the deteriorating relations between the United States and the Soviet Union.* It can of course be debated whether any single action can or should be called decisive when the general situation already exhibited such momentum toward sustained and embittered antagonism. On the other hand, Soviet officials stationed in Germany who later came to the West testified that it was "one of the pivotal events." And it provoked the first all-out postwar propaganda attack by the Russians upon American policy. Those considerations make it useful to examine the episode more fully.

It is essential first of all to realize the issue was economic. Given that, the importance and the impact of the action can best be understood by placing it in its general and specific context. At the beginning of the year, on January 5, 1946, Truman had declared that World War III was inevitable un-

---

* W. H. McNeill, in his excellent volume, *America, Britain, and Russia. Their Co-operation and Conflict, 1941–46* (London: Oxford University Press, 1953), was perhaps the first to sense the importance of Clay's action.

less Russia was "faced with an iron fist and strong language." By the end of January, Byrnes had discontinued "the practice of having private meetings with the Russians," even though "they were always eager to do so." Then, on March 5, Truman applauded from the platform as Churchill delivered his extremely violent and unrestrained anti-Soviet "Iron Curtain" speech at Fulton, Missouri.

Stalin promptly and bluntly called Churchill's performance "a dangerous act." He went on to speak of it as "something in the nature of an ultimatum: 'Accept our rule voluntarily and then all will be well; otherwise war is inevitable'." A bit later, on April 4, 1946, Stalin told the American Ambassador to Russia that in his opinion the United States had "definitely aligned itself with Great Britain against the U.S.S.R."

Clay's action on reparations was intimately bound up with American conditions for a loan to Russia. American representatives persistently tied such aid to the question of the Open Door Policy in eastern Europe. Secretary of Commerce Wallace warned Truman on March 14, 1946, that such an approach was increasing the tension. He suggested that it would be more fruitful "to talk with them in an understanding way" about "their dire economic needs and of their disturbed sense of security." Contrary to the impression created by all the vicious attacks on Wallace, he was not proposing anything that could be called appeasement. He wanted a calm and less adamant approach to economic discussions as a means of persuading the Russians to modify "many of their assumptions and conclusions which stand in the way of peaceful world co-operation." Wallace wanted neither to demand nor to surrender, but only to bargain in a mature fashion. But quite in keeping with his support for Churchill, Truman reports that he "ignored this letter of Wallace's." Note that the President does not say merely that he considered but finally rejected Wallace's analysis and proposal. He "ignored" it. In that difference lies considerable insight into the state of the cold war as of March 1946.

By cutting off reparations so soon thereafter from the western, industrial zones of Germany, Clay in effect put real and positive, as well as verbal and negative, pressure on the Russians. The Soviets no doubt interpreted Clay's actions as proof of America's double standard of judgment. For at the very outset of the four-power occupation of Germany, long before the Russians took any such steps, the French had refused to be bound by any joint Allied decisions. They handled their zone as they pleased. To the Russians, at any rate, the conclusion was obvious. Not only could they not negotiate a loan, as the French had been able to do, but they were being punished in a very vital area for the kind of behavior that, when taken by the French, was tolerated by the United States.

Clay's action was also important as background for a subsequent and very significant move by the United States. His termination of reparations came less than six weeks before the United States offered its long-heralded plan to control and ultimately share the secrets of atomic energy. The point here is not only that Clay's clamp-down on reparations squeezed a very tender Russian nerve, and thereby increased the general tension; but that it was an economic nerve that was very quickly pinched again and even harder by the American proposal on nuclear energy.

The American approach to the atom appeared first as the so-called Acheson-Lilienthal Report of March 1946. During the next three months it was transformed, under the general direction of Bernard Baruch, from a general analysis and report into a proposal involving sanctions against violators. Then, on June 14, it was presented to the United Nations. The final policy proposal is usually considered to be proof positive of American statesmanship and generosity, and its rejection by the Russians as the final evidence of their intransigence. While that matched set of conclusions can be, and has been, advanced with great power and persuasion, it nevertheless seems worthwhile to review the essential elements of the episode.

The strongest part of the generally accepted favorable interpretation concerns the point that the United States offered the proposal even though it enjoyed a monopoly of nuclear power. It is usually implied, furthermore, that America did this without any prompting or pressure. Let there be no misunderstanding on two points. It was a positive move, and there is no reason to question either the sincerity or the good intentions of American leaders. In a similar way, it can be argued that it is unrealistic and even unfair to criticize the United States on the grounds that it should have done more—or should have done differently what it did. This may be, even probably is, true in the sense of being highly improbable.

But it *is* fair to point out at the very beginning of any evaluation of the American plan that such criticism is *not* unrealistic or unfair in the sense of being made outside the context and obligations of direct governmental responsibility. For Stimson made exactly such criticism in September 1945, while he was Secretary of War.

Stimson's memorandum to Truman offers or suggests three crucial insights into the general nature of the American attitude and policy. The first stems from his blunt warning that the United States would not secure its objectives if it merely continued to negotiate with Russia *"having this weapon rather ostentatiously on our hip,"* or if it did so in a way that involved *"many small nations who have not demonstrated their potential power or responsibility."* The American proposal on atomic energy ignored and violated both those danger signals. Secondly, the rapid development of a tough American policy in the summer and fall of 1945 that prompted Stimson's memorandum also provoked serious concern and fears on the part of the British. Prime Minister Clement Attlee told Truman that the question uppermost in his mind was a fundamental one: "Am I to plan for a peaceful or a warlike world?" Attlee's subsequent visit to Washington in November 1946, was clearly undertaken to influence Truman to take the former course in connection with atomic energy, and had some effect. This British pressure has to be credited in any assessment of American action. Finally, Stimson's memorandum bears directly, and in two ways, on the whole question of American disarmament at the end of the war. The official and widely accepted view is that the United States disarmed almost completely. This conclusion seems to have stemmed from three things: the extremist rhetoric and rather frantic behavior of Secretary of Defense James V. Forrestal who replaced Stimson (and similar assertions by assorted newspaper columnists and other pundits); the annual scare campaigns conducted by the Army, Navy, and Air Force in connection with their budget requests; and various formal and pseudohistorical accounts of the immediate postwar period prepared by the State Department, other government agencies, and associated intellectuals as part of cold-war propaganda.

But the striking thing is that neither Stimson nor Truman thought that the United States stood disarmed and defenseless before the Russian bear. Neither did Churchill. The Stimson letter to Truman of September 1945, is based on the assumption that the possession of the bomb and the capacity to deliver it gave the United States a clear military advantage: it meant having "this weapon rather ostentatiously on our hip." Churchill stated the same thing very simply in March 1946: the bomb kept the Russians under control. And Truman, on July 10, 1946, in a letter to Baruch about the American control plan, phrased it with perfect candor. "We should not under any circumstances throw away our gun until we are sure the rest of the world can't arm against us."

The fact is that the United States had not disarmed just because it had demobilized the mass army created to fight World War II. Nor did its leaders think it had disarmed. Men like Forrestal merely wanted more conventional weapons to exploit the basic advantage of nuclear supremacy. Granted their assumptions, it was an intelligent proposal, but it had nothing to do with a desperate need to provide a disarmed United States with the means of its survival. Indeed, Forrestal himself admitted during his own campaign—as in his diary entry for June 10, 1946—that "the Russians would not move this summer—in fact at any time."

Truman's remark about "our gun" brings into clear focus the first of three essential points concerning the Acheson-Lilienthal-Baruch plan for the atom. The American proposal not only failed to set any time for giving up the nuclear weapons monopoly held by the United States, but it never committed the United States to do so in any firm manner. "The plan," explained the joint committee, "does not require that the United States shall discontinue such manufacture [of the bomb] either upon the proposal of the plan or upon the inauguration of the international agency. At some stage in the development that is required." * But the United States never specified the conditions of that stage. Let the motivations of the United States be accepted as stated by its protagonists and defenders, that demand for an immediate *quid* from Russia without a clear commitment to supply the *quo* by America remains a gaping weakness in the plan.

* U.S. Congress: *Senate Report No. 1211* (19 April 1946).

This suggests very strongly that J. Robert Oppenheimer was being accurate and candid in his recounting of the proceedings of the Acheson-Lilienthal committee, of which he had been a member.† He makes the second principal point about the American proposal: it was conceived in the spirit of Truman's remarks in August and October 1945. "The prevalent view," he explained, "saw in the problems of atomic energy . . . an opportunity to cause a decisive change in the whole trend of Soviet policy." "There appears to be little doubt that we yearn for the notion of a trusteeship more or less as it was formulated by President Truman in his Navy Day Address of late 1945." At that time, on October 27, the President had invoked the "righteousness and justice" of American foreign policy, and had assured the public that he would refuse to participate in "any compromises with evil."

Finally, the American plan demanded even more of the Russians than that they trust the United States with a nuclear weapons monopoly for an indefinite period. It asked in the meantime that the international authority established to administer the program should be granted extensive control over the nuclear economic affairs, and by indirection all economic affairs, of the Soviet Union. This is clearly one of the points that Oppenheimer had in mind when he spoke of the committee's idea of changing Soviet policy.

This proposed international authority was to be one, according to Baruch, "to which should be entrusted all phases of the development and use of atomic energy, starting with raw materials and including: 1. Managerial control or ownership of all atomic energy activities potentially dangerous to world security. 2. Power to control, inspect and license all other atomic activities."

Baruch seems to have understood from the beginning what this meant as far as winning approval from the Russians. For this phase of the plan amounted to applying the traditional Open Door Policy to atomic energy, and backing it up with sanctions. If this seems at first glance to be an exaggerated or mistaken analysis, it appears that way only because of the matter of timing involved. Fundamentally, the plan proposed

† J. R. Oppenheimer, "The Control of Atomic Energy," *Foreign Affairs* (January 1948).

the same kind of internationalization of the atom that Secretary Knox advocated for the Manchurian railways in 1909, and that Truman demanded for the Danubian waterways in 1945.

The Baruch plan held out the prospect of an open door for the development and use of atomic energy. The only difference was that in this case the United States was going to retain the job of doorman for an indefinite period. It was as if the United States had enjoyed monopoly control of the Manchurian railroad system in 1909, and had proposed to admit other nations to participate in the venture on American terms and according to an American timetable. At some unspecified time, the United States would remove all restrictions on share purchasing—assuming that it would retain 51 per cent of the voting stock. In the meantime, the new but still American-controlled board of directors was to have the power to prevent the construction of competing lines either across Siberia or in China proper.

That analogy should also help in understanding why the Russians refused to agree to the Baruch plan. Baruch himself explained it on June 16, 1946, as well as—if not better than—the Soviet spokesmen did in their own speeches. Russia, he commented, "has no intention of permitting a situation whereby the national economy of the Soviet Union or particular branches of that economy would be placed under foreign control." That was fair and accurate enough, but then neither did the United States have any such intention. The result was precisely what Stimson had predicted: "A secret armament race of a rather desperate character."

Secretary of Commerce Wallace had become, by September 1946, so disturbed by the tone and tempo of this race that he spoke out even more forcefully than Stimson had done exactly a year earlier. He bluntly told Truman and the American public that it was time to stop using a double standard in dealing with the Soviet Union. "We should be prepared to judge [Russia's] requirements against the background of what we ourselves and the British have insisted upon as essential to our respective security. We should be prepared, even at the expense of risking epithets of appeasement, to agree to reasonable Russian guarantees of security." He also reiterated his suggestion of March 1946, to make "a new approach along economic and trade lines."

Truman did not agree with Wallace. Neither did Secretary Byrnes, then engaged in being firm with the Russians during negotiations in Paris. Neither did Truman's other advisors, or the top men in the Department of State. And neither did the Congress. Wallace was dismissed from the Cabinet on September 20, 1946. The Russians no doubt interpreted the firing of Wallace for what it was—a resounding reassertion of the tough policy. And as if to make sure they got the point, Byrnes, on October 16, 1946, cancelled an existing Export-Import Bank loan to Czechoslovakia.

Most commentators make a great deal of Andrei A. Zhdanov's rise to power in setting and enforcing the Soviet interpretations of intellectual and political questions. He did win this authority, and he advocated a very tough and even vulgar anti-Americanism derived from his argument that the world was divided into two hostile camps. But Zhdanov did not reach his position as commissar of the party line until the same period that Wallace was fired for challenging Truman. Figuratively speaking, Wallace and Zhdanov passed each other going in opposite directions aboard their elevators in the respective power systems during the last week in September 1946. And as the Varga debates of May 1947 indicated, Zhdanov cannot really be said to have fully consolidated his position for at least six months.

In this, as in so many other aspects of the cold war, the timing of apparently disparate, incidental, and unrelated events is crucial to an understanding of what was going on inside and between the two countries. In a similar way, it is a grave error to evaluate or interpret the diplomatic moves of 1945 and 1946 in an economic vacuum. This is true in three respects. First, a good many of them were specifically economic in character. Second, all of them were intimately bound up with Russia's concern to obtain either a loan from the United States or extensive reparations from Germany and its former allies in eastern Europe. And finally, the determination to apply the Open Door Policy to eastern Europe, which led directly to the policies of "total diplomacy" and "negotiation from strength" later made famous by Secretary of State Acheson, evolved concurrently with a deep concern over economic affairs in the United States.*

This fear had never really disappeared after the Recession of 1937–38. It was even present, though in its most subdued forms, during the concentrated drive in 1942–43 to win the war by out-producing the Axis. It regained all its former vigor, and power over the thinking of American leaders, beginning with the congressional hearings of 1943 on postwar planning and economic policy. By March 1946, the *New York Times* reported that "in all groups there is the gnawing fear that after several years of high prosperity, the United States may run into something even graver than the depression of the Thirties." The Employment Act of 1946, designed to relieve such anxiety, did not seem to reassure very many people.

Perhaps an explanation was the growing feeling that the welfare state approach of the New and Fair deals had not changed the essential characteristics, or power structure, of America's corporate political economy. By the end of 1946, in any event, even government spokesmen warned that the United States might "produce itself into a bust" if it did not obtain more foreign markets and overseas investment opportunities. Complementing that fear was the increasing concern over America's "staggering" consumption and waste of raw materials. Open-door expansion, it appeared, was the answer to all problems—the Russians, markets, and raw materials.

That traditional outlook was given further support by two events early in 1947. First, the President's Council of Economic Advisors expressed concern about the probability of a serious economic slump. Second, western Europe failed to recover from the war and take its place in the American scheme of things. Hence the problem was to coerce the Russians, help western Europe, and thereby establish the reality of an open-door system throughout the world. These two themes converged during the spring of 1947 in George F. Kennan's famous policy of containment and Dean Acheson's proposal for solving the "hard task of building a successfully functioning system" at home by reinvigorating America's expansion.

* Perhaps the best single essay on these points is T. Balogh, "The Political Economy of the Cold War," in *Fabian International Essays* (ed. by T. E. M. McKitterick and K. Younger: New York, Praeger, 1957).

These and other American leaders shared John Foster Dulles' view of February 1947, that "peace lies not in compromising but in invigorating our historic policies."

Among the many ironies of Kennan's policy of containment, perhaps the greatest is the fact that he had so internalized the assumptions and principles of the Open Door Policy that he thought he was proposing a radically different program. This indeed is the final act in the transformation of a utopia into an ideology. As Kennan himself later acknowledged, containment and liberation are "the two sides of the same coin"; and it was Kennan—not Dulles—who first stressed the traditional open-door faith in America's overwhelming economic power to force the Soviet Union along a path preferred by the United States. Even in 1957, when he felt "at liberty" to admit that containment had not prevented Russian economic development, Kennan reasserted the traditional objectives of the Open Door Policy in Europe.

Kennan's condemnation of earlier exponents of the Open Door Policy who moralized about foreign policy (and other nations) provided another striking paradox. For, as a fellow foreign-service officer noted, Kennan was "constantly making moral judgments about the behavior of states." Thus, for example, he judged the Soviet system "wrong, deeply wrong," and ruled by a "conspiracy within a conspiracy." His blanket denial that the Soviets had ever considered that they could work with the United States was another such moral judgment, as well as being an error of fact.

Kennan's later remark that one of his objectives in 1947 was to counter the tendency of Americans "to take a despairing and dramatic view of Soviet relations" indicates still another facet of the ideological nature of the thought of American leaders. For he described the Soviets as moving "inexorably along the prescribed path, like a persistent toy automobile wound up and headed in a given direction, stopping only when it meets with some unanswerable force." Hence it was absolutely necessary, he warned, to "confront the Russians with unalterable counterforce at every point where they show signs of encroaching" and to block the Soviet Union with "superior force" and with "unassailable barriers in its path." This language was not only dramatic and despairing, but it had a very great deal to do with the "overmilitarization of our thinking about the Cold War," about which Kennan complained ten years later.

The policy of containment was supplemented in 1947 by the Truman Administration's stress on the necessity of economic expansion. Aware of the warning made by government economists that "without a new aid program there would be a sharp drop in American exports," the President explained and stressed that problem very candidly *before* he enunciated the Truman Doctrine. In two speeches prior to that dramatic performance, the President asserted the need to "act and act decisively" to sustain the Open Door Policy. "The pattern of international trade which is most conducive to freedom of enterprise," he pointed out, "is one in which major decisions are made not by governments but by private buyers and sellers." On the assumption that America was "the giant of the economic world," Truman announced that "the choice is ours" to sustain and expand private enterprise.

Hence it is misleading to overemphasize the differences between the Truman Doctrine and the Marshall Plan. They were the two sides of the same coin of America's traditional program of open-door expansion. As the direct descendant of Winston Churchill's militantly anti-Russia "Iron Curtain" speech of March 1946, the Truman Doctrine blamed the Soviet Union for the troubles of the world and announced the determination of the United States to halt the spread of revolutionary radicalism. It was the ideological manifesto of American strategy, described by the head of *Time's* Washington bureau as a program to promote "trouble on the other side of the Iron Curtain." As Acheson revealed to the Congress, the American Government entered upon "no consultation and no inquiry" about the possibility of achieving the stated objectives either through negotiations with the Russians or within the framework of the United Nations. The approach proceeded from the assumption, openly avowed by Harriman in 1945, and by Truman in 1946, that the cold war was inevitable.

Considered in isolation, however, the Truman Doctrine provides a one-sided impression of American policy. Some of its crusading fervor seems clearly to have been the result of a conviction, most candidly expressed by Senator Vandenberg, that it would be necessary to "scare hell out of the American people." On the other hand, it contained no references to the economic difficulties that worried American leaders. It concentrated instead on the political dangers of communism.

For his part, however, Secretary of State George C. Marshall did not initially emphasize the Russian danger. In his speech at Harvard on June 5, 1947, he offered the aid program as an expression of America's warm humanitarianism. There can be no question but that it did represent America's generous urge to help the peoples of western Europe, and that it did play a vital role in the recovery of that region. Approached solely as a humanitarian gesture, however, the Marshall Plan raises several troubling questions. China and Latin America were excluded, for example, though their needs were certainly great from a humanitarian (or even a policy) point of view. Perhaps Marshall's own testimony before the Congress provides a broader understanding of the program.

Prior to Marshall's famous address at Harvard, moreover, the Congress and the Department of State had been preoccupied with the danger of another depression. Undersecretary of State for Economic Affairs Clayton redefined *the* problem as one of disposing of America's "great surplus." "The capitalistic system, whether internally or internationally," he explained in May 1947, "can only work by the continual creation of disequilibrium in comparative costs of production." Clayton was saying implicitly what Acheson had argued explicitly in 1944: the profitability of America's corporate system depended upon overseas economic expansion. Given this consensus among American leaders, it is not too surprising that Marshall took a similar approach before the Congress: "The paramount question before us, I think, can be stated in business terms." The consequences of failing to carry through on the plan, he explained, would be to confront America, "if not [with] a trade barrier, certainly with a great detriment to our ordinary business, or commerce and trade."

Marshall and other advocates of the program also spoke openly of the parallel between their policy and America's earlier westward expansion across the continent. Marshall presented the program in those traditional terms as the way to avoid the loss of democracy at home. Assuming that it offered the only solution to America's economic difficulties, the Secretary argued that the nation faced an either-or situation.

Unless the plan was adopted, he asserted, "the cumulative loss of foreign markets and sources of supply would unquestionably have a depressing influence on our domestic economy and would drive us to increased measures of government control." By thus defining America's expansion as the key to prosperity, Marshall defined foreign policy as the key to domestic problems and to the survival of democracy at home. The intellectual continuity of his thought with the frontier thesis and the policies of John Hay, Woodrow Wilson, Herbert Hoover, and Franklin D. Roosevelt was apparent.

Other Americans were even more explicit. Secretary of the Interior Julius A. Krug defended the plan as "essential to our own continued productivity and prosperity." Another enthusiastic supporter remarked that "it is as if we were building a TVA every Tuesday." Even in the most restrained temper of judgment, this might well be the biggest "as if" in American history; for whereas TVA qualified as one of what Alvin Hansen has described as "frontiers in our own backyard," the Marshall Plan was a concerted program to sustain and expand a frontier overseas.

The testimony of liberal and conservative leaders indicated that they viewed the frontier thesis as the answer to the theories and prophecies of Karl Marx. Chester Bowles, for example, warned specifically that it "was wholly possible that within the next ten years Karl Marx's judgment will have proved correct." Concretely, he thought the United States was "heading toward some sort of recession which can be eased by quick approval of the Marshall Plan." Nelson Rockefeller explained that "with the closing of our own frontier, there is hope that other frontiers still exist in the world." Spruille Braden also saw the program as a way to "repeat what had been done in the development of our own great west."

One of Truman's Cabinet members preferred to think of the whole operation as a "logical extension of the good-neighbor policy, that the Fair Deal for all cannot flourish in isolation." Another Cabinet official saw it as the "restoration of Europe as a paying market for United States goods." And such widely different men as William Henry Chamberlain and Marquis Childs pointed directly to the analysis and program advocated by Brooks Adams in 1900 as a wise guide for 1947. Writing in *The Wall Street Journal*, Chamberlain thought it was "high time to face the problem created by what Brooks Adams called 'America's vast and growing surplus.'" Childs republished Adams's recommendations for the deployment of "America's economic supremacy" in behalf of the open door, and pointedly remarked that Adams "would have . . . to alter scarcely anything to relate his views to the world of today." Perhaps Childs, along with others, was struck by Adams's praise for Britain's traditional policy of "containing" the Russians.

From the beginning, for that matter, many American leaders stressed the desirability and possibility of making the countries of eastern Europe "independent of Soviet control" and the importance of the "struggle for the preservation of Western civilization." Even a casual reading of the *Congressional Record* makes it clear that John Foster Dulles was a latter-day missionary for the doctrine of liberation. Coupled with this thought was a general acceptance of the idea of ending Soviet rule in Russia. Hardly any American leader failed to contribute his insights to the "cheerful discussion of how America ought, and ought not, to try to remake Russia." Some thought it might be necessary, and certainly magnanimous, to allow the Russians to retain some features of socialism. Others proposed a Heavenly City of the American Century. All agreed on the morality and the practicality of the objective.

This emphasis on open-door expansion and the assumption of the inevitable downfall of the Soviet Union again indicated that American leaders were not motivated by fear of a Russian military attack. When asked point blank, *even after the Russians had tested their first nuclear bombs and the Chinese communists had defeated Chiang Kai-shek*, whether or not "our position on foreign policy with respect to communism is not relative to Churchill's in 1940," Secretary Acheson replied in the negative. "I do not mean to infer at all that there is that desperate a situation. I said I was not discouraged and was not taking a pessimistic view at all." "The problem which confronts us," he explained, "can be stated very simply: To maintain the volume of American exports which the free world needs and which it is our national interest to supply as a necessary part of building a successfully functioning political and economic system, the free world must obtain the dollars to pay for these exports."

For their part, the Russians clearly interpreted the Marshall Plan as the over-all economic equivalent of Baruch's proposal on atomic energy. It was to them an American strategy for setting and maintaining conditions on economic development in eastern Europe and the Soviet Union. That estimate prompted them first to refuse to participate, and then to embark upon a series of actions which most Americans mistakenly think had already occurred. They initiated a program of general political repression in Rumania. They sharply curtailed freedom of the press in Bulgaria, Rumania, and eastern Germany. They shot the Peasant Party leader Patlov in Bulgaria. And within the year the Communist Party in Czechoslovakia seized a monopoly of political power.

These events typified the nature of the cold war as it continued on into the 1950s. In the United States, President Truman repeatedly blamed all the troubles of the world on the Soviet Union, and American leaders in and out of government "bombarded the American people with a 'hate the enemy' campaign rarely seen in our history; never, certainly, in peace time." This American propaganda barrage prompted analyses by two government figures that received little publicity. A congressional committee headed by Representative Forrest A. Harness concluded its long study of the problem with this estimate in 1947: "Government propaganda distorts facts with such authority that the person becomes prejudiced or biased in the direction which the Government propagandists wish to lead national thinking." Exactly ten years later, General Douglas MacArthur offered an even more biting commentary on the same pattern of distortion. "Our government has kept us in a perpetual state of fear—kept us in a continuous stampede of patriotic fervor—with the cry of a grave national emergency. . . . Yet, in retrospect, these disasters seem never to have happened, seem never to have been quite real." There is ample evidence that the policy-making elite misled and manipulated the American public.

Perhaps it was true that the community of American policymakers "fell in love with its Cold War plan." That was the considered conclusion of James P. Warburg, an eminent conservative student of foreign affairs. It was more likely, however, that the ideology of the Open Door Policy had come to be so firmly believed by American leaders that they never questioned either the freedom or the necessity of their program for America and the world.

Certainly the attitude of American leaders toward the underdeveloped societies of the world suggested that explanation. Kennan, for example, took an extreme position on China, discounting almost completely its immediate significance or its potential importance. Others defined the poorer areas in the traditional open-door manner, seeing them as markets for exports and as sources of raw materials. Even when they spoke of the need to help such regions—or provided such assistance —they did so from the point of view of developing them as part of America's corporate system. It was quite normal, given that conception of the world, for American leaders to consider such regions as dependent variables of the situation in western Europe. The problems and difficulties in the underdeveloped areas could be handled through their existing ties to European empire countries. Time after time, therefore, the United States endeavored to support the crumbling ruins of eighteenth- and nineteenth-century colonialism against the impact of nationalistic and radical onslaughts.

No American leader personified all aspects of the ideology of the Open Door Policy more dramatically than John Foster Dulles, who served as a major advisor to the Truman Administration before becoming Secretary of State under President Dwight David Eisenhower. In the 1920s, he supported the Hughes-Hoover policy of expansion based on a "community of ideals, interests, and purposes" with Germany and Japan, and specifically pushed American penetration of underdeveloped areas in line with his emphasis on the necessity of markets for surplus goods and capital. He followed the same policy throughout the 1930s. Arguing that it was necessary to accept changes in the world, and asserting the Christian way of compromise, he labored diligently as late as 1939 to work out a broad understanding with Nazi Germany and a militarized Japan.

Dulles continued to advocate and practice this approach after 1945. Understandably, he worked very well as an advisor and assistant to Secretary Acheson during the early years of the cold war. His definition of compromise did not include a fundamental rapprochement and accommodation with the Soviet Union, or the acceptance of fundamental changes in the underdeveloped regions. On the threshold of his lifelong ambition to be Secretary of State, Dulles provided in 1952 the definitive statement of the Open Door Policy. Synthesizing the moral imperialism of his missionary background with the necessity of economic expansion of his banking experience, Dulles announced that he would liberate the Russians and the Chinese from "atheistic international communism" and usher in the American Century.

Perhaps Dulles himself provided the most accurate insight into the final failure of the Open Door Policy. Against the background of constant and record-breaking travels all over the world, Dulles undertook yet another mission to Latin America. He was greeted by his official host with the pleasant and gracious remark that it was "good to have you here, Mr. Secretary." "You shouldn't feel that way," Dulles replied, "for I go only where there is trouble." And trouble indeed there was for America in its policy of the open door.

A bit later, when it appeared that negotiations with Russia could no longer be avoided, Dulles inadvertently laid bare the basic flaw of the open-door conception of the world. He worried about such a meeting with the Soviet Union, he explained, because it might tempt Americans to turn their attention and energies away from the cold war. But only a view of the world which defined freedom and necessity in terms of expansion could lead to that response. For a growing number of Americans were beginning to join millions of others throughout the world in a reassertion of the elementary fact that man was born to achieve and exercise his self-knowledge in more fruitful endeavors than a cold war which persistently threatened to erupt in nuclear horror. Dulles apparently failed to realize that he felt anxiety for the wrong reasons and was pursuing a policy that had now become a denial of the spirit of man.

Though not as extreme as Dulles in their reactions, most other American leaders were slow to grasp the real meaning of the revolutions throughout the world—their ability to destroy a cherished American illusion in Asia, to manage the transfer of power in Russia, to initiate and carry through a major conference of underdeveloped societies without American leadership, and even to defy the United States to use its nuclear weapons in retaliation.

CHAPTER SEVEN

Despite the fact that they were simple people, the Russians should not be regarded as fools, which was a mistake the West frequently made, nor were they blind and could quite well see what was going on before their eyes.

JOSEPH STALIN

Revolution is not a dinner party, nor a literary composition, nor a painting, nor a piece of pretty embroidery; it cannot be carried out "softly, gradually, carefully, considerately, respectfully, politely, plainly, and modestly."

Our primary duty is, not to add flowers to the embroidery, but to send coal to the snowbound.

MAO TSE-TUNG

I want no freedom based upon the assumptions of the British. Such a freedom simply means exchanging a set of white masters for a set of black masters. If I'm against British rule, then I'm against the rule of her stooges.

BLACK MAN NUMBER ONE, IN *White Man, Listen!*
BY RICHARD WRIGHT

All day and all night they talk to us about "sound and solid

THE IMPOTENCE
OF NUCLEAR SUPREMACY

development, sound and solid education." . . . I say to hell with John Stuart Mill and John Locke. Let's make our own philosophy, based upon our own needs.

BLACK MAN NUMBER TWO, IN *White Man, Listen!*
BY RICHARD WRIGHT

The North American business interests here were sending back to the United States, during the last ten years before 1959, one hundred million dollars a year more in profits than we were receiving. The little underdeveloped country was aiding the big industrialized country. . . .

FIDEL CASTRO

So long as the U.S. army of aggression still remains on our soil, our people will resolutely fight against it.

HO CHI MINH

It is not yesterday, a tradition, the past, which is the decisive, the determining force in a nation. Nations are made and go on living by having a program for the future.

JOSÉ ORTEGA Y GASSET

At the apex of its power, the United States found itself persistently thwarted in its efforts to inspire, lead, and reform the world. This supreme paradox of American history becomes comprehensible when viewed as a direct result of the nation's conception of itself and the world in terms of open-door expansion. For America's weakness in strength was the product of its ideological definition of the world. The United States not only misunderstood the revolutions in economics, politics, color, and anticolonial nationalism; it asserted that they were wrong or wrong-headed and that they should be opposed in favor of the emulation of the American example.

When this advice was not followed, the offenders were defined as conspirators in league with Russia. When it was followed, but failed to succeed, a variation of the same theme was offered in explanation. Inherently exasperating because of its less than satisfactory results, either in theory or practice, America's definition of the world led to even deeper frustration when it was confronted by the continued vitality of the revolutions. Having mocked America's nuclear supremacy, the revolutions sustained their development outside the ideology and the empire of the open door.

These results of America's conception of itself and the world can be seen and understood most clearly by reviewing its explanation of the Soviet Union and other specific revolutions, and by examining the inability of the theory and the practice of the Open Door Policy to promote either the balanced improvement of poor societies or the acceptance of America as the leader of the world. For the Soviet Union did not develop according to the pattern of Nazi Germany, and the people of the underdeveloped regions of the world blamed the American *system* of open-door political economy for their troubles as much as, if not more than, the United States itself.

Though from time to time other estimates were offered, George F. Kennan's 1946–1947 explanation of Soviet behavior established the framework and set the tone for all but a tiny corner of the American discussion of Russian action.* His analysis, and the more extreme interpretations derived from it,

---

* For a different view see, beyond the works cited in earlier chapters, G. A. Morgan, "Stalin on Revolution," *Foreign Affairs* (1949); J. Maynard, *Russia In Flux* (New York: The Macmillan Co., 1948).

concluded that continued outside pressure could and would accelerate an inevitable process of dissolution. The thesis held that Soviet behavior resulted primarily (if not exclusively) from the necessity of Marxian revolutionaries having to resort to force to maintain the domination of an alien and evil ideology over Russian traditions and history. It asserted that the prime mover of Soviet action was a drive to maintain centralized power in the face of fundamental and persistent hostility. The weakness of the analysis is that it is a single-factor thesis which forces and limits one, in the first rather than the last resort, to a simplistic psychological interpretation of Soviet conduct. Such an approach lends superficial validity to the analogy with Nazi Germany and to the argument that Soviet Russia corresponds in reality to the sociological abstraction known as a totalitarian society.

On the one hand, therefore, Kennan's analysis spawned a vast literature which treated Stalin as no more than a psychotic and, on the other, an equally large body of comment which argued that the only effective way to deal with the Soviet Union was to apply the lessons learned from the experience with Hitler. When tested against known facts, rather than accepted on the basis of a syllogism, these interpretations and recommendations did not lack all validity. Even by their own logic, however, they pointed to ultimate failure. For, by creating in fact a real, avowed, and all-encompassing outside threat, action based upon such analysis and analogy lent substance to what Kennan originally defined as a hallucination in the minds of Soviet leaders. Having argued that they had to create imaginary foreign dangers in order to stay in power at home, Kennan concluded with a policy recommendation to create a very serious (and from the Soviet point of view, mortal) outside challenge to their authority.

Both in abstract theory and in practical fact, however, pressure of this kind on Soviet leaders served only to make them tougher at home and abroad and to spur them to redouble their efforts to match the West. The final result might indeed be the collapse of the Soviet Union, but only in the context of general nuclear war. Chester Bowles, one of the early supporters of the containment policy, ultimately recognized the consequences of that approach. "The harder the Soviet Union is pressed," he concluded in April 1957, "the more vigorously her people will rally behind their leaders. If the Kremlin is forced to the wall it will almost certainly strike out with all its very formidable nuclear capacity."

Bowles could point to a great deal of evidence in support of his observation, including such items as the speed of Russia's industrial recovery and improvement after the war, its own program of economic aid to other countries, its ruthless countercontainment in Hungary and Czechoslovakia, and the Sputniks. But neither Bowles nor the handful of other men who grasped the same point made much impression on the majority of America's policy-making elite. By and large, those men stressed the urgency of maintaining unquestioned supremacy over Russia.

Startling as it may seem, in view of the constant emphasis on Soviet military power, the central fact confronting any past or present Russian leader is the imbalance of the economic and political development of the nation. Czarist and Soviet history is the record of a continuous, all-pervading struggle to reach a minimum level of material well-being, let alone relative prosperity or actual wealth. Russia is big, but much of its territory is inhospitable to organized society, and other large sections are at best but marginally productive agriculturally and industrially. As in the case of China, the situation may be modified in the future, but at any given moment in the past or present, no Russian leader has been able to escape the gnawing knowledge of poverty and the insistent pressure to produce enough to save enough to produce more. This essential fact of Russian history provides great insight, for example, into Lenin's argument that revolution could come first in the weakest link of world capitalism, or into the long tradition of Gargantuan developmental plans—from Peter the Great to Joseph Stalin.

At the same time it has been necessary for Russia to maintain strong armed forces, urgently needed to defend open borders against the continuous threat and recurring actuality of foreign attack. This military investment always drained off a sizable segment of the savings which might have eased Russia's economic and cultural needs. The same circumstance gave the Russians little opportunity to practice and develop the skills of self-government. It is not possible to maintain seriously that Russia has no valid historical or present fears of foreign attack. And to employ a metaphor from modern technology, the present actuality of nuclear bases around its borders feeds back into, and reinforces, the historical memory of the Tatars, of Napoleon, of World War I, of the intervention against the revolution itself, and of Japanese and German military attacks from the 1930s on through World War II.

Perhaps a game of "as if" would help Americans grasp the depth, scope, and meaning of this aspect of Russian experience. Imagine, for example, that instead of conquering the Indians and establishing them on reservations, Americans had been forced to concede a stalemate and accept several ethnically and culturally defined Indian states; that instead of defeating the Mexicans once and for all, America had suffered periodic and destructive counterinvasions (and a similar relationship with Canada); and that instead of having bases on the military frontiers of the Soviet Union, America was confronted by Soviet jets manned by Russian pilots deployed throughout the Western Hemisphere. The purpose of exercising one's historical imagination in this manner is not to work up a brief for Soviet action in the cold war, but rather to grasp and understand the basic economic, political, and social consequences of living in that kind of world for generation after generation.

There are still other important facets of the interrelationship between Russia's economic and political imbalance. For in order to close the gaps in the poverty-conditioned cycle of production, saving, and reinvestment for greater production, Russia constantly found it necessary to resort to borrowing abroad; yet that additional indebtedness further weakened the country's international security and so again increased the burdens upon its citizens at home. This not only *seems* like a vicious circle; it *was* a vicious circle. And, as with all human experiences, the memory lingers on to influence the future.

This interplay of fundamental economic and political hardship was reinforced by related problems. The necessity of sustaining a major effort to overcome poverty led to early, and ultimately successful, attempts to bind many diverse ethnic and cultural units into one centralized administrative organization. This not only intensified the existing pattern of localized coercion, but it demanded even greater investments of economic and political savings (money *and* brains) to sustain the central organization in the face of sporadic struggles by various subsumed units to break away on their own or attempts by outsiders to crack off one or more of the frontier provinces.

Moscow's problem has never been the loss of just a Poland or a Hungary. To czar and commissar alike, the real issue has concerned the Baltic States, White Russia, and the Ukraine. And the same may be said of the Asian provinces, whether the illustrations are drawn from the czar's difficulties with the Maritime Province, from the Soviet's troubles with the Far Eastern Republic and the new industrial centers east of the Urals, or from the abortive Japanese intrusions of 1918 to 1922 and 1937 to 1939.

It is within the setting of poverty and centralized power that the Russians have grappled with the eternal dilemma of freedom and power. Their search for freedom took several paradoxical forms. Localized, nongovernmental, collective action was at once a means of fighting back against the system itself and of holding on to a sense of humanity and community in the face of such institutionalized power. At the same time, however, the czar, though he stood at the apex of the entire apparatus of coercion, also became the symbol of whatever immediate rewards and ultimate hopes survived the grinding, enervating, never-ending effort to conquer poverty and win respite from foreign enemies. The czar's ambivalent role was strengthened by his position as the spokesman of the religious answer to the quest for freedom in the presence of poverty and power.

In addition, however, the search for meaning and freedom also turned inward in a deep and almost desperate reconnaissance of the secular self for valid insights and viable values. It is here, perhaps, that a paradoxical similarity with America is most noticeable. For the loss of identity in prosperity led Americans toward Freud, while the similar Russian experience in the context of poverty produced Dostoevski, Kuprin, and Gogol, to name but the obvious examples. The self-knighted robber baron and the anarchist-terrorist are not, after all, so far apart. Neither is the Calvinist with a calling very far removed from the secular revolutionary driven by a historical necessity. And both experiences produce their respective sense of mission toward the world. The Russian's search for self and emphasis on community in the face of poverty and power led him to conclude that man's essential goodness emerges as a phoenix from the pyre of degradation. Hence in his mind he is best qualified to lead a similar reconstruction of all humanity. For his part, the American concluded that his achievement of prosperity and military might elected him as trustee for the same responsibility.

This review of Russian experience suggests that the sources of Russian conduct are the drives to conquer poverty and achieve basic security in the world of nation states. From these efforts developed, on the one hand, the practices and traditions of centralized power to force saving, allocate investment, and maintain security, and, on the other, the heightened domestic tension between collective action and individual identity and the ambivalence of a foreign policy at once militantly and suspiciously defensive yet characterized by a missionary and benevolent desire to help other men save themselves.

By pouring this historical experience into a Marxian mold, the Bolshevik Revolution emphasized and highlighted these Russian traditions, offered solutions for the problems of poverty and security, and suggested a resolution between the individual and his society. Given the success of the revolution, the problem becomes one of assessing the direction and extent of the impact of a Marxian revolution on the sources of czarist Russian conduct.

At the outset, clearly enough, the Bolshevik Revolution accentuated the basic problems of poverty and security. It disrupted even more completely the war-caused derangement of the productive process while at the same time encouraging England, France, Japan, and the United States to join Germany in direct military intervention. Both individually and collectively, these powers sought far more than the mere overthrow of the revolution. Each of them, although in conflict with the others, had plans for the New Russia, plans which saw the country as an area for them to develop, each according to its own particular genius. Hence the central experiences of czarist Russia continued uninterrupted.

At the same time, moreover, the Marxian conception of the

world jibed in essentials, if not in language and detail, with the prerevolutionary Russian outlook. It is all too easy, perhaps because it also is so convenient, to forget that the revolution attracted and inspired a great portion of Russian society from the end of the civil wars to the mid-1930s. It did so again, though to a lesser extent in all probability, at the end of World War II. But such forgetfulness is dangerous as well as self-indulgent, for it leads to a misunderstanding of present Soviet society.

Here it is essential to realize that Marx was four men, so to speak, and that each of them contributed a share to the final product known as Marxism. The four aspects of Marx may be described as follows: (1) Marx the romantic, who emphasized the freedom and the primacy of the individual; (2) Marx the brilliant, tough-minded economist, who not only analyzed capitalism but, even more importantly in the Russian context, also suggested the basis for policies that would effect the rapid and continuing production of wealth; (3) Marx the politician, who outlined strategy and tactics for a successful revolution; and (4) Marx the prophet, who came back from his researches in the British Museum and from his battles against poverty and carbuncles with the vision of a society in which men would live in comradely community blessed with plenty.

Each of these four aspects of Marxism paralleled and reinforced its counterpart in the existing Russian tradition. The romantic Marx offered inspiration to those Russians who emphasized the individual's central place in society. Yet he also made sense to those who stressed collective discipline and action for great domestic and international achievements. Most significantly of all, he offered theoretical and practical suggestions for solving the central problems of poverty and security. And his vision of a planned socialist society infused the Russian tradition of centralized, coercive power with meaning and promise. Whether by national accomplishment or by international revolution (or both), therefore, Marxism seemed to promise an end to Russia's perpetual struggle against poverty and insecurity, a resolution of the conflict between freedom and power, and a place in the vanguard of humanity.

For these reasons, it is dangerously misleading to stress the monolithic character and heritage of Marxism. It is in fact a most pluralistic tradition which can be described as totalitarian only by falsely isolating and dramatizing one of its particular facets. The most dangerous consequence of misconstruing Marxism in that fashion lies in the resulting conclusion that all Russian communists also follow such a single, narrow interpretation. For as the record reveals, the Russian communists have always been divided into the four groups which correspond to the four aspects of Marx. They also draw upon, identify with, and emphasize the corresponding Russian traditions. Thus Trotsky's commitment to international salvation through revolution. Thus Gorky's stubborn individualism. Thus Bukharin's emphasis on decentralization and consumer goods. Thus Stalin's single-minded concern with centralized, coercive power for saving and investment and for security. Thus Lenin's truly epic struggle to keep the Russo-Marxian traditions in dynamic balance so that the means would neither subvert the ends nor forestall forward movement toward the desired goal. And thus, too, the less poetic efforts of later Soviet leaders to redress the Stalinist imbalance and sustain the evolution.

By their very success in establishing an industrial system, moreover, Soviet leaders reinforced and extended such competing forces within Russian society. Based as it is upon an extensive and complex division of function, responsibility, and labor, an industrial society develops within it different attitudes and ideas about what can be done, what should be done, and how to do whatever is finally agreed upon. There is, to be sure, a strong pressure exerted by the system itself in the direction of a general consensus on certain basic issues; but even on these questions there are various ideas as, for example, about how to increase the production and distribution of consumer goods while it is still necessary to increase capital investment. Just such questions were raised in Russia after the battle of Stalingrad (as they had been earlier), and they are still being debated at the present time.

Differences of function also lead to competing ideas and programs. At the broadest level, there is a conflict between those who produce and those who plan and direct the process itself. Similar disagreements arise within each of those groups. Such conflicts can never be resolved once and for all, and each time they are compromised the result is a change in the previous state of affairs. Given its traditions, it is very unlikely that such conflicts in the Soviet Union would ever lead to the development of Western-style democracy. But it is quite probable, given an era of peace, that they would promote the progressive loosening up of Russian political and intellectual life.

To miss or deny the existence of these competing traditions and groups, or to interpret the struggle between them as mere vulgar wrestling for power, is to substitute a creaky mechanistic model for the reality. And that, in turn, pyramids the probability that a policy based upon such an interpretation will fail of its objective. For the problems are poverty and security, not power per se. Stalin was not Hitler. Neither is the present leadership simply a conspiracy. Policy based on such analogies, however sophisticated their logic and presentation, is doomed to failure. The reason is clear. The composite Russo-Marxian tradition has arrived at the beginning of the end of poverty and has proved its ability to match foreign technology and military power.

It would be a serious error, therefore, to misinterpret the present resurgence of the individualistic, local, and utopian traditions of Russo-Marxism as evidence of impending Soviet collapse. Their vigor is a sign of maturity and positive evolution, not an indication of decay and death. With such maturity comes an unshakable determination on the part of the people who brought it about to maintain the hard-won identity and to continue the process toward ever greater accomplishments. Such men will fight before they surrender. And they are armed with hydrogen bombs.

But America need not abandon all efforts to influence events because they cannot be controlled perfectly, or because one theory seems, in practice, to produce unfortunate results. By adopting the more modest aim of encouraging the positive forces, and undertaking the effort in line with a more subtle analysis, it would seem realistic to hope for a moderate degree of success. The key problems faced by Russia are those of poverty and security and the basic traditions are those of centralized power resisted by localized collective action and individual integrity. Hence the most fruitful approach would seem to be action designed to relieve the problems of poverty and security on the grounds that achievement in these areas would encourage the decline of centralized power—both by choice and necessity.

The effort of the United States to force more drastic changes in Russian affairs not only failed of direct success, but it subverted other phases of American policy. For unlike America, the rest of the world was not primarily interested in waging a cold war with Russia. Perhaps the majority, often criticized by American leaders as "neutralists," tried to ignore both Russia and America as much as they could in order to concentrate on developing their own societies in their own way. A sizable number of people, for example, were positively attracted to Marxism. Either they judged it relevant to their own problems, or they were impressed—despite the brutal and undemocratic aspects of the Bolshevik Revolution and the era of Stalin's terrorism—with the tremendous advances made by Russia in less than their own lifetime. Others throughout the world supported the Soviet Union, or at least did not side actively with the United States, as a check on the unrestrained expansion of America. And another group sought or accepted aid from Russia either because it was offered on good terms or because it was not available from other sources.

For their part, many Chinese were attracted by the Bolshevik Revolution and the accomplishments of the Soviet Union. Lenin's theory of imperialism provided them with an explanation of their weaknesses and backwardness which tallied with their own experience and flattered their capabilities: Western powers were to blame. The revolution in Russia renewed their confidence that the Chinese, too, could change their unhappy lot. This reaction was sustained by the help and advice provided by the Soviets, who did not seem to care very much about the color of a man's skin or his cultural and social eccentricities. It was further strengthened by the fact that the Chinese, like Sun Yat-sen and Mao Tse-tung, who turned to Marxism and the Soviet Union were more inspiring and appeared to be more effective leaders than the men like Chiang Kai-shek who followed Western—even American—ideas and advice. The Chinese communists not only had a program, they were willing and able to make it work.

These were the fundamental explanations of why the communists triumphed in China. They also were the basic reasons behind communist strength elsewhere in the world. The communists were harsh and ruthless, and during their agitation and revolutionary action against the old order they neglected or ignored many, if not most, of the more liberal traditions of Marxism as well as many of the more humane values of their own cultures. But as indicated by developments after 1952 in Russia, and by the events of 1956 in Poland and Hungary, communists began to return to, and reassert and act upon, those values.

It is crucially important to realize, and actually to integrate into one's thinking, that those changes were initiated by communists. For this means not only that they were demonstrating the pluralism of the Marxian tradition, and exhibiting great personal dedication and courage in doing so, but also that the communists were the most likely source of such improvements in communist countries short of war.* There is inherent in the American policy of containment, after all, a deep callousness and indifference to the very Western values that it asserts and proclaims as absolutes. Its logic rests on the proposition that the act of forcing hardships on people through outside pressure will ultimately provoke them to action in behalf of those Western values. It may or may not do so, and the evidence is that the communists hold those values as part of their own Marxism (which is, after all, a philosophical heresy born in the West), but in any event the means employed by the policy of containment can hardly be defended as being appropriate to the ends.

These considerations are also pragmatically significant because they are understood, and their implications appreciated, by men and women throughout the rest of the world. They realized that the communists worked hard, and progressively more effectively, to improve conditions in their own societies.

---

* One of the best, short introductory surveys of the Polish and Hungarian revolutions is in Fleming, *The Cold War*, Vol. II. In addition to the materials he cites for further reading, no serious student can afford to neglect R. L. Garthoff, "The Tragedy of Hungary," *Problems of Communism* (Jan.–Feb., 1957). It is in many, many ways the single most important study.

To many, many people, who had known little beyond survival, cruelty, and ridicule, this dedication and the increasing successes of the communists seemed more important than their failure to operate according to the highest Western standards of democracy. Indeed, the character and consequences of two centuries of Western predominance and leadership had little impressed those men and women.

Most American leaders failed to grasp the importance of these considerations. Instead, they continued to think and act according to their traditional assumption and belief that Marxism, the Soviet Union, and communists in general were wholly evil and incapable of maturing into something more humane. In one form or another, therefore, Americans operated on the premise that most of the difficulties in the world were caused by the Soviet Union or agents, fellow travelers, and dupes of the Kremlin. This initial attitude was reinforced and given emotional intensity by the victories of the communists in China, southeast Asia, and other parts of the world. Perhaps it was understandable, under these conditions, that Americans overlooked or neglected the important role of other ideas and developments in producing such changes. They also failed to consider whether or not their own Open Door Policy had anything to do with the difficulties they encountered. It was difficult to decide which of these consequences was the most damaging, for they interacted upon each other in a way that compounded the crisis.

By concentrating on the communists so much, for example, Americans underestimated or discounted such realities as world poverty, the fantastic increase in world population, Western society's persistent discrimination against other races and ideas, and the continued vigor of man's ancient urge toward self-definition and creative activity. In a similar way, America's stress on the communists amounted to a rather arrogant slap in the face to the millions of people who were not communists but who wanted and acted for a better life in the here-and-now. Giving the communists most of the credit for such agitation had two unfortunate results. First, it encouraged others to accept that misrepresentation of the facts. Second, it implicitly said that nobody else was capable of doing that kind of work. This result of the American attitude was only heightened when the United States went on to assert—or imply—that at least nobody else but Americans could do it.

Many people throughout the world might have forgotten that insult, or at least not let it rankle in their hearts and minds, if American diplomacy actually produced such highly favorable results. The trouble was that it did not. After fifty years of the Open Door Policy, twenty-five years of the Good Neighbor Policy, and more than a decade of a crusade against communism, conditions throughout most of the free world did not verify either the assumptions, arguments, or promises of the policy of the open door.*

It is vital at this point to differentiate between the motives, the specific results, and the over-all consequences of American policy. The question is whether or not America has in fact translated its ideas and ideals into programs and policies which serve to realize its objectives. America's motives are not evil. Neither are all of its actions wrong or fruitless. Indeed, many of them have literally made the difference between life and death to hundreds of thousands of people throughout the world. The Marshall Plan in Europe and other assistance to less developed nations clearly benefited many human beings in those areas.

The difficulty arises from the general view of America and the world in which these specific policies are formulated and put into operation. America has defined assistance to other people far too much in terms of anti-Russian and counter-revolutionary objectives, and as a necessity for the continued functioning of the existing system in the United States. In the realm of ethics and politics this point of view has led America to define legitimate behavior almost solely as anti-Russian conduct. In practical affairs the result has been to define as acceptable only those means which do not seriously challenge the American economic empire of raw materials and markets.

But neither of these definitions is valid. A nation can act in many ways and yet become neither a satellite nor a dupe of the

* Illuminating are J. Levinson and J. de Onis, *The Alliance That Lost Its Way* (Chicago: Quadrangle Books, 1970); D. Green, *The Containment of Latin America* (Chicago: Quadrangle Books, 1971); and E. Friedman and M. Selden (Eds.), *America's Asia* (New York: Vintage Books, 1971).

Soviet Union. Nor would the United States stagnate or go bankrupt, for example, if Venezuela nationalized its oil reserves and then sold petroleum to American corporations in an open market. The tragedy of American diplomacy is not that it is evil, but that it denies and subverts American ideas and ideals. The result is a most realistic failure, as well as an ideological and a moral one; for in being unable to make the American system function satisfactorily without recourse to open-door expansion (and by no means perfectly, even then), American diplomacy suffers by comparison with its own claims and ideals, as well as with other approaches.

In this vital respect, at any rate, America's high standard of living is only part of the story. On the one hand, the United States relies, in its own thinking as well as in practice, upon a great imbalance in its economic relations with poorer and weaker countries to achieve that standard of living. Even then, moreover, there are great extremes of wealth and power within American society.* And, on the other hand, American foreign policy has not produced either the kind or the degree of military security that policy-makers have asserted to be desirable and necessary. The basic question raised by these failures is not, as so often is asserted, one of how to implement the existing policy more efficiently, but is instead whether or not the policy can—because of its inherent nature—ever produce its avowed objectives. The evidence indicates that it cannot.

The Open Door Policy has failed because, while it has built an American empire, it has not initiated and sustained the balanced and equitable development of the areas into which America expanded. When it increased the gross national product of an area, for example, it did so under conditions which immediately removed much of the added wealth of the United States. Little of what remained was invested in the development of the political economy, let alone distributed among the population. Finally, the basic change that occurred over the period of American penetration was an intensification of the tensions and conflicts within the other society. What the Catholic Archbishop of Caracas said of Venezuela on May 1,

---

* On this point, begin with M. Harrington, *The Other America. Poverty in the United States* (New York: Macmillan Co., 1962); and H. P. Miller, *Rich Man, Poor Man* (New York: Crowell, 1971).

1947, applied elsewhere with but minor modifications: "Nobody will dare affirm that wealth is distributed in a manner that reaches all the Venezuelans, since an immense mass of our people are living in conditions that cannot be qualified as human." Even in countries where conditions were better, the Open Door Policy did not produce balanced and dynamic economic development. Neither did it contribute much to investing life in such areas with a sense of purpose. American action and intervention failed to initiate and sustain either kind of improvement on a broad and fundamental basis.*

Soviet and other communist leaders could be criticized far more severely. Their revolutions extracted a terrible price in terror and hardship. Many of their subsequent policies—Russian intervention in Hungary and Czechoslovakia, for example —warrant harsh judgments. But to concentrate exclusively on these points is to neglect others of considerable importance. Most significant of all, perhaps, is the fact that life in the communist countries has improved. The picture is one of brutality *and* betterment, not simply one or the other. And it was that consideration which exercised a persuasive influence on men and women who had known little improvement under the American Open Door Policy or the imperialism of America's

* The literature on the nature and problems of underdeveloped countries, and their relations with the advanced nations, is so vast that any short list of recommended reading is almost certain to seem either biased or superficial. The following provide an introduction to the subject, and all have bibliographies. R. E. Asher, *Grants, Loans, and Local Currencies. Their Role in Foreign Aid* (Washington: Brookings Institution, 1961); P. A. Baran, "On the Political Economy of Backwardness," *Manchester School Economic and Social Studies* (1952); B. F. Hoselitz, *Sociological Aspects of Economic Growth* (Glencoe: The Free Press, 1960); B. F. Hoselitz, et. al., *Theories of Economic Growth* (Glencoe: The Free Press, 1960); J. L. Levin, *The Export Economies. Their Pattern of Development in Historical Perspective* (Cambridge: Harvard University Press, 1960); W. A. Lewis, *The Theory of Economic Growth* (London: Allen and Unwin, 1955); D. A. Morse, *Report of the Director-General, Seventh Conference of American States Members of the International Labour Office. Economic Growth and Social Policy* (Geneva: International Labour Office, 1961: in many ways the best single introduction for the general reader); and two volumes by G. Myrdal: *An International Economy* (New York: Harper & Bros., 1956), and *Rich Lands and Poor* (New York: Harper & Bros., 1957). My *Contours of American History* is an effort to reconstruct the way that early American leaders dealt with these problems.

European allies. Pain and poverty they knew, but never as the price of progress in their own lifetime. Hence the communists, as examples and leaders of such development, gained stature and influence throughout much of the world.

A great deal has been said in America about the "revolution of rising expectations" under way in the underdeveloped areas of the world, but it has often been overlooked that such a revolution is powered by a willingness to pay a high price for the realization of those aspirations. By appearing to be a nation which refused to let other peoples pay a price they thought justified, as well as a nation which did not extend itself to reduce that cost, the United States did more than merely forfeit leadership to radical (or even conservative) nationalists. Such action made it seem as though the United States was the major obstacle to the revolution of rising expectations. To many throughout the world, therefore, the Open Door Policy appeared to confront them with a door closed to their own progress.

As a result, America found itself impaled on the traditional dilemma of empire. It could resort to war or it could disengage, safeguarding its strategic position by formulating a new outlook which accepted the reality of a world in revolution and devising new policies calculated to assist those revolutions to move immediately and visibly toward their goal of a better human life.

CHAPTER EIGHT

Were half the power, that fills the world with terror,
Were half the wealth, bestowed on camps and courts,
Given to redeem the human mind from error,
There were no need of arsenals or forts.

HENRY WADSWORTH LONGFELLOW,
"THE ARSENAL AT SPRINGFIELD"

It is not the primacy of economic motives in historical explan-
ation that constitutes the decisive difference between Marxism
and bourgeois thought, but the point of view of totality.

Whatever the subject of debate, the dialectical method is con-
cerned always with the same problem: knowledge of the his-
torical process in its entirety. This means that 'ideological' and
'economic' problems lose their mutual exclusiveness and merge
into one another.

GEORG LUKÁCS, *History and*
Class Consciousness

THE TERRIFYING
MOMENTUM TOWARD DISASTER

Though a few Americans began at the end of the 1940s to recognize and face the necessity of undertaking a thorough reevaluation of existing foreign policy, the decision makers either discounted the need for such action or were carried along by the momentum of the long commitment to expansion and to reforming the world in the image of the United States. The elite remained limited by the outlook that had crystallized during the 1890s: organize the world according to the principles of the Open Door Policy and reap the benefits of benevolent and liberal empire. The scene recalled Alice in Looking-Glass Land running as fast as she could to stay under the same tree—with the vital difference that she was not succeeding in her effort.

The power of that belief prompted the Truman Administration to intervene, immediately and without public debate, when the North Koreans launched their effort on June 25, 1950, to unify and revolutionize that divided country. The first major statement of policy suggested that the leaders of the United States were willing, at least for the time, to content themselves with reestablishing the South Korean Government that had been created under American direction. As he so often did, Secretary of State Acheson sounded reassuring: the military intervention had been undertaken "solely for the purpose of restoring the Republic of Korea to its status prior to the invasion from the north."

Within three months, however, that apparent moderation had been proved illusory. President Truman approved military operations north of the 38th parallel on September 11, 1950, very probably on the assumption that General MacArthur's landing at Inchon, scheduled for September 15, would be a success. Orders transmitting the President's decision to MacArthur were sent on the day of the invasion. When his brilliant and difficult operation at Inchon did turn the tables on the North Koreans, MacArthur advised Secretary of Defense Marshall of his proposed directive to troops crossing the parallel. Marshall promptly ordered the General to withhold the document. "We desire that you proceed with your operations without any further explanation or announcement and let action determine the matter. Our government desires to avoid having to make an issue of the 38th parallel until we have accomplished our mission."

The mission, as Acheson later revealed, was to realize one of the earliest, turn-of-the-century objectives in the strategy of the Open Door Policy. Put simply, it was to free Korea of Russian as well as Japanese influence. World War II had accomplished the latter; the Korean conflict would finish the job. Under American leadership, the United Nations General Assembly on October 7, 1950, approved a resolution authorizing "all appropriate steps to be taken to ensure conditions of stability throughout Korea."

Secretary Acheson was later asked the key question during a congressional investigation:

SENATOR HARRY CAIN: What, may I ask, were our United States forces doing on the shores of the Yalu River last November if it was not in an attempt to crush the aggressor and to unify Korea by force?

ACHESON: General MacArthur's military mission was to pursue them and round them up . . . and, as I said many times, we had the highest hopes that when you did that the whole of Korea would be united. . . .

SENATOR CAIN: If, sir, the Red Chinese had not entered the war, and our allied forces would have rounded up all those who were a party to the aggression in Korea, we would then have unified Korea by force; would we not?

ACHESON: Well, force would have been used to round up those people who were putting on the aggression . . . unifying . . . it would be through elections, and that sort of thing.

Force would have played a part. . . .

The attitude toward China that was an inherent part of the open door outlook served to subvert the effort to apply the strategy of the Open Door Policy to Korea. The United States assumed that it could unify Korea by force because it did not believe, despite many indications to the contrary, that the Chinese Communists would intervene. The assumption of over-weening power, developed at the grass roots as well as within the elite during the 1880s and 1890s, remained a vital—and dangerous—part of the American outlook in the 1950s.

Secretary of State Dulles believed in that power and sought to use it (directly and as a threat) to consolidate (and hope-fully extend) the American imperium when he took office in January 1953. But if he is evaluated only on the basis of his militant and overblown rhetoric, Dulles is easily misunder-stood. Realizing that the policy of containment trapped the United States in a defensive posture, he wanted to seize the initiative and thereby sustain the momentum of American ex-pansion. That might have been possible, at least for a time, if Dulles had been willing to concentrate on developing and im-proving the global system that had been created since the 1890s. Former President Herbert Hoover had pointedly ad-vised the country in December 1950 to follow that course, even pulling back to the Western Hemisphere: otherwise, he warned, the nation would become overextended and risk the loss of freedom at home as well as disaster abroad.

That approach was too defeatist for Dulles (and other mem-bers of the elite), and he launched his diplomacy with ex-treme proposals for subverting the communist governments of Eastern Europe, with bold talk about threatening nuclear war in order to guarantee peace, and with supreme confidence in the ultimate breakdown of the communist systems in Russia and China. Several factors forced him to retreat on all fronts.

One was the quiet but effective opposition that had developed in the United States against the interminable intervention in Korea. This resistance has often been overlooked or discounted for two reasons: it was not the dramatic and increasingly fundamental kind of dissent later generated by the intervention in Vietnam, and it was successful in the short run without changing the essentials of traditional policy. It encouraged and enabled President Dwight David Eisenhower to end the war, and it served as a persistent warning to Dulles that he needed to move carefully lest he revive such antagonism.

Even though the war in Korea was ended, and the critics stilled on that issue, Dulles sustained the hard core of opposition (and periodically roused a larger coalition) with his fervent rhetoric about striding to the brink of nuclear war in order to convince the communists and other revolutionaries that he meant what he said. However much they opposed what they had been told was communism, most Americans drew back, for moral as well as pragmatic reasons, from a policy that stressed a willingness to risk catastrophe. Such a policy seemed pointless in dealing with revolutions in small countries and, though it might be effective for a time against China (then a weak nation trying to reorganize itself to achieve its own objectives), few people wanted to live with an ultimatum to Russia. In an ironic sense, therefore, Dulles was limited by the effectiveness of the long campaign by policy-makers to picture the Soviets as totally evil. Such people could not be trusted, after all, not to use whatever nuclear weapons they possessed when they were challenged—even though they knew they would lose.

A third element that limited Dulles involved the continuing upsurge of revolutionary activity around the world. For, if nuclear weapons were irrelevant and immoral in dealing with such events, traditional military intervention required an expansion of conventional forces. And that was politically risky for Republicans who held the White House for the first time in two decades, as well as expensive for conservatives who opposed large budget deficits. Thus Dulles had to rely very largely on economic weapons and political pressure. When those proved to be of limited effectiveness, and the revolutions consolidated their power without causing dire consequences for the United States, Dulles and his supporters lost some creditibility.

Finally, and despite various appearances to the contrary, Dulles was limited by Eisenhower's deep reluctance to involve the United States in another major military intervention. The President was not a true cold war crusader. And while he accepted a large role for America in the world, he was not an active expansionist. He had an honest, informed concern for the security of the United States. He understood that the economy required a routine relationship with the world marketplace. And he was advised—pushed—by men who advocated the orthodox answers to those problems. That factor is the key to Eisenhower as President. He had assembled and trained, as Supreme Commander in the European Theater during World War II, one of the best staffs in the history of warfare. He mistakenly assumed that the civilian elite around him was intellectually as tough (and as self-critical), and on that basis he delegated too much authority.

Even so, had he been as weak as his critics charge, then the United States would have been at war several times during the eight years he served as President. But Eisenhower did control Dulles and he did slow the momentum of the interventionist "total diplomacy" evolved by Truman and Acheson. His personal traits and philosophical outlook combined to give the United States a breathing space from the burdens of empire. World War II clearly deepened his inherent aversion to organized violence, and his approach stressed the idea of giving Americans a chance to explore their individual capacities, and to act together to improve their society.

Eisenhower emerges as a true conservative in the traditional sense. He clearly seems to have sensed that the era of American expansion was coming to an end. He did not fully comprehend what that meant, let alone understand how to act as a civilian general on the insight he enjoyed, but he was not mesmerized by the vision of a New Frontier and he did not think that the United States could determine the future of the world. His greatest mistake in foreign policy was the failure to follow through on his decision against a massive air strike to help the French avoid defeat in Vietnam.

After the French were driven from the country, the peace

settlement negotiated in Geneva included a provision to hold
national elections in Vietnam in 1956. But the anticommunist
clique that took control of the southern part of the country
(below the 17th parallel) became increasingly reluctant to
honor that commitment. The United States chose not to intervene to force those men to comply with the Geneva Agreement. That decision could be—and can be—defended by citing
the principle of self-determination: men make their decisions
and take the consequences. And American policy-makers had
given the South Vietnamese elite an opportunity to make such
a choice. If Eisenhower had at that point ceased all active and
covert involvement in Vietnam, he would have avoided any
responsibility for the terror that followed. Indeed, he might
have rejuvenated the principle of self-determination. He did
not. He acquiesced as Dulles maneuvered to transform the
South Vietnamese elite into a viable government. And so continued the tailspin to disaster.

Yet even then a new President could have said *no*. But John
Fitzgerald Kennedy was only a powerful man. He was not
strong in the sense of breaking with tradition. More exactly,
he was a Lochinvar who revived orthodoxy. Kennedy charted
his course by the star of empire and generated the confidence
that sustained the interventionist momentum. No one will ever
know if he was gaining a stronger grasp on reality at the time
he was murdered. If so, he would have needed much time and
great will to counter the imperial thrust he generated between
his inauguration and his assassination. For the aura of terror
about American foreign policy, created both by what was
done and by how it was done, increased sharply under Kennedy. He was an elitist with great elan and charming style.
Both characteristics served to mask the continuing and serious
reduction of general—or even limited—involvement in decision making during his reign.

First came his campaign for election, in which he stressed
the need to cast aside Eisenhower's caution and move boldly to
realize America's destiny as the leader of the world (first by
terminating the threat posed by Castro's Cuba, and next by
overcoming what he publicly claimed to be a dangerous Russian lead in intercontinental missiles—though he knew that
such a crisis did not exist). Then he approved the disgraceful

(and absurd) invasion of Cuba. And out of that action came a fateful escalation of the terror.

The Kennedy Administration concluded that the failure to topple Castro did not represent a basic flaw in outlook and policy, but was only the result of mistakes in execution. Kennedy further insisted that he had to recover the lost ground to avoid losing power at home, and concluded that he could not retain office through a candid discussion of the need to recognize and adapt to the waning of the American empire. Most of what followed between 1963 and 1971 emerged from that frightening logic.

Thus, for example, the decision to invest great resources (and many lives) in counter-revolutionary warfare. That represented a full acceptance of Winston Churchill's recommendation for dealing with the Bolshevik Revolution in 1917: strangle the baby at birth. And that outlook led directly to crossing the threshold of major intervention in Vietnam. It may even be, for that matter, that the Kennedy logic and actions played a significant role in causing the Cuban missile crisis. No one outside Russia knows the full story of that grisly moment of terror for all mankind. Perhaps we shall never have the true account. But the standard explanations leave one with the uneasiness that demands further inquiry.

One analysis stresses the causal importance of Kennedy's weak performance during his encounter with Soviet leader Nikita S. Khrushchev in Vienna. That is supposed to have led Khrushchev to believe that he could overawe the young president in confrontations involving Berlin and Cuba. A more sophisticated interpretation adds that Khrushchev was in serious political trouble at home because of the failure of his domestic programs, and argues that both motives combined to produce the Cuban missile ploy.

Those explanations arise from the skepticism that is ingrained in all serious historians and political scientists: they strongly discount contemporary public explanations of any action offered by the protagonists. There is sound reason for such caution. But there are exceptions. For in times of *great* crisis, men often speak much of the truth about their thoughts and actions. If we approach the Cuban missile crisis with that awareness, we find a different history that must be considered.

It begins with Cuba and Russia deeply concerned about another invasion, or a projected assassination of top Cuban leaders. It truly makes no difference whether or not such actions were planned (though there is evidence that they were being considered). One acts on what one believes to be reality. Russian leaders are also fearful, knowing full well their inferior nuclear striking power, that Kennedy means to act upon his imperial rhetoric because he knows the United States enjoys a great relative advantage.

The Soviets conclude, in those circumstances, that placing missiles in Cuba offers a way of dealing with both problems. (And, if the strategy succeeds, of gaining resources for domestic programs.) Such weapons say two things: "No second invasion," and "You must realize that we will use what weapons we have, even if we know we will lose, so give up the idea of a nuclear *Pax Americana* for the world." There are many clues, indirect as well as overt, in the published documents and other comments by the protagonists, that support such an analysis of the confrontation. And so, of course, does the openness of the Russian operation in creating the missile sites in Cuba. Perhaps therein lies the key to the mystery—it seems probable that the Russians miscalculated because they assumed that the Kennedy Administration would respond rationally by opening negotiations about *all* such foreign bases for nuclear weapons.

And there was, it appears, a moment when that was considered the proper course of action. Secretary of Defense Robert S. McNamara (and perhaps others) pointed out, almost by reflex, that *Russian missiles in Cuba did not in any way change the existing balance of nuclear power*. There was a corner, a turning point in history, which was recognized, and yet no one moved the wheel. Instead, Kennedy alerted all Americans to the possibility of being ready to die for their traditional policies. And therein lies the final question about the crisis. No one has offered a convincing explanation of why the Kennedy Administration declined, at least initially, to deal with the issue in private discussions.

And therein more terror. For the elite refused, even after the event, to explain and accept responsibility for its actions. One thinks of the anchor on a battleship: once it begins running free into the sea there is nothing one can do until it hits bottom. And so it was with American foreign policy. From "victory" over Khrushchev—he *did* withdraw the missiles— Kennedy moved on to take a crucial step in Vietnam. The trail was there, blazed by Truman and kept open by Dulles, but Kennedy committed a significant number of American troops to a situation in which they would be exposed to enemy action. That was the fateful decision. Then he acted, through involvement in a coup that ended in the murder of President Ngo Dinh Diem, to make sure that the South Vietnamese government self-determined itself according to America's conception of America's self-interest.

Thus all the elements of the terror inherent in the tragedy of American diplomacy had appeared before Kennedy was assassinated. First, the elitism that led to life-and-death decisions being made by a tiny group of leaders without any pretence of engaging in debate about actions that involved military operations. Second, the passivity and even indifference of most elected representatives. Third, the loss of the capacity to think critically about reality, and about individual actions. And, finally, the application of traditional attitudes and analyses in a situation that called for a drastically different approach.

The murder of Kennedy, an act that dramatized the terror and the related rush toward disaster, jarred many Americans into a greater awareness of their predicament than they had exhibited since the end of World War II. It served to heighten their recognition of the weaknesses of domestic society, as well as to arouse their concern about the consequences of a foreign policy that stressed counter-revolutionary interventions around the globe. The election campaign of 1964 was marked, in consequence, by a general (if also vague) opposition to further involvement in Vietnam. The elite was forced to speak to the issue, and Lyndon Baines Johnson did so with the touch of a master.

Johnson talked peace, but at the same time he unequivocally reasserted the necessity of acting forcefully to honor America's traditional policies. He was perfectly sincere. He simply did not comprehend the contradiction involved: for him, as for countless others, American policy was peace. There could be no true peace until historic American principles were honored by all.

And so, quite naturally, once again to war to uphold the principle of self-determination, to secure the necessary access to the world marketplace, and to help the poor and the weak.* And, again quite naturally, to war covertly without any dialogue with the citizenry and without any Congressional declaration of war. Intervention had become a way of life, as President Johnson underscored in April and May 1964 by dispatching more than 20,000 troops to overturn a revolutionary government in Santo Domingo.

Perhaps such terror and disaster were necessary in order to change the tragic course of American diplomacy. Perhaps the American people were too deeply enmeshed in the traditional policy that had become a belief (and hence too easily and too effectively manipulated by an elite that used that same faith as its primary instrument of control) to break free of the dead past until the dead themselves became omnipresent. One would prefer to think not, but that is the way it finally became possible to talk with some measure of hope about the transcendence of the tragedy.

For it was the horrible reality of the ever increasing death and devastation in Vietnam that galvanized growing numbers of Americans to demand an end to the terror. The pulverizing destruction of a tiny nation in the name of self-determination, and the related barbarization of the once proud American Army, were gruesome and shameful ways to learn the nature of disaster. The final terror would come to be if ending the war did not lead to fundamental changes in the American outlook, in American society, and hence in American foreign policy.

---

* See, for example, the following documents in *The Pentagon Papers* (New York: *The New York Times*, 1971): National Security Council Statement (1952), "United States Objectives and Courses of Action With Respect to Southeast Asia," p. 27; Eisenhower's Instructions of May 12, 1954, p. 42; Joint Chiefs of Staff Memo on "U.S. Forces in South Vietnam," May 10, 1961, p. 125; L. B. Johnson, "Mission to Southeast Asia, India, and Pakistan," May 23, 1961, p. 127; and R. S. McNamara, "South Vietnam," March 16, 1964, p. 278.

CONCLUSION

CONCLUSION: THE WISDOM OF AN

The tradition of all past generations weighs like an Alp upon the brain of the living.

KARL MARX

It is not my duty as a historian to predict the future, only to observe and interpret the past. But its lesson is clear enough; we have lived too long out of contact with reality, and now the time has come to rebuild our lives.

CALLITRAX, HISTORIAN OF LYS, *In the City and the Stars*, BY ARTHUR C. CLARKE

Yes, strictly speaking, the question is not how to get cured, but how to live.

MARLOW TO STEIN, IN *Lord Jim*, BY JOSEPH CONRAD

OPEN DOOR FOR REVOLUTIONS

The students, teachers, and other dissenters who initiated and led the movement to end the war in Vietnam understood that the pattern of intervention was ineradicably entwined with other inequitable and destructive aspects of American society. Many had been early foot soldiers in the on-going battle to end racism and discrimination against Black Americans. Others had concentrated on the problem of poverty, or on the stultification of high school and college education. A few were dedicated pacifists, and some had given much effort to help workers improve their lives. Most of them had become aware, whatever their age, of three other deeply disturbing developments in America: the steady loss by the individual of his ability to self-determine himself in postwar society; the loss of almost all sense—as well as the reality—of a community in an increasingly managed and manipulated system; and the decline of a commitment to being moral (or, conversely, the increasing hypocrisy).

The recognition of those failures gradually created, during the long and difficult struggle to end the war, a conviction that existing American society had to be changed. Otherwise there would be more interventions and more deterioration at home. Not all of the millions who came to oppose the war in Vietnam developed that kind of understanding or commitment. But many did come to sense the necessity of going beyond the question of ending the war. As a result, the beginnings of a true social movement appeared for the first time since the turn of the twentieth century.

Much of that process was reinforced by the continuing success of revolutionary movements throughout the world. The dedication and determination of the Vietnamese to truly self-determine their own lives forced many Americans to confront the implications of trying to sustain traditional American foreign policy. They sensed, even if they did not fully understand, that such a course would involve its own kind of drastic changes in the United States. It would mean ever less freedom and ever more enforced work and privation. It would mean living with the death of friends and loved ones as a routine experience. And it might well mean the death of all.

Even in its existing unfocused and unorganized state, that awareness among the citizens first forced the elite to manifest a new degree of caution and circumspection. During that phase of its response, the elite clothed its maneuvers and manipulations in the traditional rhetoric of victory for a free and peaceful world. Then the reality of massive death-counts in Vietnam and the increasing strength of the opposition in the United States forced President Johnson to withdraw from the election of 1968. Finally, the growing recognition of the true nature of the terror began to affect the thinking of some erstwhile imperial-minded leaders (like Robert F. Kennedy) and led others (like President Richard M. Nixon) to attempt to stabilize the existing empire by cutting losses in Vietnam and by negotiating an interim *modus vivendi* with Russia, the People's Republic of China, and various other revolutionary governments.

Hence the meaning of the title of this chapter has changed since I wrote it in December 1961. Then I was primarily concerned, having tried to show how History offers a way of learning, to do what I could to break the terrifying momentum toward disaster that ultimately carried us into Vietnam. Thus I emphasized the methods by which we could change our traditional ways of dealing with other peoples. I see no reason to alter anything in the list of suggestions I offered at that time, except to drop the device of the rhetorical question.*

---

* Which I used, despite my strong dislike of the form, in the hope of giving the general reader a sense of the relevance of History, and of engaging him in a serious reevaluation of his existing outlook.

It is time to stop defining trade as the control of markets for our surplus products and control of raw materials for our factories. It is time to stop depending so narrowly—in our thinking as well as in our practice—upon an informal empire for our well-being and welfare.

It is time to ask ourselves if we are really so unimaginative that we have to have a frontier in the form of an informal empire in order to have democracy and prosperity at home. It is time to say that we can make American society function even better on the basis of equitable relationships with other people.

It is time to stop defining trade as a weapon against other people with whom we have disagreements. It is time to start thinking of trade as a means to moderate and alleviate those tensions—and to improve the life of the other people.

It is time to stop trying to expand our exports on the grounds that such a campaign will make foreigners foot the bill for our military security. It is time instead to concern ourselves with a concerted effort to halt and then cancel the armaments race.

It is time to stop saying that all the evil in the world resides in the Soviet Union and other communist countries. It is time to admit that there is good as well as evil in those societies, and set about to help increase the amount of good.

It is time to admit that our own intelligence reports mean that the Russians have been following a defensive policy in nuclear weapons. It is time to take advantage of that attitude on their part, break out of our neurosis about a Pearl Harbor attack, and go on to negotiate an arms control measure.

It is time to admit, in short, that we can avoid living with communist countries only by embarking upon a program that will kill millions of human beings. It is time, therefore, to evolve and adopt a program that will encourage and enable the communist countries to move in the direction of their own utopian vision of the good society as we endeavor to move in accordance with our own ideals.

Nor do I see any reason to modify the following passages:

Once freed from its myopic concentration on the cold war, the United States could come to grips with the central problem of reordering its own society so that it functions through such a balanced relationship with the rest of the world, and so that the labor and leisure of its own citizens are invested with creative meaning and purpose. A new debate over the first principles and practices of government and economics is long overdue, and a statement of a twentieth-century political economy comparable to *The Federalist* papers would do more to enhance America's role in the world than any number of rockets and satellites. The configuration of the world of outer space will be decided on the cool green hills of earth long before the first colonizing spaceships blast free of the atmosphere.

Having structured a creative response to the issue of democracy and prosperity at home, the United States could again devote a greater share of its attention and energy to the world scene. Its revamped foreign policy would be geared to helping other peoples achieve their own aspirations in their own way. The essence of such a foreign policy would be an open door for revolutions. Having come to terms with themselves—having achieved maturity—Americans could exhibit the self-discipline necessary to let other peoples come to terms with themselves. Having realized that "self-righteousness is the hallmark of inner guilt," Americans would no longer find it necessary to embark upon crusades to save others.

In this fashion, and through a policy of an open door for revolutions, Americans would be able to cope with the many as yet unknown revolutions that are dependent upon peace for their conception and maturation. Only in this way can either the general or the specific tragedy of American diplomacy be transcended in a creative, peaceful manner.

To transcend tragedy requires the nerve to fail. But a positive effort to transcend the cold war would very probably carry the United States and the world on into an era of peace and creative human endeavor. For the nerve to fail has nothing at all to do with blustering and self-righteous crusades up to or past the edge of violence. It is instead the kind of quiet confidence that comes with and from accepting limits, and a concurrent understanding that accepting limits does not mean the end of existence itself or of the possibility of a creative life. For Americans, the nerve to fail is in a real sense the nerve to say—and mean—that we no longer need what Turner called "the gate of escape" provided by the frontier. It is only in adolescence or senility that human beings manifest a compulsive drive to play to win. The one does not yet know, and the other has forgotten, that what counts is how the game is played. It would actually be pathetic rather than tragic if the United States jumped from childhood to old age without ever having matured. Yet that is precisely what it will do unless it sloughs off the ideology of the Open Door Policy and steps forth to open the door to the revolutions that can transform the material world and the quality of human relationships.

Perhaps it is by now apparent to the reader that there is a basic irony involved in this conception and interpretation of American foreign policy as tragedy. This irony arises from, and is in that sense caused by, the truth that this essay is in two respects written from a radical point of view.

First, it is radical in that it seeks to uncover, describe, and analyze the character and logic of American foreign policy since the 1890s. It is therefore critical in the intellectual sense of not being content with rhetoric and other appearances, and of seeking instead to establish by research and analysis a fuller, more accurate picture of reality.

Second, it is radical in that it concludes from the research and reflection, that American foreign policy must be changed fundamentally in order to sustain the wealth and welfare of the United States on into the future. This essay recommends that the frontier-expansionist explanation of American democracy and prosperity, and the strategy of the Open Door Policy, be abandoned on the grounds that neither any longer bears any significant relation to reality.

This essay also points toward a radical but noncommunist reconstruction of American society in domestic affairs. And it is at this point that the irony appears: there is at the present time no radicalism in the United States strong enough to win power, or even a very significant influence, through the processes of representative government—and this essay rests on the axiom of representative government. Hence, ironically, the radical analysis leads finally to a conservative conclusion. The well-being of the United States depends—*in the short-run but only in the short-run*—upon the extent to which calm and confident and enlightened conservatives can see and bring themselves to act upon the validity of a radical analysis. In a very real sense, therefore, democracy and prosperity depend upon whether the New Frontier is defined in practice to mean merely a vigorous reassertion of the ideology and the policies of the past or to mean an acceptance of limits upon America's freedom of action.

The issue can be stated as a very direct proposition. If the United States cannot accept the existence of such limits without giving up democracy and cannot proceed to enhance and extend democracy within such limits, then the traditional effort to sustain democracy by expansion will lead to the destruction of democracy.

We now know that the conservatives did not act upon a radical analysis. Yet the proposition remains true: that was the only way the disaster in Vietnam could have been avoided. And it remains true in the deeper sense that short-term palliatives devised from selected portions of the radical critique will serve at most to postpone—not avoid—further such terrors.

And so now we confront another irony. There is today the beginning of a social movement that could change America in a radical way, and thereby realize our most cherished ideals and aspirations. Hence we must recognize the wisdom of including in our outlook the idea of an open door for such a revolution in America.

Chile has demonstrated the possibility of choosing that course in a democratic election. Perhaps we Americans, whose votes have mattered increasingly less in recent decades, can restore the integrity of our own franchise through a similar display of self-determination.